Pro .NET 2.0 Extreme Programming

Greg Pearman and James Goodwill

Apress®

Pro .NET 2.0 Extreme Programming

Copyright © 2006 by Greg Pearman and James Goodwill

ISBN-13 (pbk): 978-1-59059-480-3

ISBN-10 (pbk): 1-59059-480-0

Printed and bound in the United States of America 9 8 7 6 5 4 3 2 1

Lead Editor: Dominic Shakeshaft
Technical Reviewer: Jason Lefebvre
Editorial Board: Steve Anglin, Ewan Buckingham, Gary Cornell, Jason Gilmore, Jonathan Gennick, Jonathan Hassell, James Huddleston, Chris Mills, Matthew Moodie, Dominic Shakeshaft, Jim Sumser, Keir Thomas, Matt Wade
Project Manager: Sofia Marchant
Copy Edit Manager: Nicole LeClerc
Copy Editor: Marilyn Smith
Assistant Production Director: Kari Brooks-Copony
Production Editor: Kelly Winquist
Compositor: Lynn L'Heureux
Proofreaders: April Eddy, Lori Bring
Indexer: Carol Burbo
Artist: Kinetic Publishing Services, LLC
Cover Designer: Kurt Krames
Manufacturing Director: Tom Debolski

Distributed to the book trade worldwide by Springer-Verlag New York, Inc., 233 Spring Street, 6th Floor, New York, NY 10013. Phone 1-800-SPRINGER, fax 201-348-4505, e-mail orders-ny@springer-sbm.com, or visit http://www.springeronline.com.

For information on translations, please contact Apress directly at 2560 Ninth Street, Suite 219, Berkeley, CA 94710. Phone 510-549-5930, fax 510-549-5939, e-mail info@apress.com, or visit http://www.apress.com.

The source code for this book is available to readers at http://www.apress.com in the Source Code section.

To my wife, Simone, my soul mate; to my daughter, Ashley, and my son, Austin. Thank you for making my life complete. I love you with all my heart.

—Greg Pearman

To my girls Christy, Abby, and Emma.

—James Goodwill

Contents at a Glance

Contents

PART 1 ■ ■ ■ XP Introduction

PART 2 ■ ■ ■ XP Tools

PART 3 ■■■ XP in Action

About the Authors

GREG "HAP" PEARMAN is the founder of Spotted Dog Software LLC, located in Littleton, Colorado. He has more than 18 years of experience in architecting and developing enterprise software solutions. Formerly a senior architect and developer at Qwest Communications, Greg was a leading member of a small, elite team that developed and implemented Extreme Programming (XP) practices for the entire Qwest IT organization. This team worked with each Qwest IT project team to teach them XP and to follow up with those teams in the field after their training. This experience gave Hap the unique opportunity to stress-test XP under multiple and varying circumstances as an XP coach and mentor.

Greg has also architected and developed small to large enterprise systems using technologies such as J2EE, .NET (C#), Cocoa, and C++ for various companies, including IBM, EPA, US West Direct, Hertz, VeriSign, and ABC/Disney.

JAMES GOODWILL is a renowned technologist and experienced open source leader. James is a member of the JSR-152 Expert Group and is a frequent speaker at major conferences such as ApacheCon, Comdex, and multiple Java Users Groups. He has provided technical and business leadership to many Global 2000 organizations, including QualCOMM, BellSouth, MCI, and BEA Systems. Books that James has authored include *Mastering Jakarta Struts* (John Wiley and Sons, 2002), *Apache Jakarta-Tomcat* (Apress, 2001), and *Apache Axis Live* (SourceBeat, 2004).

About the Technical Reviewer

JASON LEFEBVRE is vice president and founding partner of Intensity Software, Inc. (www.intensitysoftware.com), which specializes in providing custom Microsoft .NET applications, IT consulting services, legacy system migration, and boxed software products to a rapidly growing set of clients. Jason has been using .NET since its alpha stages in early 2000 and uses Visual Studio and the .NET Framework daily while creating solutions for Intensity Software's clients. Jason has been a participating author for a number of books and has written numerous articles about .NET-related topics.

Acknowledgments

First and foremost, to my personal Lord and Savior, Jesus Christ, through whom all things are possible. I would like to give a big thanks to Paul Karsten (The Big Kahuna) for being a great role model. You are the XP coach of all XP coaches. Thanks goes to the rest of the original Piranhas (Carl Podlogar, Charles Kastner, Joel Fredrick, Ken Conway, Rebecca Germain, Andy Ochsner, and Roger Burnett), too. You guys made XP fun and real for me.

Thanks to Owen Rogers for all your help with NMock. You guys at ThoughtWorks are doing a great job for the development community.

Thanks to Gina Jackson for all her hard work on creating legible user story cards for the book. You always had a smile for me when I asked you for just one more set of cards.

Lastly, I would like to thank my dad. You gave me the character, values, and strength I have today. I miss you.

Greg Pearman

I would like to thank the people who made this book a success. They are the people who took my words and shaped them into something that I hope will help you use Extreme Programming to its fullest. I would like to especially thank everyone at Apress for their patience during the development of this text. Each and every person made this book what it is today.

On a closer note, I would like to thank everyone at my company, Virtuas Solutions, LLC, for their support while I was completing this text. The entire "UNREAL" staff contributed by picking up my assignments when my plate was too full. I want to also thank Hap for his contribution to this text. It was a lot of fun working with a qualified coauthor.

Finally, the most important contributors to this book are my wife, Christy, and our daughters, Abby and Emma. They are the ones who really sacrificed during the development of this text. They are the ones who deserve the credit for this book. With their support, I can do anything.

James Goodwill

PART 1

XP Introduction

■■■

CHAPTER 1

Introducing XP

Many books cover the theory of Extreme Programming (XP). This is not one of them. If you are picking up this book hoping to learn about the philosophy of XP, you will be disappointed. This book concentrates on the practical, not the theoretical. We hope to leave you with the knowledge of how to implement XP in a practical manner. But before we do this, we need to give you a clear, no-nonsense definition of XP.

To put XP in context, we'll begin by looking briefly at the waterfall and Agile methods of software development. Each methodology has many books dedicated to it, of course. Here, we will give you just enough information to understand how and why XP came to exist.

Then we'll answer the question "What is XP?" We'll look at all of the specific key values, principles, and practices of XP. You'll know what XP is after you have read this section!

Next, we'll offer you a comparison between XP and some other current Agile methods. Finally, we'll address when it's best to use XP.

The Waterfall Methodology

The waterfall methodology is a software development process that is broken up into a series of distinct phases, with each phase existing as an autonomous phase with respect to all subsequent phases. In a waterfall project, all phases of the process have a distinct beginning and end. When a phase is over, the subsequent phase begins. This stepped approach continues throughout the remaining phases of a project until it reaches completion.

Several characteristics of the waterfall methodology often create some undesirable results:

- Each phase of a waterfall project must be complete prior to moving to the next phase. This approach makes it difficult for you to learn and adjust to changes in the project requirements.

- The waterfall methodology is very heavily focused on process. This approach often causes the team to concentrate more on managing the waterfall processes, as opposed to fulfilling the goals of the project.

- The waterfall methodology is focused on documentation as one of its primary forms of communication. Unfortunately, software development is often a complicated matter and is difficult to capture entirely on paper. Additionally, what is not said, or written in this case, can be as powerful as what is said, but that type of information is not captured in a document.

- Extensive documentation is also used as a means of trying to control scope. In the analysis phase, requirements documents are used as contracts between software developers and the project stakeholders. This requires the project stakeholders to know exactly what they want and to have those needs and wants remain constant throughout the development life cycle. This is rarely the case.

- The waterfall methodology assumes that a project can be managed by a predefined project plan. Months are spent perfecting the plan before any work on the project really begins. A lot of work is put into maintaining the plan throughout the project, and often the plan is out of date with the current status of the project. The end result is the project plan tends to be more of a historical document than a working guide to the development team. Planning is not the problem; the problem is trying to predict and plan for the future.

While the waterfall approach does have problems, it did start with the best intentions—bringing order out of chaos. When waterfall methods were first employed, there was no software process at all in place. Having some processes, documentation, and a plan is not a bad thing. Unfortunately, the waterfall methodology swung the pendulum too far to the right. Software projects need to be manageable, but without becoming too brittle or complicated to implement—which is exactly what the first waterfall methods created. This swing resulted in the development of another group of methodologies, known as Agile methods.

The Agile Methodologies

Agile methods were born out of the frustration software development teams were having with the waterfall approach. These software developers were not seeing the results they felt were necessary to deliver successful projects on a regular basis. They saw several shortcomings with this heavy emphasis on process and documentation.

Several developers who shared the same frustrations with waterfall approaches got together and formed the Agile Alliance. The alliance members agreed on four key values that they felt all Agile projects should have in common. They called the compilation of these values the Agile Manifesto (http://agilemanifesto.org). The values of the Agile Manifesto are as follows:

Individuals and interactions	*over*	Processes and tools
Working software	*over*	Comprehensive documentation
Customer collaboration	*over*	Contract negotiation
Responding to change	*over*	Following a plan

The idea is that by focusing on the values on the left, you shift your approach to software development. It's not that the items on the right are wrong or bad, but that the items on the left should be more important.

With the increasing popularity of the Internet and e-commerce, businesses are migrating to the Web in alarming rates. With this migration comes the need for rapid deployment of software. In addition, changes in the economy have required development teams to do more with less. Handling these changes gracefully is the focus of the Agile methods.

We'll return to Agile methods as a group at the end of the chapter and see when it's best to use XP over the various other Agile methods.

What Is XP?

Extreme Programming, XP for short, is an Agile software development methodology that is made up of a collection of core values, principles, and practices that provide a highly efficient and effective means of developing software. At the core of XP is the desire to embrace the change that naturally occurs when developing software. XP differs from other Agile methodologies because it defines an implementation strategy for practicing the four core Agile values on a daily basis.

Four XP Values

XP defines four key values. These values are important because they form the foundation on which all XP principles and practices are built. Each of these values is described in the following sections.

XP Value 1: Communication

One of the key factors of software development teams that are highly successful is their ability to communicate effectively. Teams that communicate often in an open and honest environment are able to make effective decisions and mitigate problems more quickly than teams that don't have that type of communication.

Communication comes in several forms: written, spoken, gestures, and body posture. Traditionally, these types of communications can be executed in several fashions: formal documentation, e-mail, telephone, video conferencing, and face-to-face conversation. While all of these forms of communication are useful, XP favors face-to-face communication.

XP Value 2: Simplicity

Another key factor of software development teams that are highly successful is their ability to make what they do as simple as possible. This includes the code they develop, the documentation they produce, the processes they use, and the form of communication they choose. Simplicity forces the team to build what is needed to satisfy requirements as they are defined today, as opposed to building unnecessary features that may never be needed.

The result of keeping things simple is a reduction in code, processes, and documentation, which, in turn, leaves additional time to incorporate more features into the system. After all, the project stakeholders are paying for system features, not code with functionality they did not request.

XP Value 3: Feedback

Feedback is the XP value that helps the team members know if they are on the right track. This is why feedback needs to be highly repetitive and frequent. In XP, feedback comes not only from individuals and their interactions, but also from the automation of tests, the progress charts that the tracker generates, and the successful acceptance of user stories.

Note User stories are an XP component used to capture project requirements. We will describe user stories in detail in Chapter 3.

Constant feedback keeps the development team from missing the project target. It ensures that the software the team is developing is high quality and stable. Feedback also gives the project stakeholders the confidence that what they will receive is what they need and expect.

XP Value 4: Courage

It takes an enormous amount of courage to try something new. That is because individuals seem to naturally resist change and fear the unknown. XP teams need courage when they encounter resistance to what they are trying to do.

It also takes courage to expose your weaknesses. That is what developers are doing when they pair-program.

Note Paired programming is when two developers work on a task together. It is one of the XP practices, as described in the "XP Practice 3" section of this chapter.

It takes courage for the development team members to tell the project stakeholders that they are not going to complete all of the user stories in a given iteration.

Fifteen XP Principles

While the XP values are bold and can influence your team's development mind-set, they are a bit too vague when it is time to start selecting practices that implement these values. To bridge the gap between values and practices, XP needed a set of principles that built on the values. Fifteen principles are derived from the four XP values. These principles are the focus of this section. The first five of these are the fundamental XP principles.

XP Principle 1: Allow Rapid Feedback

The principle of rapid feedback enhances the value of feedback by pumping the received feedback back into the XP environment as quickly as possible. The business receives rapid feedback in days and weeks, and developers receive rapid feedback in seconds and minutes. This is all accomplished by selecting XP practices that provide this type of feedback.

For example, acceptance tests are written during an iteration starting with the first iteration. In a waterfall approach, these tests would not be available until the end of the project. Acceptance tests provide the business with rapid feedback in days and weeks, instead of months or years.

Another example of rapid feedback is unit tests, which we will discuss later in this chapter when we cover the seventh XP practice of testing. This provides the developers with rapid feedback in seconds and minutes, instead of a waterfall approach where this type of feedback may not be available for weeks or months.

XP Principle 2: Assume Simplicity

The second principle supports the basic value by treating every problem as if it could be solved with ridiculous simplicity. That's not to say that every problem is ridiculously simple, but to trust your ability to add complexity in the future where needed. This principle encourages you to solve your current problems by keeping things simple.

XP Principle 3: Make Incremental Changes

XP promotes incremental changes. When you make a large change and then encounter a bug or problem, through compilation or testing, you have a large area of code to search. Making smaller, incremental changes will help you identify new problems. This approach will also build confidence when making changes.

XP Principle 4: Embrace Change

Kent Beck's initial XP book is titled *Extreme Programming Explained: Embrace Change* (Addison-Wesley, 1999). This is a key aspect of all the Agile methodologies. If you can develop applications and systems that preserve options and solve only the problem or need at hand, you can effectively manage change.

XP Principle 5: Deliver High-Quality Work

There is no point in developing software if the end result is not a high-quality product. You could have a software product that has all the features anyone could imagine, but if that product is bug-ridden and unstable, who needs it? Take pride in your work and insist on delivering only high-quality code.

The other ten principles are less central to mapping practice to values, but they can be helpful in deciding what to do in specific situations.

XP Principle 6: Teach Learning

You could just dictate that your development projects follow XP like sheep—not actually understanding what they are doing or why. But that would not be very effective. XP encourages you to teach your development teams not only what XP is, but why these concepts and practices are valuable.

XP Principle 7: Make a Small Initial Investment

Because customers will sometimes bring projects that are large in scope, it can be tempting for the development organization to build a large team from the start and try to tackle all of the scope. The small initial investment principle of XP says to keep your initial resources and work load small. If you absolutely must grow bigger, do it as the project progresses; don't start off large.

XP Principle 8: Play to Win

Do what it takes to make the project succeed. Some teams play not to lose by doing the bare minimum to say they followed XP. These types of teams don't get the spirit of XP. Create a team that plays to win.

XP Principle 9: Conduct Concrete Experiments

Create tests that continually prove you are on the right track. Don't create tests just for testing's sake. Build tests on tests that demonstrate that the prior test's assumptions were correct.

XP Principle 10: Promote Open, Honest Communication

You can have an XP team communicating face-to-face, but if the culture and environment do not encourage open and honest communication, then the value is lost. So, make sure your team respects and encourages open and honest communications.

XP Principle 11: Work with People's Instincts, Not Against Them

If you have selected team members with positive attitudes, they already have the desire to do the right thing, so let them. Trust them and their instincts.

XP Principle 12: Accept Responsibility

Don't dictate the team's tasks; let the team members choose their tasks. This will create a sense of ownership, and they will be more committed to getting the tasks done.

XP Principle 13: Adapt As Necessary

You will never work on two projects that are exactly alike. Each project has its own unique characteristics and challenges. So adapt as needed, but only do so with a firm understanding of what needs to be adapted and why.

XP Principle 14: Travel Light

Don't go overboard on process, documentation, or tools just for the sake of it. Use process, documentation, and tools where they make sense, and get rid of them as soon as they no longer make sense.

XP Principle 15: Measure Honestly

Pick metrics that make sense for the given team and project. Don't gather metrics on a project just for the sake of having metrics.

Harnessed with the understanding of XP's values coupled with its principles, you are ready to add in the XP practices. These practices will take the concepts and ideas of the values and principles and make them come to life.

Fourteen XP Practices

Now that you have seen the foundation on which XP is based, you need to take a look at the practices that implement these values and principles. The practices defined by XP are actually "best practices" that successful software development projects have implemented for years. The big difference in XP is that it combines all of these practices into a single methodology. This is an advantage for XP because the practices are not based on theory like many other methodologies. Combining all of these practices together creates a synergy that produces a greater whole. It is these practices that you will use in your day-to-day life, and it is these practices that make XP unique.

Traditionally, there are 12 practices in XP, but we offer you here the 14 practices we have most success with in our work.

Note XP sometimes uses the terms customer and stakeholder interchangeably. We will use the term customer to apply to both.

XP Practice 1: On-Site Customer

Traditional development takes an approach where requirements are defined at the beginning of the development life cycle, without the presence of the developers who will actually develop the project. To compensate for the absence of the developers, extensive documentation is generated to communicate the intent of the customer's wants and needs. This requires the customers to know exactly what they want and need at the beginning of the project. It also requires that those wants and needs remain constant throughout the development process.

Traditional development also has the customers wait until the end of the project to perform acceptance tests. Since this is the first time the customers have seen the system, they are often shocked at the results. In many cases, the requirements are misinterpreted or missed completely.

XP address these issues by asking the customer to be more involved throughout the entire development process. The more involved the customer, the more likely the development team will deliver what the customer wants.

XP believes that the best way to get the customers engaged is to have them sit with the development team, allowing them to give and receive feedback and communicate with the development team members.

Note Usually, the development team will need to convince the customer that sitting with the development team is the right thing to do, as the customer will usually resist such a request. Your team will need to describe the benefits to the customer. These benefits should include the customer's ability to make changes throughout the development process, to receive rapid feedback as to what is going on with the project, and to make better decisions concerning the project. If you are unsuccessful in convincing your customers that they need to sit with you, you will have a difficult time working effectively as an XP team.

XP Practice 2: Sit Together

Putting the team together in the same work area is an implied XP practice that we are adding explicitly to make it clear that it is a best practice. A core value of XP is communication, preferably face-to-face. In XP, creating large, open areas where the development team can work together facilitates this. Sitting together also supports feedback, because developers and customers can talk to each other without needing to track each other down. Additionally, sitting together discourages distributed teams. (XP projects experimenting with distributed teams have had different degrees of success.)

At first, this work area may seem counterproductive because of the increased noise level and perceived distractions. This is a common fear, but don't give in to it. Adjustment to the noise level is very quick (hours to a few days), and any perceived distractions will quickly disappear.

XP Practice 3: Paired Programming

Code reviews are a good thing. They provide a learning experience for all individuals involved and create consistency throughout the project. The issue with code reviews is that they take a significant amount of time and are often skipped in order to meet deadlines.

Paired programming makes code reviews an everyday activity. In addition, when a development issue or uncertainty comes up, instead of a developer taking significant time trying to solve the problem on his own, his pair jumps in to give him ideas and support. This helps developers resolve their problem much more quickly. Lastly, with paired programming, developers have someone else to keep them focused on the task at hand—keeping the system as simple as possible.

XP Practice 4: Collective Code Ownership

Traditional development teams often divide an application by assigning ownership of components or subsystems to specific individuals. These divisions create bottlenecks that hinder development when the component or subsystem owner is swamped with work. The result is a backlog that affects other team members. The backlog also adds to the stress of the component owner, as she is aware of the bottleneck she is creating.

Collective code ownership eliminates this bottleneck by granting the right to change or enhance any code within the application to any developer. In addition, collective code ownership promotes the transfer of knowledge among all the developers. With the transfer of knowledge, you don't have to worry about when a given individual on the team suddenly becomes unavailable. So, collective code ownership removes yet another bottleneck or risk to the project and improves the development team's communications.

XP Practice 5: Coding Standards

If all the developers are working on the same code, as is the case with collective code ownership, you don't want them changing the code appearance to suit their individual styles. This would be a tremendous waste of time. So, by agreeing on a coding standard at the beginning of the project, you will increase the productivity and communications of the team.

XP Practice 6: Refactoring

XP doesn't favor large up-front design phases, as waterfall methodologies do, but it does promote design, through the practice of constant refactoring. In *Refactoring: Improving the Design of Existing Code* (Addison Wesley, 1999), Martin Fowler defines refactoring as "the process of changing a software system in such a way that it doesn't alter the external behavior of the code yet improves the internal structure." An example of refactoring is moving a section of duplicated code into a method where it could be reused with a simple method call, as opposed to having it proliferated throughout the application.

To facilitate system design without needing to perform it all up front, you should use refactoring techniques. Fowler's book is a great place to learn about refactoring.

XP Practice 7: Testing

One of the biggest advantages of XP is that it stresses high quality through up-front testing. This happens with both test-driven development and acceptance testing. What really makes this practice worthwhile is that it doesn't wait until the end of development to create or even run the tests.

Test-Driven Development and Unit Tests

Test-driven development (TDD) promotes the writing of tests prior to writing the code that is being tested. This allows you to focus on your interface and what you expect from your code prior to focusing on its particular implementation.

The testing components for implementing a test-driven development plan are known as *unit tests*. Unit tests are small pieces of code that are written to exercise autonomous "units" of your implemented classes. When developing these tests, you usually focus on the public interfaces of your classes. A common test-driven development sequence looks something like the following:

1. Create a unit test that will exercise the class that you intend to create.

2. Compile your unit test. It will fail to compile, because the code you're trying to test doesn't exist.

3. Write just enough functionality to allow the unit test to compile.

4. Run your test. It will fail, because you haven't actually implemented the class.

5. Write your class implementation.

6. Run your test again. You should now have a test that passes. (If it doesn't, back up one step and try again.)

Test-driven development gives developers the confidence to make changes to the system, because they know that the tests will tell them if they have broken anything and where in the application the break occurred. This is one of the most effective feedback mechanisms that the development team can have for ensuring stability and high quality.

Another advantage to test-driven development is that it assists in keeping the code simple. When developers take a code-first approach to development, they have a tendency to design as they code, without having a clear picture as to what they want to achieve. They basically let the creative process lead them to a design while they are coding. This often does not result in the most straightforward solutions. In fact, in many cases, it results in an overly complicated design. Test-driven development forces developers to think about the outcome of what they are developing, and then simply code until the test passes, which leads to a simpler design. This is called *development by intention*.

Acceptance Testing

Acceptance testing in parallel with coding also provides a huge benefit to the project. Often, nuances about a user story (which will be covered in more detail in Chapter 3) that weren't apparent during the creation of the user story are discovered during acceptance testing. Developers can catch such issues early in development and make the necessary changes immediately. In traditional development life cycles, these issues would be caught later and would require more complicated and costly changes.

These testing practices will deliver production-ready code at the end of every iteration. Customers can deliver the system to production as soon as they feel there is enough business functionality. Using traditional development methodologies, this would never be possible because this type of testing does not occur until the end of the development life cycle.

XP Practice 8: Continuous Integration

Most applications are complex and consist of many components and/or subsystems. These components need to be integrated to make the application whole. Unfortunately, in a traditional development process, integration of application components or subsystems happens late in the development life cycle—usually in an effort to overcome the unforeseen bottlenecks that occurred during the development phase. The end result is usually a nightmarish effort of trying to piece the application together at the last minute.

With continuous integration, you can address any integration issues early and can resolve these issues as they arise. In XP, you will be integrating every time code is checked into the source code repository.

XP Practice 9: The Planning Game

The planning game, which is a part of release planning, usually takes a day or two to complete. The idea of this practice is to get to the big picture—what the customer wants and how much it's going to cost—as fast as possible. This way, the customers can decide if they want to proceed with the project. If they choose not to, then they have invested only a week, as opposed to the months they might invest using a traditional approach.

Customers often want everything under the sun, unaware of the cost of their requests. They don't usually have realistic expectations as to the level of effort needed when building software. They just define what it is they want and the date they expect it to be delivered.

With waterfall-type methodologies, this all happens during the analysis and requirements phases and usually takes months to complete. This phase is long because the customers who are requesting the features are not involved during the development phase. Therefore, all of the customers' thoughts and ideas must be captured in written documents. Unfortunately, this also requires the customers to know everything they need and want from the onset of the project. It also requires that nothing change between the time the requirements are defined and when the system is delivered.

In addition, the requirements in a waterfall project often form the contract between the customer and the development organization. This is how the development team knows that the team has completed what the customer requested. The contract is used to discourage change, because changes usually result in renegotiation.

XP gathers these requirements, in just a few days to a couple of weeks (depending on the complexity of the project), during release planning. Everyone is present during this time (developers, testers, and customers), so the need for written documentation decreases. Costing of the requested features is done immediately and on a feature-by-feature basis.

XP Practice 10: Small Releases

The sooner customers can start to use the software, the sooner the customers can receive a return on their investment. Projects that develop systems in small increments prove to be more successful than those that have long delivery dates.

This is where the practice of small releases is invaluable. By selecting just enough business functionality and setting that as the target release, the whole XP team has a more visible target. Additionally, small releases allow the XP team to gain a greater sense of accomplishment when compared with projects that take many months or years to reach a release date.

Ideally, a release should be due in 30 to 180 days. This is negotiated with the customer during the planning game.

XP Practice 11: System Metaphors

Imagine if every time you wanted to describe what your application does, you needed to have a two-hour conversation. You would quickly find yourself tiring of explaining it over and over. There is a lot of room for error in explaining complex systems repeatedly.

The solution is to find a simple yet complete way of explaining your application through the use of metaphors. Albert Einstein was fond of saying, "Explain it to me like I'm a four-year-old," and you should keep that idea in mind when you're communicating concepts.

System metaphors create a way for everyone on the XP team to share a common vision of what the system is. If the customer tells the development team that the system needs a shopping cart feature (a metaphor), she should not need to go into significant detail as to what a shopping cart is or does.

The system metaphor is also another way that XP incorporates system design into the process. The key difference between the XP and waterfall methodologies is that the design is kept to a high level, with just enough design for the whole XP team to understand the system.

XP Practice 12: Simple Design

Traditional software projects take the approach of a large up-front design that can take weeks or months to create. This approach makes the assumption that everything about the system can be designed from the beginning; little to no change will occur throughout the development life cycle.

Change will occur during the development life cycle, and that change will not only affect requirements, but it will impact the design as well. If that change is significant, the up-front design will also change significantly, and the time spent on that design will have been wasted.

With XP, the practice of simple design keeps the developers from trying to predict the future and forces the design to be just enough to meet what is known about the system today. Often, a quick high-level design is created during release planning. The detailed design is started with the first iteration and evolves with each subsequent iteration.

XP Practice 13: Sustainable Pace (40-Hour Week)

Traditional development projects are usually rampant with overtime and heroic efforts to deliver by the promised due date. The result is a team that is drained and less productive, so quality drops dramatically.

Overtime and heroic efforts are signs of bigger problems, including overcommitted deliverables, poor estimation, lack of resources, and so on. Many organizations just accept this as the norm.

XP addresses these issues by making sure that the development teams do not take on more work than they have proven to be capable of completing. This is the technique of using *yesterday's weather*. However much work the development team successfully completed last iteration is how much work the team is allowed to sign up for this iteration. This is always done at the beginning of the iteration and with the customer's full understanding.

The result is higher quality. Because the development team owns its estimates (someone else, such as the project manager, didn't dictate the estimates), the team is more confident of completing the work on time. The stress of the team members is reduced, because they have a manageable schedule.

XP Practice 14: Journaling

Journaling is a practice that we suggest adding to your XP toolkit. It is the other practice that we added to the standard 12.

Every day, you should spend about 15 minutes or so writing down what happened that day. This can be your thoughts, observations, or just general notes as to the day's progress. The idea is to write about whatever is on your mind that day.

Journaling can be an effective tool for finding positive and negative patterns within the XP team. You can use this information as a lessons-learned type tool. Also, journaling can be a way to collect your thoughts so you can communicate more effectively. You might even find it humorous when you review your journal after the project is over.

By now, you should start to see that the practices are very interdependent. Figure 1-1 shows that interdependency. Removing one or more practices will have a negative impact on the remaining practices. For example, if you choose not to practice test-first development, you will impact collective code ownership because the developers will not have the confidence that the tests would have given them when they change code.

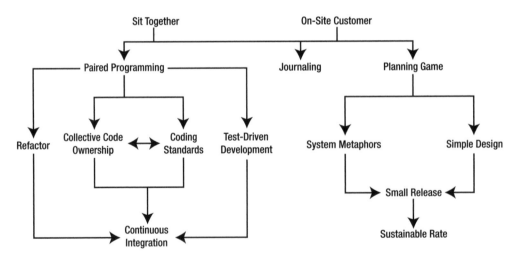

Figure 1-1. *The XP practices are interdependent.*

The bottom line is that all of these XP practices are good. These are practices that all developers start out wanting to exercise, but because of project deadlines and unforeseen circumstances, they are dropped in favor of completing promised system functionality.

XP believes that these practices are too valuable to let slide, regardless of the promised functionality.

Other Agile Methodologies

As we mentioned earlier, a good number of other Agile methodologies are available. These include Lean Development, Dynamic Systems Development Method, Adaptive Software Development, Crystal, Scrum, and Feature Driven Development (FDD). We include a brief description of each of these methods, since they all compete with XP.

Lean Development

Lean Development is a strategically oriented methodology created by Bob Charette. It is based on concepts introduced at Toyota and used for improving the production of automobiles. It centers around 12 principles:

- Satisfy the customer.

- Always provide the best value for the money.

- Success depends on active customer participation.

- Every Lean Development project is a team effort.

- Everything is changeable.

- Domain—not point solutions.

- Complete, don't construct.

- Deliver 80 percent of the solution today versus 100 percent of the solution tomorrow.

- Minimalism is essential.

- Needs determine technology.

- Product growth is feature growth, not size growth.

- Never push Lean Development past its limits.

Bob would say you are not doing Lean Development unless you are developing at one-third the cost, one-third the time, and one-third the defect rate.

Dynamic Systems Development Method

Dynamic Systems Development Method (DSDM) is an outgrowth from the Rapid Application Development (RAD) practices and iterative development. At the heart of this methodology are three core cycles that include functional modeling, design and build, and implementation.

A dedicated consortium develops this methodology. In order to use DSDM, you must sub-scribe to the organization that supports it. For the cost of your subscription, you receive manuals, training courses, accreditation programs, and such.

Adaptive Software Development

Adaptive Software Development (ASD) is a methodology founded by Sam Bayer and Jim High-smith. At the heart of ASD are three nonlinear overlapping phases: speculation, collaboration, and learning. The six basic characteristics of the ASD life cycle are mission-focused, feature-based, iterative, time-boxed, risk-driven, and change-tolerant.

Crystal

Crystal is a family of methodologies developed by Alistair Cockburn. The reason Crystal is a family is because Alistair believes that different kinds of projects require different kinds of methodologies.

Crystal has a graph with two axes. On one axis is the number of individuals on the project. On the other axis is the degree of consequence of error. Based on these two values, you can plot which Crystal family is appropriate for your project.

Scrum

Scrum was introduced at OOPSLA 1996 (the annual conference on object-oriented program-ming systems, languages, and applications). It focuses on incrementally building software in 30-day sprints. Scrum provides empirical controls that allow for development to occur as close to the edge of chaos as the development organization can tolerate. Establishing an open and honest relationship with the customer is the most important aspect of Scrum.

Feature Driven Development

Feature Driven Development (FDD) was developed by Jeff De Luca and Peter Coad. It focuses on short, iterative cycles of development (two weeks in length) that produce deliverable functional-ity. The five key FDD processes are to develop an overall model, build a features list, plan by feature, design by feature, and build by feature. Only the last two processes are done iteratively.

Is XP the Best Agile Method?

Just like XP, each of the Agile methodologies described in the previous section embraces the core Agile values. They have their own strengths and weaknesses as well. But, with the excep-tion of DSDM, they all lack specific detail as to how they are used and incorporated in the day-to-day life cycle of software development.

■**Note** Due to the restrictive nature of getting specific information concerning DSDM, it is not possible to tell how well defined the methodology is compared with XP.

Through its practices, XP does define the day-to-day development life cycle with roles and responsibilities. In fact, most (if not all) of the other Agile methodologies are now trying to sell their methodology with some portion of XP incorporated.

XP is not a silver bullet, however. It does not talk about business processes and their interaction with the XP processes. XP does not directly address deployment issues or activities. XP does not address the issue of managing multiple projects and their possible interdependencies.

While XP does have some gaps, it is currently the most comprehensive Agile software development methodology available. We leave it to you to further explore the relative merits of the other methods. We will now move forward with XP as our chosen method, with the caveats described in the next section.

When Shouldn't You Use XP?

Are there times when XP is not the right choice? Certainly there are. As you've learned, communication is a key value of XP. The larger the number of individuals directly involved in a project, the more difficult it gets to manage face-to-face communication. Therefore, it would seem that XP is not well suited for projects with extremely large teams. But note that our experience has indicated that large project teams are rarely, if ever, a good idea.

Another instance where XP might not be the best choice is for a project with requirements that will never change. This phenomenon is rare indeed, and we have not seen such a project in all our years of experience. Industry sectors such as space or military may fall into the solid requirements category.

Finally, remember that XP requires a significant amount of customer involvement. If your customer is not willing to invest the necessary amount of project time, you will be hard-pressed to successfully execute XP.

Summary

XP is one of several Agile methodologies. It has 4 core values, 15 principles, and 14 practices (since we added to the traditional 12 practices). The principles of XP build on the values of XP, and the practices build on the principles. Although there are many other Agile methodologies to choose from, none of them define software development practices to the level of XP.

In the next chapter, we will get started with XP. We will look at assembling an XP team and setting up a workspace (environment) for that team.

CHAPTER 2

∎∎∎

Assembling the Team

In this chapter, our goal is to help you build your XP team and your working environment. We will begin with a discussion of the team roles and responsibilities. Keep in mind that XP is very much a team activity, and picking the right team members is extremely important.

We'll then move on to describe the environment in which your XP teams will be working. Creating the right environment is almost as important as having the right team members, in the XP mind-set.

XP Roles and Responsibilities

In Chapter 1, you learned that XP focuses on the people, implying that the team is more important than the process or tools. While you can leverage processes and tools, the team members, with their collective experiences, will actually build the software. In this section, we will describe the roles of an ideal team.

In later chapters, where we walk you through the actual implementation of a project, we will address issues that can arise when some of these ideals aren't met by the people you have assembled. But right now, what's most important is that you understand what kind of team you are trying to create!

The Customer

The *customers* of an XP team are the project stakeholders that are requesting the software being built. They are responsible for defining, with the guidance of the rest of the team, the functionality that will go into the developed software. The customers are expected to be available during the entire development process. This is the most important requirement of the customers. If the customers are not part of the actual development process, it will be very difficult to succeed. The following are some of the responsibilities and expectations assigned to customers:

Drive the direction of the team: The customers make up the group that will define the product being developed. They are responsible for setting priorities and defining the business value of the project.

Answer developer questions: One of the most important roles of customers is to answer the questions of the developers. This is why customers must be available during the entire project. This way, the developers will be able to let the customers make a decision during development, as opposed to waiting until project delivery. When the customers are not available during the development process, developers will find their own answers.

Write stories: The customers are responsible for writing all of the project's user stories (which, for now, you can think of as single requirements; we'll explain user stories in detail in the next chapter). They are responsible for prioritizing these stories and for splitting a story when it needs to be simplified.

Declare stories complete: The customers are the only team members who have the authority to declare a story complete. They wrote the stories and are therefore responsible for their acceptance. The customers are also responsible for determining when a story can be moved to another iteration or dropped altogether.

Write acceptance tests: The customers are responsible for defining the project's acceptance criteria. They do this by writing acceptance tests for all of the project's stories. These acceptance tests will be written in parallel to the development work.

Accept the release: The customers are responsible for determining when a release is complete. They must decide whether the current release has true business value, according to their defined needs.

As you read through the description of the customer role, you may have gotten the impression that the customer functions like a project manager. This is not the case—a traditional project manager is focused on project plans and tracking the status of those project plans, while a customer is focused on the definition and development of the product.

The Development Coach

The XP *development coach* assumes the second most important role in an XP team. The customers have the most important role because, without them and their needs, there would be no project. The development coach is the person responsible for the team's adherence to the XP practices.

■**Note** Traditionally, XP has just a single coach role. We separate the coach role into two separate roles: the development coach and the business coach (described next). The traditional role of the XP coach is what we refer to as the development coach. In our experience, we have found that the addition of a business coach really increases the productivity of the customers, which ultimately helps the productivity of the entire team. If no business coach is available, developers and customers will go to the development coach when they have questions about the XP process.

Because the XP development coach is so important to the XP process, we recommend that you look for the following characteristics when identifying people to fill this role:

A thorough understanding of the XP process: The development coach should have a very good understanding of the XP process. This coach will be the point person for the entire XP team.

Professional development experience: The development coach should have professional development experience in many diverse areas. The coach should be able to answer some of the more common questions related to the technologies or programming languages being leveraged on the development project. The coach will also be expected to use his experience to explain how, why, and when XP works.

Leadership experience: The development coach should have leadership qualities and experience. If the development coach has true leadership abilities, the team will respect him, and the project is more likely to succeed.

The following are some of the responsibilities and expectations assigned to the development coach:

Get the developers and testers to adhere to the values and practices: This is the development coach's most important responsibility. The development coach is the team member that makes sure that the team is following the proper XP practices.

Assume a leadership role for the development and testing teams: The development coach is responsible for leading the team through the entire XP process. He will help the team resolve conflicts. He will work with the team in the tasking process.

Pair with other developers and testers as needed: The development coach is responsible for pairing with an unpaired developer, when necessary. This is one of the reasons a development coach must have the appropriate technical experience. However, while able to pair with other developers, the development coach cannot sign up for tasks.

The Business Coach

The XP *business coach* is probably the next most important role in an XP team. The business coach acts as the guide and representative of the team's customers. The business coach should have some knowledge and experience with the business domain and purpose of the project. Customers will go to the business coach when they have questions about the XP process.

Like the XP development coach, the business coach is very important to the XP process. Therefore, we recommend that you look for the following characteristics when identifying people to fill this role:

A thorough understanding of the XP process: The business coach should have a very good understanding of the XP process. She will be the point person for the team's customers.

Professional project/analysis experience: The business coach should have professional project/analysis experience in many diverse areas. She should be able to answer some of the more common project questions. The business coach will often set the expectations for the customers. This coach will also act as a conduit to the development team.

Some of the responsibilities and expectations assigned to the business coach include the following:

Assume a leadership role for the customers: The business coach will act as the guide to the customers. She is responsible for guiding them through the entire XP process, including release and iteration planning.

Assist customers in the story writing process: The business coach will lead the customers during the story candidate development and eventual story process, while not actually writing the stories. This coach must have a very solid understanding of what a story is and how stories are developed.

Assist customers in the acceptance test writing process: The business coach is expected to help the customers develop the appropriate acceptance tests, while not actually writing the tests, and assist with the automation of the developed acceptance tests.

We have run XP teams without a business coach, but we have found that having this extra coach guiding the customers can be invaluable to the team's success.

The Developer

The XP team *developers* are the actual programmers who will build the software. They will work with the customers to create the software product. Some of the responsibilities and expectations assigned to developers include the following:

Estimate stories: The developers are expected to estimate the level of effort required to complete each of the defined stories. They will estimate this length in *ideal days*. Ideal days are an XP unit of measure representing a focused day of development. We will describe ideal days in more detail in the following chapter.

Brainstorm tasks: The developers are responsible, as a group, for breaking down each story into manageable tasks and estimating the level of effort required to complete each of the defined tasks.

Develop unit tests: The developers are responsible for writing unit tests and automating these tests, whenever possible. As discussed in Chapter 1, test-driven development uses a unit testing approach, where you write the tests before you write the code.

Develop the tasks: The developers are responsible for developing the tasks that they undertake. Developers own their tasks and the estimates that go with them. No one else tells a developer what task to work on or how long that task will take to complete. This way, developers learn to refine their estimation skills and have the opportunity to select work that interests them.

Refactor the code: The developers are responsible for refactoring the code. This is part of collective code ownership—any developer can change any piece of code. When developers see code that needs to be refactored, they take the responsibility to do the work, instead of leaving it for someone else.

Communicate with customers when questions arise: The developers are expected to communicate with the customers whenever questions about a story or task arise. When the developers have a question, they have a conversation with the customer. If the customer is not available, the developers will find answers elsewhere or assume an answer. In either case, the developer may come to the wrong conclusion. Use your customers and use them often. Also, don't forget that XP is a team effort. Communication needs to happen with the whole team, not just the customers.

The System Engineer/Business Analyst

The *system engineers* and *business analysts* are the *subject matter experts* (SMEs) of the team. They are responsible for helping the rest of the team with project domain questions. The following are some of the responsibilities and expectations assigned to these SMEs:

Help the customers define intelligent stories: The SMEs of an XP project are responsible for helping the customers understand the domain of their business. They often are the only ones with the detailed knowledge that the customers need.

Act as a proxy for the customer: The SMEs can also act as a customer proxy, when the customer is not available. This responsibility must be approved by the customer prior to any decisions being made.

The Tracker

The *tracker* of an XP team is responsible for monitoring and reporting the progress of the development team. The tracker is often referred to as the conscience of an XP team, because he focuses on the honest status of the project. Some of the responsibilities and expectations assigned to the tracker include the following:

Collect development metrics: The tracker is responsible for recording the real level of effort for each developer task. The tracker will record this length in ideal hours.

Produce reports indicating the team's progress: The tracker is responsible for creating reports based on the collected development metrics. These reports should detail the current status of the development team.

Communicate the team's historical velocity: The tracker is responsible for communicating the historical velocity of the team. *Velocity* is a calculation used to determine the amount of work a team can accomplish in a single iteration. (Velocity is discussed in detail in the following chapter.) For example, the tracker may say to either the team or an individual something like, "Your most recent estimates were way too conservative." This kind of feedback helps team members to estimate their next set of tasks with a higher degree of accuracy.

Communicate the status of the team's progress: The tracker is responsible for providing the team status reports to the customer, coaches, and parties outside the team.

The Tester

The *testers* of an XP team are responsible for the software quality. They work with the customers to develop all of the acceptance tests and the test plan for the software being developed. Some of the responsibilities and expectations assigned to the testers include the following:

Ensure that a story is testable: The testers are responsible for making sure that each of the stories written by the customers is testable. This guarantees that each individual story's completion is quantifiable.

Assist the customers with writing acceptance tests: The testers will assist the customer in acceptance test writing. These tests are used to validate the completeness of each story.

Run the acceptance tests: The testers are expected to continually run the collection of acceptance tests. They are also expected to automate the running of these acceptance tests, if possible.

The Big Boss

The *big boss* of an XP team is responsible for the overall success of the XP project. His role begins at project inception and ends when the project is complete or has been terminated. Some of the responsibilities and expectations assigned to the big boss include the following:

Build the XP team: The big boss is responsible for assembling the entire XP team. The boss will often employ other resources, such as technical interviewers, when determining the qualifications of each team member.

Get the necessary equipment: The big boss is responsible for acquiring the tools and equipment that the team needs to be successful. These tools can be anything from software licenses to office furniture.

Assemble the team's workspace: The big boss is responsible for assembling the XP team's working environment. This could include anything from acquiring the necessary office real estate to getting the appropriate desk/cube environment built.

Act as a conduit to the outside world: The big boss acts as a conduit to anyone outside the XP team. This responsibility can also require the boss to act as a buffer from outside distractions, which can slow the team's progress.

Team Assembly

Here is the critical path to putting the team together:

- It starts with the big boss, of course.

- Next comes the customer. If you can't get at least one customer on the team, there isn't much point in going any further! That's an essential part of the XP mind-set.

- Once you have your customer, you need to have at least one experienced development coach and preferably one business coach. These coaches need to be experienced because they will have to defend XP throughout the development process.

- Then you will need to add the developers and testers to the team. Remember that in order to communicate effectively, you need to keep your XP team small. So, select between four and twelve developers and two testers.

- You can now select a tracker. The tracker role will be a part-time role and may be a person who is shared among two XP teams.

- The SMEs or business analysts can be added as needed, but don't forget to keep your team small. You can also bring in other experts as needed throughout the development process.

When you have identified all the players on the team, you will be ready to start the project. So, now let's take a look at your XP environment. Your assembled team needs the right place to work.

Your XP Environment

The physical XP environment can ensure that your XP team communicates effectively. It can just as easily, with a closed working environment, act as such a communications dampener that it can threaten the success of your entire project.

To allow effective team communications, you need to make sure that your physical environment is open and conducive to the sharing of information. This means that you need to knock down any barriers that impede communications. The space should be big enough for everyone to be located in it without feeling crowded, but still small enough that anyone can eavesdrop on anyone else's conversation from any point in the space.

In our opinion, the best XP environment should include low-walled cubes or open bullpens, a side conference room for private conversations and brainstorming sessions, and places that allow team members to get away from the process.

When we were assembling our XP environment, we were in the fortunate situation of having outgrown our current office and in the process of looking for new facilities. This allowed us to look for space that would suit our XP needs. We were able to find a space that was, with very little effort, a very practical XP environment. You can see the layout of our space in Figure 2-1.

As you can see, we have a very open environment that is surrounded by everything the team needs. At the center of our setting we have the common XP room, which consists of 16 workstations that easily accommodate paired programming. This room allows for easy communications from any location.

To the right of the common room is a full kitchen stocked with snacks, sodas, and, of course, some very strong coffee. It is very important to have these "essentials" nearby. These conveniences allow the team members to grab a soda or snack without having to wander too far from the action.

To the bottom left of our common room is a conference room, which is dedicated to the XP team. It allows the members to gain some privacy for phone conversations, brainstorming sessions, informal design sessions, or lunch.

To the top left of the common room is one of our most popular rooms: the Xbox room. This is where team members can get away from everything and play a quick video game. One thing to note about this room is that it has a door—while you do want to provide an escape, you don't want to disturb the other team members. Many people think that a video game room is a bit excessive, but we have found our team members to be very responsible with their time. They don't often want to blow their team's velocity for a few extra minutes of Halo.

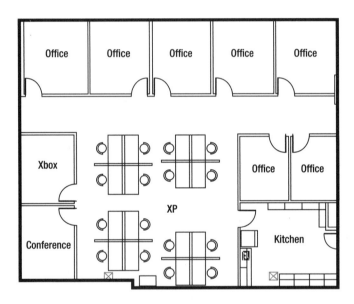

Figure 2-1. *The layout of our XP environment*

Finally, the perimeter of our common area contains a collection of offices that allow private work to be completed, when necessary.

That is all there is to it. We have found this space to be very effective and conducive to our team's needs.

Summary

In this chapter, we discussed two very important XP topics: the team and the environment. We covered the roles and responsibilities of the entire XP team. We highlighted the characteristics of the important XP roles of the development coach and business coach. Then we looked at the best order in which to assemble your XP team. Finally, we took a look at an effective XP working environment for that team.

In the next chapter, we are going to take a look at release planning, the place where you and your team's XP adventure will begin.

CHAPTER 3

■ ■ ■

Release Planning

In XP, an application or system is developed in the context of a project. A project defines all the features of the application or system.

Release planning happens at the beginning of each project. In XP, a project is broken up into one or more releases. Each release must deliver enough features to be of value to the business. As noted in Chapter 1, an XP practice is to do small releases, so you want to select just enough business functionality and set that as the target release.

A release represents a collection of user stories that provide the features. If the collection of user stories in the release is a subset of the total user stories for the whole project, then the project will have multiple releases.

The interval between releases is usually 30 to 180 days. Only the current release is planned in recognition of the changes that can occur on a project. It's quite possible that a business change would be significant enough to invalidate any plans of the future releases.

Release planning involves two phases: exploration and the planning game. In this chapter, we will look at both of these phases. You'll learn what the phase activities are and what value they provide to the software development life cycle.

The Exploration Phase

The *exploration phase* of release planning is where analysis, requirements gathering, and initial design occurs. The goal of the exploration phase is to get a high-level understanding of what the customer is requesting and to associate a development cost with those requests. This phase should last from a few days to a week. The more complicated the project, the longer it will take to explore.

All of the activities in this phase are kept at a high level, including requirements and design. Detailed requirements will be flushed out in iteration planning, which is discussed in the next chapter. The design will evolve as the project evolves, and as more information is gathered along the way. For the exploration phase, you need to know only enough to be able to give confident estimates.

■Note Within a release, the team will deliver production-ready code in even shorter cycles called iterations. Iterations allow a team to break up a release into more manageable chunks. Iterations should be a consistent length (two weeks is a good iteration length). Iterations are discussed in detail in Chapter 4.

The customer will define requirements as user stories. These user stories will be brief, which will shorten the time it takes to define all the features of the system. By keeping the stories at a high level, the team is able to cover many user stories in a short amount of time.

The end result of the exploration phase is a collection of high-level requirements captured as user stories. You will see a practical example of the exploration phase in Chapter 11.

User Story Writing

So, if a user story is roughly equivalent to a requirement, what's the difference? We have already stated that user stories are brief, but what does that mean?

A user story is so short that it fits on an index card. In fact, we highly recommend index cards as the tool of choice for capturing user stories for several reasons:

- Index cards are very tactile. You can pick up one feature, pass it around, and tear it up when it is no longer appropriate. Try doing that with a requirements document!

- Index cards are just the right size. It is difficult to get complex on a 3 × 5 index card. So, index cards drive simplicity.

- Index cards make it easy to prioritize user stories from 1 to n. If there are many user stories, trying to prioritize requirements in a document can be cumbersome.

The user story card has a title and a few sentences that describe the user story. The few sentences that describe the user story are there to serve as a reminder to the customer as to the story's purpose. It is often said that a user story is "a promise for a future conversation."

Each user story contains one and only one business feature. Look at Figure 3-1 for an example of a user story.

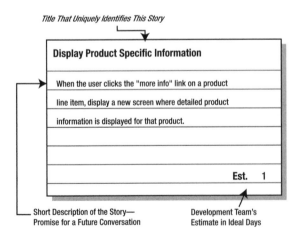

Figure 3-1. *Components of a user story*

Story writing is in contrast to the traditional approach, where each requirement is written out in painstaking detail. Traditional requirements are intentionally verbose in order to convey to the individual fulfilling the requirement the intent of the requirement. This level of detail is needed because the customer is not usually available to interpret the requirement.

Many newcomers to XP worry that the details of user stories will be lost if they are not captured completely. This fear can be overcome when you realize that there are many individuals involved in this phase who are all on the XP team. The chance that they will all forget an important detail is minimal. In addition, there is no rule that forbids people from taking notes to remind themselves of any information they feel is important. But most important to remember is that each user story will be revisited again in the iteration that it is selected to be a part of. During that iteration, details of the user story will be brought to bear again if needed.

Who Writes the User Story?

In XP, all user stories are written and owned by the customer. This restriction exists because the customer is the one responsible for interpreting the user story. If someone else wrote the user stories, the customer might not be able to understand what that other person wrote or meant by the choice of words. Having customers write the user stories also ensures that they will use terms they understand and increases the odds that they will be able to recall the purpose of the user story.

The analysis portion of the project happens as the user stories are being created. The customer starts to describe a certain feature of the system. As the customer describes the feature, everyone else starts asking questions to make sure they understand what is being requested. Many newcomers to XP don't believe that XP supports analysis, but in truth, it happens naturally and with everyone present.

What if a customer already has a set of requirements? Does the customer still need to create user stories? Yes! The customer can create user story candidates from the existing requirements. Then the user story candidates should be read to the whole XP team to determine if they are truly valid user stories.

What Makes a User Story Valid?

During story creation, two important questions are considered for each user story:

- The developers are deciding if they can estimate the user story.

- The acceptance testers are considering if they are able to test the user story.

If either of these groups cannot say yes to their respective questions, then the user story is not well defined.

Sometimes, the developers may say that they do not know if they can estimate the user story. This can be the case if the developers are unfamiliar with the aspect of the technology they plan to use or the business domain in which they are working. In these cases, the developers will tell the customer they will need to *spike* the user story.

The purpose of the spike is to give the developers some level of understanding as to what it will take to implement a user story. The developers generally break off from the rest of the team and investigate the requirement. The developers should try to find experts who can help them understand the solution. As a rule, the spike should not take more than a day or two to research.

User Story Examples

Perhaps the best approach to understanding user stories is to look at a few and decide if they are good or bad and why. Look at the user story in Figure 3-2. It has a title and a short description. It also has just one feature. But this user story is too vague. The developers will find it difficult to estimate, and the testers will not be able to test it.

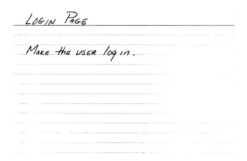

Figure 3-2. *A user story that is too vague*

How about the next example in Figure 3-3? It has the proper form. It is limited to one business feature. The problem with this user story is that it defines implementation details. What reason or advantage does the user story have defining the use of Dreamweaver and Tomcat? Does the customer really care? Probably not.

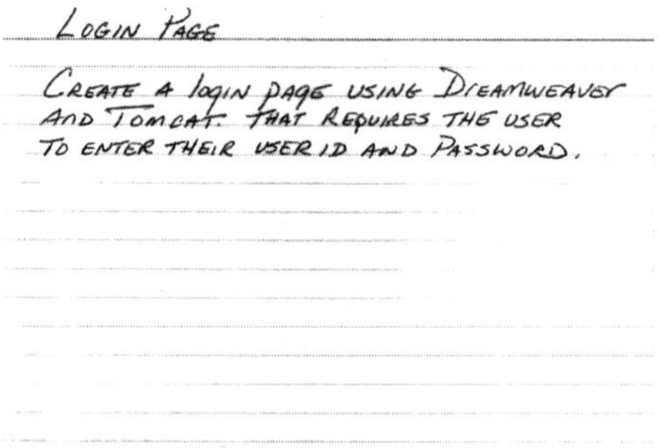

Figure 3-3. *A user story with too many details*

Figure 3-4 shows another attempt at the same user story. It has good form. Is it estimatable and testable? Yes! It looks like we may have got it this time.

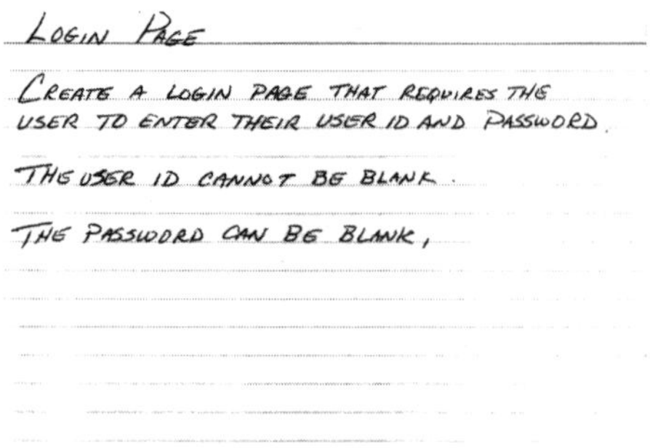

Figure 3-4. *An acceptable user story*

Figure 3-5 shows another user story. Is this a good story? Unfortunately, this user story has more than one business feature: both search and selection functionality.

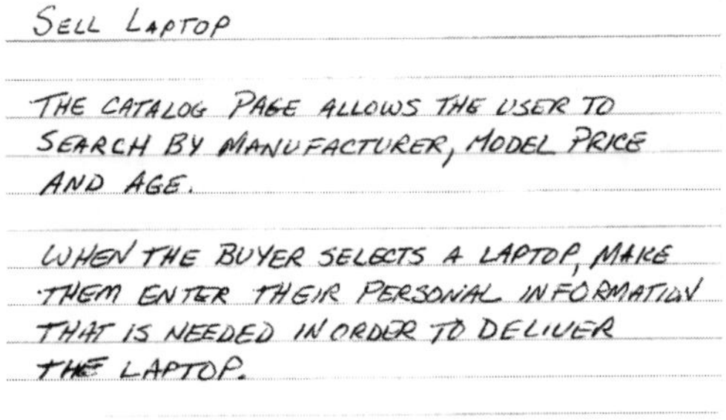

SELL LAPTOP

THE CATALOG PAGE ALLOWS THE USER TO SEARCH BY MANUFACTURER, MODEL PRICE AND AGE.

WHEN THE BUYER SELECTS A LAPTOP, MAKE THEM ENTER THEIR PERSONAL INFORMATION THAT IS NEEDED IN ORDER TO DELIVER THE LAPTOP.

Figure 3-5. *A user story with too many features*

The solution to the problem with the story in Figure 3-5 is to ask the customer to split the user story and create two new stories, with each feature captured on a different card. Figure 3-6 shows the user story for the search feature.

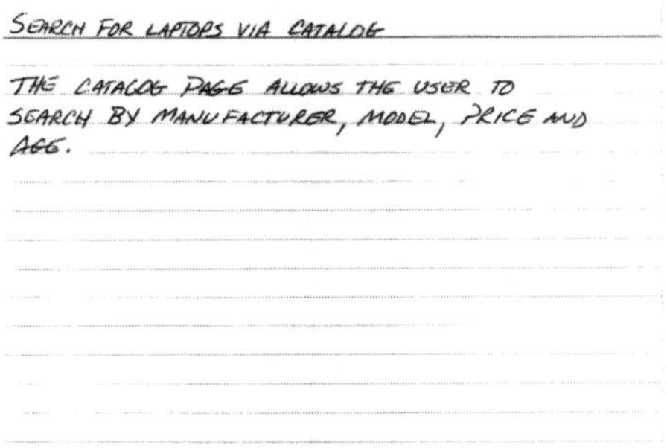

SEARCH FOR LAPTOPS VIA CATALOG

THE CATALOG PAGE ALLOWS THE USER TO SEARCH BY MANUFACTURER, MODEL, PRICE AND AGE.

Figure 3-6. *One user story resulting from a split*

Figure 3-7 shows the other user story split from the example in Figure 3-5, which focuses on gathering information about the buyer. Notice that it doesn't list all the data you would expect to gather. Remember that a user story is brief and a promise for a future conversation. When the developers implement this user story, they can get all the specifics at that time. If the amount of detail on the user story is adequate to estimate and test, that is all you need.

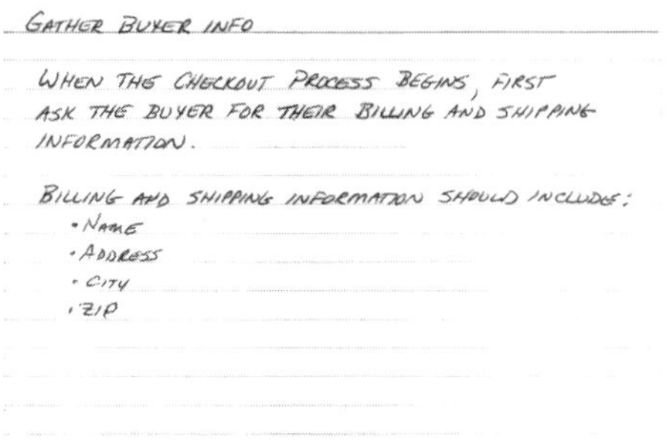

GATHER BUYER INFO

WHEN THE CHECKOUT PROCESS BEGINS, FIRST
ASK THE BUYER FOR THEIR BILLING AND SHIPPING
INFORMATION.

BILLING AND SHIPPING INFORMATION SHOULD INCLUDE:
• NAME
• ADDRESS
• CITY
• ZIP

Figure 3-7. *A user story with enough information*

Let's look at one more example. See if you can determine what is wrong with the user story in Figure 3-8. What do you know about the packing label printer? You probably don't know too much about it. Interfacing to this printer may be an issue. This user story is a good candidate for a spike.

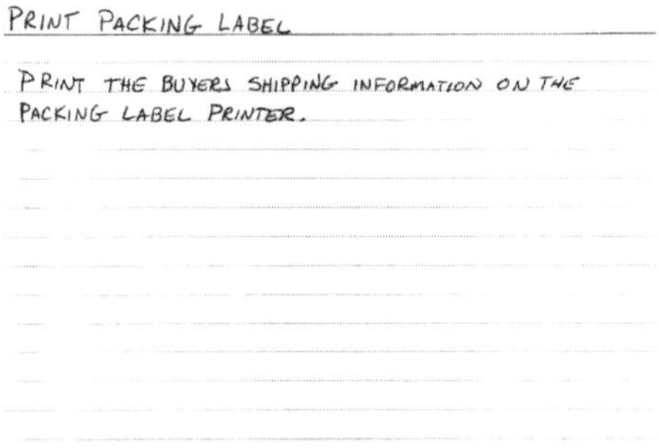

PRINT PACKING LABEL

PRINT THE BUYERS SHIPPING INFORMATION ON THE
PACKING LABEL PRINTER.

Figure 3-8. *A user story that is a candidate for a spike*

User Story Estimating

User story estimating is where the developers on the XP team work collectively to estimate each user story at a high level.

All estimates are in *ideal days* and referred to as *story points*.

What's An Ideal Day?

Have you ever seen a pig fly? How about if you never had to go to another meeting, answer your phone or e-mail, or be interrupted in any way? What if you only had to write code? That is an ideal day. Have you ever had one? More than likely, you have never had one and you never will.

So why do we estimate in ideal days? You can never predict all the things that will rob time from your day, so why even try. Your team and its individual velocity, which we will discuss in the upcoming "Velocity Determination" section, has already been adjusted to account for an average amount of activities that will rob each of the team member's time. If the reality is you have fewer distractions than average, then you should finish your work early and you will be able to ask for more work. Your velocity will go up as a result. If the reality is you have more distractions than the average, the opposite will happen.

The main point to keep in mind is that you should not pad your estimates. Estimate for what your experience tells you. You don't need to pad for paired programming, stand-up meetings, or any other noncoding activities.

Why Are Estimates in Terms of Story Points?

Estimates are in story points because you don't want to get hung up on days and hours. One story point is equivalent to one ideal day. When you think in terms of story points, they are just points—no more and no less. The developers work collectively to estimate because none of them know which user stories they will be working on, so it is important that they all agree.

The Planning Game

The *planning game* phase is when the customers go shopping. The customers have defined the features they need, in the form of user stories, and the developers have assigned a cost to each user story. Now it is time to select the stories to be delivered.

Story Prioritization

The customers will start by prioritizing the user stories they have defined. Priority is from 1 to *n*, not buckets of high, medium, and low. The reason you don't prioritize stories as high, medium, or low is that most customers will lump the majority of their user stories into the high category. After all, if a user story wasn't important to them, they would not have brought it up in the first place. The idea here is to help the customer decide in what order the user stories are important.

Velocity Determination

Now that all of the user stories are prioritized, you need to decide how many of these stories can be completed. To do this, you determine your team's *velocity*.

The XP team's tracker determines the team's velocity based on the release date selected and the number of full-time development resources assigned to the project. You can also use part-time development resources and their associated velocity, but the majority of the development resources should be full-time. Part-time resources can be unpredictable because their priorities are split and a conflict often results.

The team's velocity is a product of the team's history. In other words, whatever the team members successfully completed in the last release is what they get to sign up for in this release. This value is represented as the number of story points the team can sign up for in the release.

If the team does not have history or certain team members do not have history, you can calculate the team's initial velocity. To do this, first calculate the velocity of a single iteration with this formula:

(*No. of Developers/Load Factor* × *Length of Iteration in Business Day*) (Truncated) = *Iteration Team Velocity*

For example, for eight developers with a two-week iteration, the calculation is as follows:

$(8/4 \times 10)$ (Truncated) = 20

In this example, you take the number of developers on the project and divide them by 4. The 4 is the load factor used to account for all the time developers spend doing activities other than coding for their own task (such as attending meetings, communicating through e-mail, paired programming, and such). Then you multiply the result of that division by the length of the iteration. The length of the iteration is in working days. Then truncate the result of that calculation, and you get the iteration velocity for the team. Here, the result is 20 ideal days in the iteration.

To get the release velocity for the team, you take the iteration velocity and multiply that number by the number of iterations you plan to have in your release. Do not include any iterations that will not have development coding in them, such as an iteration for just testing or setting up the development environment. The formula looks like this:

No. of Development Iterations in a Release × Iteration Team Velocity = Release Team Velocity

So, using the previous calculation of 20 ideal days as the iteration team velocity, for six development iterations, the velocity calculation is as follows:

$6 \times 20 = 120$

The result is 120 ideal days in the release.

Please don't mistake velocity for an indicator of how fast a team is completing work. Velocity is an estimating tool used to help teams and individuals refine their estimates to match reality. A team's velocity should never be used to compare two or more teams or individuals.

User Story Selection

At this point, each user story has a declared number of story points, and the development team has a declared number of story points that the team can complete in a release. Now the customer will need to select a collection of user stories that do not exceed the total number of story points allocated to the team.

Customers will often start by selecting their highest priority user stories, but they are not restricted to this selection method. In fact, when they try to balance the number of story points allowed for the release, they will more than likely need to select some user stories that have a low story point estimate and lower priority.

The Release Plan

The end result of release planning is a release plan that consists of a set of user stories that have story points associated with them. Given that much information, the customers should be able to determine if they want to proceed with the project or not.

The most beneficial point of the release plan is that they have arrived at a conclusion in about a week. Had they taken a traditional approach to software development, they would just be getting started with the analysis phase. So this approach has already resulted in a reduction of cost for the customer.

Summary

Release planning has two phases: an exploration phase and a planning game phase. During the exploration phase, analysis is conducted and requirements are gathered in the form of user stories. As each user story is created, developers are asking if the user story is estimatable and testers are asking if the user story is testable. The user stories are also estimated in the exploration phase. If the user story is too big, it is split. If the user story is not estimatable, because the developers don't know how to estimate it, the user story is spiked.

During the planning game phase, the customer prioritizes the user stories from 1 to n. The tracker will declare the number of story points that can be completed in the release. The customer will select user stories that do not exceed the number of story points declared by the tracker. If the user stories selected have enough business features to be valuable, then the project continues.

The next chapter moves on to the next step: iteration planning.

CHAPTER 4

■■■

Iteration Planning

Assuming the customer chooses to continue the project after release planning, your next activity is iteration planning. Equipped with the knowledge from the release plan, you are ready to plan an iteration. Iteration planning breaks the overall release plan down into a manageable set of user stories, known as the iteration plan, that the development team can focus on and deliver to the customer in a very short period of time. Iteration planning usually takes less than a day to complete.

Whereas release planning is all about understanding the high-level requirements of the customer, iteration planning is about understanding a detailed subset of those requests. As you will learn in this chapter, iteration planning has all the usual pieces you would expect to find in a planning process: features, level of effort, and scope.

Iteration Velocity

The first step in selecting which user stories are going to be included in the iteration plan is to declare the number of story points that are allowed. This will be based on the number of story points successfully completed last iteration. Always use historical data as the basis for what you should do today. If you don't have any history, then you can calculate *one time only* the team's iteration velocity based on the formula given in the previous chapter.

The overall goal of using the team's iteration velocity is to prevent team members from signing up for more work than they can reasonably complete within the iteration.

Story Subselection

Once the number of story points allowed for the iteration has been declared, the customers select which user stories to include in the iteration. They start with all the user stories included within the release plan. Usually, customers pick their highest priority user stories first.

During this time of user story selection, the development team will help the customers understand where synergies exist between user stories. This will help the customers choose stories that might benefit each other. Of course, the final decision as to which stories are selected is up to the customers.

Task Determination

One of the activities of iteration planning is to determine the detailed tasks of each story selected for the given iteration. These are the tasks that are needed in order to complete the story. The tasks are written down on the back of the user story index cards.

The following are some examples of tasks:

- Build customer database table.

- Create initial login screen.

- Create credit card validation web service.

This activity is carried out by the development team working together as a group. Everyone on the development team should understand what each task involves and why. This is necessary because the developers are not sure which tasks they will do yet. Therefore, the developers need to be prepared to sign up for and estimate any given task. Additionally, this approach takes advantage of all the experience of the team.

The customers are involved during this activity to ensure that their needs are accurately interpreted. The customers are not expected to understand all the details that the developers are describing, but they should have a general understanding of what the developers are planning to do. Also, the customers are needed during this activity to answer questions concerning the stories they have selected for this iteration. Remember that a story is a promise for a future conversation, and this is one of those times that the customer will need to fulfill that promise.

Task Assignment and Estimation

After all the stories for the iteration have had their tasks defined, developers select tasks. Each developer assigns his name to a given task, and then applies his estimate in ideal hours (described shortly) to the task.

Developers own their estimates. Although a developer may solicit feedback from other developers, asking their opinion for an estimate, the developer who owns the estimate has the final say.

It is recommended, but not dictated, that developers should try to sign up for all of the tasks on a given story. This helps reduce the dependencies that can occur when you have multiple developers working on a single story. You can recognize this type of dependency if you have one developer waiting for another developer to complete a given task on a given story before the first developer can start her task on the same story.

Task Points and Task Point Velocity

The level of effort for each task is in the form of *task points*, which represent *ideal hours*. Like an ideal day, an *ideal hour* is a fictitious amount of time when you have no interruptions and you are able to just write code. Also like an ideal day, it is impossible to determine ahead of time what activities and events are going to take away from the time you would have spent writing code. A typical approach is to pad your estimate with time in an effort to account for the unexpected. Using an ideal hour, you don't have to do this with every task, as the ideal day already tries to account for the unexpected. So, the ideal hour estimate should reflect the time you believe it would take to complete the tasks if you did not have to deal with anything else.

Each developer is assigned an individual *task point velocity*. This is the number of task points the developer successfully completed last iteration. If the individual has not completed a previous iteration and therefore does not have a history, his individual task point velocity is calculated one time only. Thereafter, the developer's velocity will be based on his history from the prior iteration. Here is the formula for calculating the velocity of an individual:

No. of Hours in Workday × Length of Iteration / Load Factor (Truncated) = *Individual Velocity*

The length of the iteration is in business days. The load factor accounts for other, nondevelopment, activities. The individual velocity is in ideal hours. For example, the following uses an 8-hour workday with a 2-week iteration and a load factor of 4:

$8 \times 10 / 4 = 20$

The result is 20 ideal hours in the iteration for the developer.

Task Sign-Up

Developers can select tasks in a number of ways. One method is to go round-robin, where each developer signs up for one task at a time. This approach gives developers an equal chance to select tasks that they want.

Another method is to post all the tasks up on the wall by story and allow the developers to make a mad dash all at once until they use up all of their individual task points. While this approach can provide a significant amount of entertainment, it can also be difficult for some less aggressive developers to have a chance to sign up for tasks they prefer.

Having developers sign up for their own tasks has several advantages:

- The developers have a greater level of commitment and buy-in.

- The team's skill level as a whole will increase, and as a result, the team will be more flexible and produce higher-quality work.

- It removes the roadblock of only a given individual being able to work on certain types of tasks because that developer is the only one who possesses that skill.

Some managers and customers worry that developers will be signing up for tasks that they are not necessarily skilled at in an effort to learn new skills at the customer's expense. In reality, developers tend to work on tasks with which they feel comfortable. The few developers who do sign up for work outside their skill set tend to be the more advanced developers and are more likely to be successful in fulfilling those tasks. Also, developers are pairing together, and one of the pair is likely to be familiar with the chosen task. Ideally, a developer who wants to try her hand at a task that is outside her current skill set would ask to pair with a more experienced individual who signed up for that task.

Iteration Balancing

After the developers estimate and sign up for tasks, you may have one of the following situations:

- Some tasks remain unassigned. This happens when all the developers have used all of their allotted task points and some tasks are still not chosen. This is an indication that the initial high-level estimates that the development team assigned to the user stories using story points were too optimistic.

- All the tasks are assigned, but some developers still have individual task points available. This is an indication that the initial high-level estimates that the development team assigned to the user stories were too conservative.

Either case is a natural result of the task assignment process. Remember that the estimate given for the user stories during release planning were just high-level estimates. The purpose then was to get a general idea of how big the user stories were, so everyone could have a sense of how much work was being requested. The task-level estimates are much more detailed, and therefore more refined and granular.

But what should happen when there are more tasks to complete than signed up for or there are more individual task points available? The answer has to do with balancing the iteration.

One of the fundamental goals of XP is keep the development team from overcommitting to the amount of work they can reasonably accomplish in the given time frame. In the case where there are outstanding tasks, the customer will need to either split the user stories with partially assigned tasks or remove the user stories entirely from the iteration plan. In the case where there are developers with additional tasks points available, the customer will need to add more user stories to the iteration plan.

Either way, the team is not allowed to exceed its allotted number of task points. If the team members were allowed to do this, they would be effectively saying to the customer that they are knowingly accepting more work than they can accomplish in the given time frame. It is never advisable to take this approach, even if you think you can accomplish the overallotment of tasks using overtime. If something unexpected should come up during the iteration, and the team is already overexpended, you are most likely doomed in your attempt to successfully complete the iteration.

The Iteration Plan

The end result of iteration planning is, of course, a plan—a course of action that the team can act on to deliver concrete business features. The iteration plan should not include more work than the team can reasonably complete within the iteration time frame.

The iteration plan allows the team members to focus on a reasonably sized target that they can complete in a short amount of time, giving them a feeling of success and accomplishment. Building upon successive iterations will give the entire team the feedback needed to indicate progress.

Summary

Iteration planning involves selecting a subset of user stories, defining tasks, and then estimating and assigning tasks. The development team can focus on the resulting iteration plan and deliver features to the customer in a very short period of time.

The subset of stories selected for the iteration plan should be the customer's highest priority user stories, so that the team is delivering the most important business features to the customer. The user stories selected for the iteration plan are broken down into detailed tasks. Developers sign up for and estimate tasks. If there are outstanding tasks that have not been signed up for or there are outstanding task points, the iteration plan must be balanced so that the team is not overcommitting its time.

The next chapter will guide you through an iteration. It will show you how to take the iteration plan and apply it to the team's day-to-day activities.

■ ■ ■

CHAPTER 5

The Iteration

This chapter covers the day-to-day activities of an XP team. This process is better known as an *XP iteration*. So, first we'll look at precisely what an iteration is, and then discuss the common activities it involves: design sessions, stand-up meetings, paired programming, coding, testing, tracking, and coaching.

What Is an Iteration?

An iteration has the following features:

- It contains a subset of user stories taken from the release plan.

- It begins immediately after the iteration planning.

- It is equal in length to all other iterations within the same release, usually two weeks in duration.

The iteration involves the entire XP team: customers, developers, testers, and so on. Everyone is an active participant from the iteration's beginning to end. Experts and other individuals who are not dedicated to the team can be brought in as needed.

Design Sessions

Right after you finish your iteration plan is a good time to have a design session. This will help start out the iteration by getting everyone on the same page.

You can't develop software without some type of design to guide your efforts. But instead of creating a comprehensive and time-consuming design up front, you should build on the high-level design you created during the release plan. Focus on the part of the design that applies to the work associated with the current iteration.

When you have other design sessions throughout the iteration, try to grab some or all of the developers right after the stand-up meeting (described next). Keep the design session focused and brief—no longer than an hour. You can repeat this as much as needed throughout the iteration, so you don't have to solve all of the world's problems in a day. You can address just the problems you are currently facing.

Stand-Up Meetings

You will have a stand-up meeting at a regularly scheduled time every workday of the iteration. Mornings usually work better than afternoons. Everyone should attend the stand-up. Keep the stand-ups brief—no longer than 15 or 20 minutes.

Some other XP resources talk about giving individual status during the stand-up. A better use of the stand-up is to bring up issues and concerns. Don't try to solve the issues or concerns in the stand-up; just have someone accept responsibility and handle it after the stand-up. Taking this approach keeps stand-ups brief, which is one of their major goals.

Use the tracker's data to generate visual graphs and charts to show status, and then hang them up in the XP space. You can also make these graphs and charts available via the Web for those individuals who are not able to attend the stand-up at the XP space.

Stand-ups are also a great opportunity to use your journal. You can check your journal immediately before the stand-up to jog your memory about issues you ran into the day before or something cool that you discovered. One XP team we know used this time to announce new objects that were available for other developers. You can keep track of that type of information in your journal, too.

Paired Programming

After the stand-up meeting, and after the design session if you have one that day, you need to pair up before you start developing. When selecting a pair, it is good to find someone who can complement your skill set and preferably has expertise in your task.

It is also important to switch who you are pairing up with multiple times during the day. This will facilitate the transfer of knowledge that makes paired programming a worthwhile activity, as well as give you different perspectives on a given solution to a task.

A good rule of paired programming is that you cannot refuse to pair with someone who asks you. You can delay pairing with someone so you can finish working on something you have already started, but you need to set a reasonable time frame to pair with the person requesting your assistance. Keep this time frame to a few hours at most.

Pairs need to be active, not passive. If you are driving (the one on the keyboard), you need to make sure your pair is following along with what you are typing and understands what you are doing. The same goes for the pair who isn't driving. If the developer on the keyboard is not communicating what she is doing and why, you need to ask her to stop and explain.

Test, Code, and Refactor

After you have your pair and understand the design you are working on, you are ready to implement a solution. Start by getting the most current source code from the source code control system. During this process, you will check out code from the source code control system and add new code into the source code control system as needed.

But before you dive in and code the solution, you need to think about how you will test to the solution. This will help you know when you have completed the task successfully. This will also help you formulate a cleaner design, as you will be forced to think through the solution before you implement it.

Building Tests and Refactoring

When building the tests, start with a testing framework such as NUnit. The NUnit tool, covered in Chapter 7, comes with a Getting Started document and a good tutorial, which are helpful at this stage. Think about the expected outcomes that should occur when you run the tests, and don't forget to build both positive and negative tests. These tests will not only demonstrate that the code you developed meets the requirements, but it will also show other developers how to use the functionality you created. This is a simple example of self-documenting code.

Don't leave out the team testers either. They can help you think of tests you might not consider. This will benefit the testers, too, because they can reuse some of your tests in the acceptance tests they create with the customer.

When you have written one or more tests, you are ready to implement the code the test will run against. Implement just enough code to make the tests pass. As you write more tests, you will expand the code to support those tests.

As the code builds, you will start to see areas where you can refactor. Keep in mind that refactoring does not change the overall behavior of the system—it just enhances the design and understanding of the code.

■**Tip** If you need to learn more about refactoring, read Martin Fowler's book, *Refactoring: Improving the Design of Existing Code* (Addison Wesley, 1999). This is one of those skills you will need in your tool belt during your entire career.

You should use iterative development throughout this process. It is a repetitive process: test, code, refactor, test, code, refactor, and then test; then code and refactor some more. Use this iterative cycle to build up system functionality.

Never go home with code checked out. So, make small incremental changes that are less time-consuming to complete. Check in code at least every one to two hours, or more often if you can. The more you can do this, the better. This will help you develop an incremental and iterative work style that will benefit you throughout your career.

When all your tests are passing and you are ready to check in the code, you should pull down the latest version of the system from the source control system, merge it into your existing code, and run all the tests again, for the entire system, to make sure nothing is broken. If everything is good to go, you are ready to check in your source code and continue.

■**Note** It is best to run an integration build on a workstation that is dedicated to integration builds after you have checked in your updates. We will be covering such a tool in Chapter 9: CruiseControl .NET.

Also, don't forget to notify the team tracker when you have completed a task. The tracker will come around a couple of times each week to ask you about your progress, but there is no reason you cannot be proactive and give the tracker an update sooner, especially when you have good news, like that you've completed a task or a story.

Keeping the Customer Involved

As you code, test, and refactor, you should keep one more thing in mind and practice it often: XP requires a high level of customer involvement. Don't forget to take advantage of this fact.

When you have a question about a task or story, go ask the customer. This is one way the customer stays engaged during the iteration process. Another way to keep the customer engaged is to show him what you are working on early and often. When you are ready to create a screen, grab the customer and have him sit with you as you lay out the design. This will save you a lot of time, because you won't need to go back later and adjust the layout because the customer wanted something else.

Acceptance Testing

When the iteration starts, the first thing the testers do is meet with the customer and define what the acceptance tests are for the user stories selected for the iteration.

Acceptance testing happens in parallel with development and should be decoupled as much as possible. If the acceptance tests are ahead of development (test features not yet implemented but scheduled to be implemented within the current iteration), that is fine. The acceptance tests will fail at first, but they make an excellent target for the developers as they bring those features online.

Each acceptance test will indicate when a user story has been successfully completed from the customer's point of view. Business analysts, systems engineers, and subject matter experts will assist in this area as well. The developers are testing from a functional and integration level, but it is the acceptance test that represents testing from the user's perspective. The customer is ultimately responsible for defining the acceptance test criteria.

■**Note** New information may be discovered during the creation of acceptance tests. When this happens, the customer needs to immediately communicate the new information to the rest of the XP team.

The acceptance testers will automate the acceptance tests as close to 100 percent as possible. Acceptance tests that cannot be automated must be manually verified. The acceptance tests should also be set up to run whenever an integration build occurs. In most cases, you will need to stage or build data to set up the correct system state to test the system. Automate as much of the data setup and creation as possible, too.

Tracking

The tracker should visit all the developers on the team about twice a week, asking two questions:

- How much actual time have you spent on the tasks you have signed up for?

- How much ideal time (in ideal hours) do you estimate you still need?

This means that the developers must keep track of their time—the actual time they spend working on the tasks they chose to do. This isn't elapsed time, but actual time spent working on their selected tasks. Specifically, it does not count time spent pairing with other developers on their tasks, reading e-mail, going to stand-ups, and any other activities.

■Tip Here is one more use for your journal. Keep track of the time you spend on development tasks in your journal. Then, when the tracker comes by for status, you can easily refer to your journal for this data.

The tracker will use the information that she collects to build charts and graphs that will communicate the progress of the team. If the data indicates that the team is not going to complete all the user stories selected for the iteration, then the coach will need to call a steering meeting with the entire team. In that steering meeting, the customer will ultimately decide what to do. Possible solutions are to split user stories to make them less complicated or to remove user stories entirely from the iteration.

The data may indicate that all the user stories will be completed and accepted prior to the end of an iteration. If this is the case, then the steering meeting can be used to select additional user stories for the iteration. The goal is to maximize all the team's resources without overcommitting.

Coaching

Coaching during an iteration is a full-time activity. While development coaches are not allowed to sign up for user story tasks, they can and will sit down with other developers and work with them throughout the iteration. Along the same lines, business coaches will not write acceptance tests, but they will help the customers develop them. Both coaches should keep a watchful eye on their respective groups to make sure everyone is participating and following the XP practices.

An excellent development coach friend of ours, Paul Karsten, developed five key questions every development coach should ask:

- What task are you working on?
- Where is your pair?
- Do you have a unit test for that?
- Did you talk with the customer about this?
- Can you describe your design/solution?

These five questions help the development coach understand the behavior that is occurring on the team and expose negative and positive behavior that may need to be addressed.

Similarly, the business coach should ask a set of questions when the customer has a problem:

- Which user story are you working on?
- Is this a new user story?
- What is the acceptance test for this user story?
- Have you talked with the rest of the XP team about this?

- Are you ready for the next iteration planning/release planning session?

- Can you describe this user story?

The purpose of these questions is to help guide the team member back on to the XP path without being too overbearing. The answers to these questions will help the business coach understand the behavior of the team and what might need to be corrected.

Summary

This chapter covered the basics of day-to-day activities within an iteration. All team members should be involved throughout the iteration and should understand their role and responsibilities. If any team members are unsure what they should be doing, the coaches should step in to help them understand their role.

The outcome of the iteration should be completed user stories that are unit and acceptance tested. As a result, the features delivered should be of production quality. That doesn't mean the features should be deployed to production—more features are most likely needed before that happens. It just means the code could be released to production if needed.

This completes your introduction to XP. The next section of this book will cover software tools that you should set up in your development environment to assist you in your Agile development. These tools will provide your team with a unit testing framework, a simulation framework, an automation process, and refactoring assistance. We will start with the unit testing framework: NAnt.

PART 2

XP Tools

CHAPTER 6

Build Environment Tool: NAnt

When working in a team environment, you will find it helpful to build the source code you are developing in an automated fashion. This will allow your team members to receive consistent feedback on the integration of their source code. Without a constant and automated build process, your team members may not remember to do their builds consistently on their own. This is especially true when the team gets overburdened.

One of the tools that will assist you in automating your build process is NAnt. By itself, this tool doesn't automate the build process for you, but it does help you define what and how you want to build your source code.

You might be asking, "Doesn't Visual Studio .NET already build my source code for me?" Yes, but while Visual Studio .NET will build your source code, Visual Studio .NET is not easily automated.

This chapter will not cover all the aspects of NAnt, but it will give you enough information and direction so that, when coupled with the tools covered in the following chapters (NUnit, NMock, and CruiseControl.NET), you will be able to create an environment ready for automated builds.

What Is NAnt?

NAnt is essentially a tool that lets you define components of your build and their dependencies. The components are called *targets*. For example, checkout may be a target (component) of your build process where your source code is checked out of a source code repository. You might also have another target, compile, that is dependent on the checkout target. In this case, the compile target should not do its thing until the checkout target has first done its thing.

NAnt uses an XML formatted file to define these components. As such, there are XML tags that come with and are specific to NAnt. You will use these tags to form the NAnt build file.

A working example should help with your understanding of the usefulness of this tool. We'll examine a simple NAnt build file and test it in this chapter. But first, you need to install NAnt.

Note The lead developers for the NAnt project are Gerry Shaw, Ian MacLean, Scott Hernandez, and Gert Driesen. Visit http://nant.sourceforge.net for more details about NAnt.

Installing NAnt

Installing NAnt is a very straightforward process. Here are the steps:

1. Download the latest version, which you will find at `http://nant.sourceforge.net`.

2. Extract the downloaded zip file's contents to your desired location on your local system.

3. Add the NAnt `bin` directory to your system path. On Windows XP, open the System applet in Control Panel, select the Advanced tab, and then click the Environment Variables button. Double-click the Path entry in the System Variables section. Either at the very beginning or the very end of the Path's Variable value string, enter the location where you unzipped NAnt. Make sure to include the `bin` directory, which is just inside the location where you unzipped NAnt. An example of what your path string might end with is shown in Figure 6-1.

Figure 6-1. *Adding NAnt to your system path*

You can test your NAnt installation by launching a command-line window, entering `nant -help`, and pressing Enter. You will see the version of NAnt that you have installed, along with a bunch of usage information if your installation was successful, as shown in Figure 6-2.

```
C:\>nant -help
NAnt 0.84 (Build 0.84.1455.0; net-1.0.win32; release; 12/26/2003)
Copyright (C) 2001-2003 Gerry Shaw
http://nant.sourceforge.net

NAnt comes with ABSOLUTELY NO WARRANTY.
This is free software, and you are welcome to redistribute it under certain
conditions set out by the GNU General Public License.  A copy of the license
is available in the distribution package and from the NAnt web site.

Usage : NAnt [options] <target> <target> ...
Options :

  -defaultframework:<text>        use given framework as default (Short format: /
k)
  -buildfile:<text>               use given buildfile (Short format: /f)
  -v[erbose][+|-]                 displays more information during build process
  -debug[+|-]                     displays debug information during build process

  -q[uiet][+|-]                   displays only error or warning messages during
build process
  -find[+|-]                      search parent directories for buildfile
  -indent:<number>                indentation level of build output
  -D:<text>                       use value for given property
  -logger:<text>                  use given type as logger
  -l[ogfile]:<filename>           use value as name of log output file
  -listener:<text>                add an instance of class as a project listener
  -projecthelp[+|-]               prints project help information
  -nologo[+|-]                    surpresses display of the logo banner
  -h[elp][+|-]                    prints this message

A file ending in .build will be used if no buildfile is specified.

C:\>
```

Figure 6-2. *Checking your NAnt installation*

Once you have a working installation of NAnt, you are ready to create a build file.

Creating a Build File

The NAnt build file is a configuration file of sorts. It tells NAnt what to build and which order and dependencies to use for the build. Listing 6-1 shows a very basic implementation of an NAnt build file.

Listing 6-1. *A Basic NAnt Build File*

```xml
<?xml version="1.0"?>
<project name="My Great Project" default="test">
  <property name="basename" value="MyGreatProject"/>
  <property name="debug" value="true"/>

  <target name="clean">
    <delete>
      <fileset>
        <includes name="${basename}-??.exe"/>
        <includes name="${basename}-??.pdb"/>
      </fileset>
    </delete>
  </target>

  <target name="compile">
    <csc target="exe" output="${basename}-cs.exe" debug="${debug}">
      <sources>
        <includes name="${basename}.cs"/>
      </sources>
    </csc>
  </target>

  <target name="test" depends="compile">
    <exec program="${basename}-cs.exe" basedir="."/>
  </target>
</project>
```

Understanding the Build File

The build file contains many different XML tags, each representing some aspect of the build. The build file defines the targets for the build.

■**Note** Covering all the tags that NAnt supports would take an entire book. We will cover only a few of the more important tags here. Refer to the documentation that came with NAnt for thorough coverage of the tags.

Build File Tags

The sample build file in Listing 6-1 starts with an XML declaration because build files are XML-based files. All well-formed XML-based files include this as the first line of the file.

The next tag is the `project` tag:

```
<project name="My Great Project" default="test">
```

The `project` tag's purpose is to define one and only one project for this build file. The `project` tag also defines a `name` attribute and a `default` attribute. The `name` attribute will be used in the output from the build as NAnt runs. The `default` attribute tells NAnt which target listed in the build file should be run if a target is not specified on the command line when NAnt is invoked. In other words, if you just type `nant` in a command-line window while you're in a directory that contains a build file, you have invoked NAnt without a build target. Specifying a build target is covered in the next section.

Next, two `property` tags are defined:

```
<property name="basename" value="MyGreatProject"/>
<property name="debug" value="true"/>
```

The `property` tags are somewhat like variables. The property consists of a name, which is represented by the `name` attribute, and a value represented by the `value` attribute. Once a property has been defined, you can reference the property's value by using the following form:

```
"${basename}"
```

The reference uses double quotation marks because a well-formed XML attribute value is always enclosed in a pair of double quotation marks.

The benefit of defining a property comes when you use its value multiple times throughout the same build file. If you need to change its value, you make the change only in one place. If you used the explicit value rather than a defined property, you would need to change the value everywhere you used it in the build file.

The next major tag used in Listing 6-1 is the `target` tag. The `target` tags are defined with `name` attributes, which must be unique within a build file. When NAnt is executed with a specified target or no target (in which case, NAnt uses the defined default target), it locates that target by name in the build file. If the target cannot be located, the output shows an error stating that the specified target was not found.

Once the target has been located in the build file, NAnt checks to see if the target has any dependent targets defined via a `depends` attribute. If dependent targets are defined, those targets are executed first before processing of the current target continues.

Build File Targets

The sample build file in Listing 6-1 defines three targets: `clean`, `compile`, and `test`. Only the `test` target has a dependent target, which is the `compile` target. Therefore, when the `test` target is executed, the `compile` target will be executed prior to any processing of the `test` target.

The `clean` target's purpose is to remove files that are generated when you build this project. It will be helpful sometimes to remove these generated files before you build the project so that you are sure you are starting from scratch and that all the source files truly generate the expected project you have defined.

```
<target name="clean">
  <delete>
    <fileset>
      <includes name="${basename}-??.exe"/>
      <includes name="${basename}-??.pdb"/>
    </fileset>
  </delete>
</target>
```

The delete tag inside the clean target tag tells NAnt that the build should delete something from the file system. What is deleted is defined using the fileset tag. The fileset is further defined by setting which files should be included. This is essentially filtering which files to include in the file set. Here, the build file is specifying any files that have a filename that starts with the value you have defined in the basename property, followed by a dash, then any two characters, and finally a file extension of either .exe or .pdb. With this information, the delete tag is able to select only a specific set of files and leave everything else untouched.

The compile target defines what should be compiled and how it is to be compiled.

```
<target name="compile">
  <csc target="exe" output="${basename}-cs.exe" debug="${debug}">
    <sources>
      <includes name="${basename}.cs"/>
    </sources>
  </csc>
</target>
```

The csc tag invokes the .NET Framework command-line compiler. The target attribute of the csc tag tells the csc compiler that it should create an application as output, with a name composed of the basename property's value followed by a dash, the characters cs, and finally the file extension of .exe. The debug attribute tells the csc compiler to compile with debug turned on or off, based on the value set by the debug property.

As with the delete tag of the clean target, the compile tag needs an identification of the files to use for compiling. The sources tag specifies which files to include. The build file in Listing 6-1 specifies that any file that starts with the basename property's value and ends with a file extension of .cs should be compiled.

The last target in Listing 6-1, test, is used to run the application. This will let you know if your project is able to be executed successfully.

```
<target name="test" depends="compile">
  <exec program="${basename}-cs.exe" basedir="."/>
</target>
</project>
```

This target uses an exec tag, which will execute any command you would normally be able to execute from a command line. The program attribute specifies the name of the executable, and the basedir attribute specifies in which directory the command should be executed. A value of . (dot) for the basedir attribute indicates the current directory.

Saving the Build File

You need to save your build file in the same directory as the source file it will build against. NAnt automatically looks for a build file that ends with a file extension of .build when it runs. Save the build file shown in Listing 6-1 and name it default.build.

■**Note** If you have chosen to hide file extensions (the default) in Windows Explorer, you will not see the .build file extension when you view the file via Windows Explorer. If you used Notepad to create the build file, you should enclose the filename in double quotation marks to prevent Notepad from appending a .txt file extension to the end of the filename.

Testing the Build File

Listing 6-2 shows a basic C# source file you can create and save in order to test the sample build file and see how NAnt works.

Listing 6-2. *A File for Testing NAnt*

```
public class MyGreatProject {
  static void Main() {
    System.Console.Writeline("This is my great project.");
  }
}
```

Make sure you save the source file in Listing 6-2 in the same directory as the NAnt build file you just created. Save this file with a filename of MyGreatProject.cs. Then open a command-line window and navigate to the directory that has both the default.build NAnt build file and the MyGreatProject.cs C# file. Execute the NAnt build file using the default target by typing nant on the command line and pressing the Enter key. You should see output similar to what is shown in Figure 6-3.

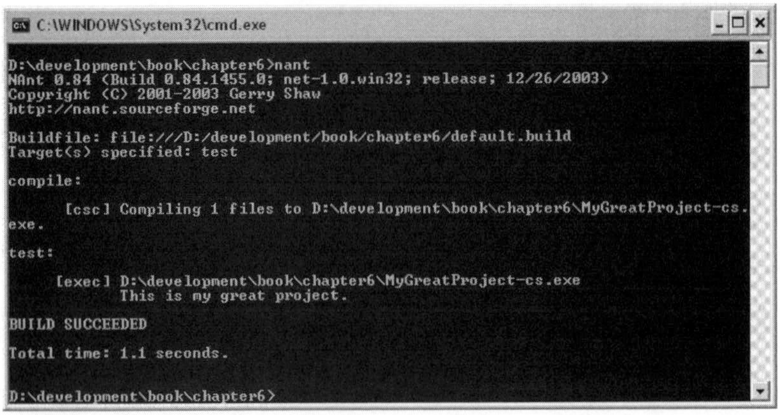

Figure 6-3. *Testing the NAnt build file*

Try playing around with the various other targets defined in the build file. For example, you can have NAnt run the `clean` target by entering `nant clean` on the command line.

Summary

This chapter has just begun to scratch the surface of what you can do with NAnt. Its purpose was to help you understand some basic aspects of an NAnt build file and to give you an idea of what you might do with such a tool. There hasn't been anything here that automates the build process by itself. You need to couple NAnt with a few other tools to set up automated builds. One of these tools is NUnit, which is the subject of the next chapter.

CHAPTER 7

Test Environment Tool: NUnit

The previous chapter introduced NAnt, a build environment tool. Now you will extend your XP tool set to include a unit testing tool.

Unit testing tools allow you to build tests at a functional level (at the method-calling level) of your application. This lets you see if the methods you are creating are working in the manner you expect. Another benefit of a unit testing framework is that it allows other developers to see how your application is expected to work at a functional level. Other developers can see what criteria (parameters) you are expecting to receive for a given call to a given method, coupled with actual data and any criteria you are expecting to return. The data passed to the application method is set up in either a special method of the unit testing framework or directly within the call from the unit testing framework to the application method.

You will be creating both positive tests (tests that you expect to pass) and negative tests (test that you expect to fail). These positive and negative tests indicate the boundaries of what is expected by the called method in your application and help developers understand those boundaries.

This chapter will cover the basics of using NUnit to create unit tests. You will then see how to integrate your NUnit test with NAnt.

What Is NUnit?

NUnit is the C# version of the unit testing framework originally made popular by Erich Gamma and Kent Beck.

If you will recall from the first part of the book, test-first is a key XP practice. NUnit is the tool you will use to implement that practice. With the help of the NUnit tool, you will develop the skills to create a unit test first, based on your ideas about how a particular application method should and should not behave. Then you will create the application method that satisfies your understanding of the method.

You should also recall that one of the four key values of XP is feedback. NUnit provides significant feedback by telling you if your application is behaving in the manner you expected. If your unit tests are failing (not a negative test that you expected to fail, but either a positive test you expected to pass but didn't or a negative test you expected to fail but didn't), you know immediately that something is wrong, and you have a good indication as to where it might be wrong.

Every time you discover behavior in your application that you did not expect (otherwise known as a bug), you should first create a unit test that reproduces the bug. The unit test should fail until you fix the actual bug. This will help you determine when the bug is fixed and also help you test for the bug in the future to make sure it does not come back. Once you have written a unit test to reproduce the bug, you should then fix the method call until the unit test passes.

As you build up unit tests, the goal is to have 100 percent of the application tested from a functional level. With this type of unit test coverage, any developer who needs to modify the application will be able to do so with greater confidence. Developers know that if their changes adversely affect the application, the unit tests will start failing.

A key point to remember is to always make changes in small increments. This is important because if you should introduce a bug, you want to have the smallest amount of code to look through to find the bug. If you make many changes at once, you will increase the amount of places and code you will need to look through to find the bug.

In this chapter, you will work through an example of building a unit test. If you have not yet followed the instructions in Appendix A, follow the steps in the next section to install NUnit.

■**Note** NUnit is developed by James W. Newkirk, James C. Two, Alexei A. Vorontsov, Philip A. Craig, and Charlie Poole. Visit www.nunit.org for more details about NUnit.

Installing NUnit

You will be using NUnit and the associated unit testing framework extensively when working through the examples in Part 3 of this book. Step-by-step installation and setup instructions for those later examples are included in Appendix A. For this chapter, you will not need to set up NUnit to work with Visual Studio. You should follow the steps here for installing and setting up NUnit if you have not already completed the procedures outlined in Appendix A.

1. Download the installer for the NUnit tool from www.nunit.org.

2. Locate the NUnit installer you just downloaded and double-click it to install the tool. You can accept all the standard defaults when prompted.

3. When you have completed the installation successfully, you should see an icon for NUnit on your desktop (the default). Double-click the icon to test your installation and make sure that the NUnit tool launches successfully. You can exit the tool after it has launched.

When you launch the NUnit tool from your desktop, you see a GUI version of NUnit. From this GUI, you can select which tests or groups of tests you would like to run. The GUI will provide feedback to you as the test or tests are running via colors and text. Green means that the test succeeded. Red means that the test failed. Several tabbed panes on the right side of the GUI give you text feedback as well. This includes error messages and a list of tests that did not run.

For the exercises in this chapter, you will be using a command-line version of the NUnit tool. In the later chapters of the book, you will be using the GUI version, which you will integrate with Visual Studio. See Appendix A for details on integrating the GUI with Visual Studio.

Building a Unit Test

When building unit tests with NUnit, you need to create two classes that are in the same namespace, using any text editor you prefer. One class will contain the unit tests that you will create, and the other class will contain the application method you create and are going to test against.

Let's say you need to build a class that will behave like an airline reservation system. One of the operations (methods) that an airline reservation system needs to perform is to schedule flights. (To keep this example simple, we're ignoring many aspects of a reservation system.)

Creating the Test Class

Using a test-first approach, you start by creating a test class using the same namespace as the actual class you will create. Listing 7-1 shows the code for the sample test class.

Listing 7-1. *A Basic NUnit Test Class*

```
using NUnit.Framework;
using System;

namespace Reservation
{
  [TestFixture]
  public class ReservationTest
  {
    private Flight denverToHouston;

    [SetUp]
    public void Init()
    {
      denverToHouston = new Flight(4332, "DEN", "IAH", 80);
    }

    [TearDown]
    public void Destroy()
    {
      denverToHouston = null;
    }

    [Test]
    public void ScheduleFlight()
    {
      DateTime departure = new DateTime(2005, 2, 11, 8, 25, 0, 0);
      DateTime arrival = new DateTime(2005, 2, 11, 11, 15, 0, 0);

      denverToHouston.ScheduleFlight(departure, arrival);
      Assert.AreEqual(departure, denverToHouston.Departure);
      Assert.AreEqual(arrival, denverToHouston.Arrival);
    }
  }
}
```

First, you must specify that you will be using the NUnit framework in this class:

```
using NUnit.Framework;
```

Next, you specify that this class is a testing class. In Listing 7-1, this is indicated by the [TestFixture] attribute above the class declaration. This is how NUnit is able to determine that this class is intended as a test class. A class that is tagged as a test fixture needs to contain at least one test case indicated by a method with the [Test] attribute above the method signature. If the test class has more than one test case defined, each test case will be run in the order specified in the test class.

The test class may also contain other special NUnit methods that are tagged with identifying attributes above their method signatures. Two such methods are declared in Listing 7-1: a setup method and a teardown method.

The Setup Method

The setup method follows the class declaration. It is indicated by the [SetUp] attribute above the method signature. When NUnit sees this method, it will run whatever code is inside it before running every test case defined elsewhere in the test class. The setup method is very handy when you need a known state of data defined before each test case is run. There should never be more than one setup method in a test class.

Listing 7-1 defines a Flight object that has a flight number of 4332, a departure airport of "DEN", an arrival airport of "IAH", and that the flight seats 80 passengers.

The Teardown Method

The opposite of the setup method is the teardown method. This is indicated by a method with the [TearDown] attribute above it. The teardown method will be called after each test case is run. This allows you to reset the system back to a known state before another test case is run. There should never be more than one teardown method in a test class.

In Listing 7-1, the teardown method simply sets the Flight object to null so that it can be disposed of when the system needs to reclaim memory.

The Test Case

Finally, Listing 7-1 has a test case defined by a method with the [Test] attribute above it. This tells NUnit the test case to run.

The sample test case declares two dates with timestamps. One date indicates the day and time of departure, and the other date indicates the day and time of arrival.

The test case then calls the ScheduleFlight method of the Flight object that was created in the setup method, passing the dates of the departure and arrival. You know the Flight object exists because the setup method is called before each test case.

The real testing part of the test case happens when you check that the departure and arrival dates that you set up for the flight equal the departure and arrival dates that you defined. The NUnit testing framework has special Assert methods that allow you to check things like equality. The example checks that the flight's departure date equals the defined departure date. If the dates are not equal, the test case fails. If the dates are equal, the test case passes. In either situation, the test class would continue on to the next test case and so on, until all the test cases have been run.

Listing 7-1 defines only one test case. Of course, in development, you will add more test cases to this class as you build more and more functionality.

You should also remember to create negative test cases in addition to the positive test cases. The test case in this example is a positive test case because it defines data that you expect the application method (ScheduleFlight) to accept successfully without error. A negative test case would define data that you expected the application method to not accept, such as a departure date that is several days after the arrival date. In this case, you would want to enhance the ScheduleFlight method to check for such a situation and throw an appropriate exception, so it may be handled in a graceful manner.

Creating the Application Class

Now that you have a test class with a test method defined, you need to create an application class that has a method that satisfies the test. You should define the minimal class and associated method that will satisfy your test. When you have done that, you are ready to build and run the test. If the test completes successfully, you are ready to create another test case, followed by enhancements to your application class, and then rebuild and run your tests again. This continues over and over throughout the development cycle.

Listing 7-2 shows the minimal code for the sample application class.

Listing 7-2. *A Basic Application Class*

```
using System;

namespace Reservation
{
  class Flight
  {
    private int flightNumber;
    private string originatingAirport;
    private string destinationAirport;
    private int numberOfSeats;
    private DateTime departure;
    private DateTime arrival;

    public Flight(int flightNumber,
                  string originatingAirport,
                  string destinationAirport,
                  int numberOfSeats)
    {
      this.flightNumber = flightNumber;
      this.originatingAirport = originatingAirport;
      this.destinationAirport = destinationAirport;
      this.numberOfSeats = numberOfSeats;
    }
```

```
    public void ScheduleFlight(DateTime departure, DateTime arrival)
    {
      this.departure = departure;
      this.arrival = arrival;
    }
    public DateTime Departure
    {
      get
      {
        return this.departure;
      }
    }

    public DateTime Arrival
    {
      get
      {
        return this.arrival;
      }
    }
  }
}
```

This application class defines a constructor that takes a set of parameters that are used to initialize the object. This constructor is called in the setup method of your test class. The ScheduleFlight method is the application method called from your test case in the test class. The two properties defined in the application class are also called from the test case method of the test class.

With the application class in Listing 7-2, you now have just enough defined to build the source code successfully and to run your test to see if it passes. In the previous chapter, you used NAnt to build your application. You will do the same here.

Integrating with NAnt

To run the sample unit test, you will create an NAnt build file similar to the one you created in the previous chapter (Listing 6-1). An important difference it that you will change the test target so that it uses NAnt tags that are specifically for running NUnit tests.

Set up a new folder on your local workstation named Chapter7NUnit. In that folder, save both the test class and the application class defined in Listings 7-1 and 7-2. Name the test class ReservationTest.cs and the application class Flight.cs. Then create the build file shown in Listing 7-3 and name it default.build. Save the build file in the same location as the two class files.

Listing 7-3. *NAnt Build File for the Sample Unit Test*

```xml
<?xml version="1.0"?>
<project name="NUnit Testing" default="test" basedir=".">
  <property name="basename" value="ReservationTests" />
  <property name="debug" value="true" />

  <target name="clean">
    <delete>
      <fileset>
        <includes name="${basename}.dll" />
        <includes name="${basename}.pdb" />
      </fileset>
    </delete>
  </target>

  <target name="compile">
    <csc target="library" output="${basename}.dll" debug="${debug}">
      <sources>
        <includes name="ReservationTest.cs" />
        <include name="Flight.cs: />
      </sources>
      <references>
        <include name="System.dll" />
        <include name="System.Data.dll" />
        <include name=" C:\Program Files\NUnit 2.2\bin\nunit.framework.dll" />
        <include name=" C:\Program Files\NUnit 2.2\bin\nunit.extensions.dll" />
        <include name=" C:\Program Files\NUnit 2.2\bin\nunit.util.dll" />
        <include name=" C:\Program Files\NUnit 2.2\bin\nunit.tests.dll" />
      </references>
    </csc>
  </target>

  <target name="test" depends="compile">
    <nunit2>
      <formatter type="Plain" />
      <test assemblyname="${basename}.dll" />
    </nunit2>
  </target>
</project>
```

In this build file, the clean target has been changed from the one in Listing 6-1 to remove artifacts specific to this build.

The compile target has been modified to create a C# library instead of an executable. If you look at the application class you created, you will see that it does not define a main method. Therefore, you cannot create an executable (.exe) because there is nothing for the Windows operating system to execute. You add a references tag to tell the csc compiler where to find the NUnit library (.dll) files. If you don't define these, the compile will fail since the csc compiler knows nothing about NUnit without a reference.

The test target is where you integrate NUnit into the NAnt build. This target is using NUnit-specific tags that are already integrated into NAnt. The formatter subtag allows you to determine how you would like the results of the unit test to be output. In this example, you indicated "Plain", so that you can see the results in the command-prompt window when you run NAnt. The next subtag, test, is where the unit testing really happens. You are specifying where (assembly name) the unit tests are stored. In the example, the unit test is bundled together with the class library you created (.dll) when you ran the compile target.

Running the Build File

Now you are ready to run the build file. Open a command-prompt window and navigate to the directory where you saved the files in Listings 7-1, 7-2, and 7-3. Then execute nant to run the build. Figure 7-1 shows the command and results in the command-prompt window.

■**Note** Later, when you automate the build using CruiseControl.NET in Chapter 9, you will output the test results as XML to a file that will be read to determine success or failure of the test in an automated fashion.

Figure 7-1. *Results of the sample unit test*

Summary

In this chapter, you started to get your feet wet with unit testing and test-first development. Don't worry if this approach to development doesn't feel quite right yet. You will be practicing these skills throughout Part 3 of the book.

On the NUnit website, you'll find a downloadable Quick Start document (www.nunit.org/index.php?p=quickStart&r=2.2), which covers the basics of developing test cases in NUnit. This document explains many useful types of test cases.

By coupling the NUnit tool with the NAnt tool, you have created a way of calling your unit tests for your application without needing to invoke the NUnit tool yourself. This will become important when you get to the CruiseControl.NET tool (in Chapter 9), which will automate NAnt and NUnit for you.

In the next chapter, you will add another important tool to your XP tool set, NMock. NUnit will take advantage of the NMock objects that you will create to test parts of your application that work with other resources, such as databases and legacy systems that are outside your application.

■ ■ ■

CHAPTER 8

Simulation Environment Tool: NMock

So far, you have a build tool that allows you to configure what is to be built and how to build it (NAnt, covered in Chapter 6). Your tool set also includes a unit testing tool to provide rapid feedback on the quality of the code you are writing and the validity of your assumptions about how that code works (NUnit, Chapter 7).

A standard philosophy of all Agile methodologies is to build for what you know today. Many times, you will need to build a part of your application that will depend on other resources that you don't have access to today. To handle parts of the system that may not exist or to emulate your external systems, you can use a simulation tool. NMock is such a tool.

This chapter describes how to use NMock to create mock objects and use them in your tests.

What Is NMock?

The developers of NMock describe it as a dynamic mock-object library for .NET. So what is a *mock object*, and what makes it dynamic?

To understand what a mock object is, you need to understand its purpose and what it does. A mock object's purpose is to solve a problem that arises when you start to develop any application that has a sizable amount of scope and/or complexity. You will find that you need to break up the solution for building the application into small pieces. This helps to simplify the development of the application and to make it easier to focus on various aspects of the application, without getting bogged down in the details of other areas of the application.

However, it may become difficult to create tests for the portion of the application that you are focusing on because of dependencies with resources that are either internal or external to your application. Internal resources are those other areas of the application that are not currently the focus. External resources are resources that are not readily available, such as databases, legacy applications, hardware, or new systems that are still in development.

One approach is to use stub code within your application that will act as a buffer between this portion of the application and the other resource. In object-oriented terms, this is often referred to as *mediation*. These objects that you create mediate to and from these other resources. While the stub code can be written in such a way to provide this layer of mediation, the stubs themselves are not intended to assist testing. To make the stubs viable for your testing purposes, you would need to add test-specific code to the stub. You would also need to add code to set up certain conditions that the other resource might represent. And you would need to add code to interpret the interactions that occurred and the specific results of those interactions. This amounts to a significant amount of code that does not apply to the actual implementation. In the actual implementation, you will test at a more abstract level.

For example, while testing, you may want to know how many times a certain method was called. This might be good to know for testing purposes but not for implementation purposes. So, you could create your stub with this testing code in it, but you would need to remember to either remove it or comment it out later. As more and more test-specific code creeps into the stub, the code becomes less manageable and it's more difficult to understand what the actual implementation is all about.

Mock objects were designed to address the issue of the test code in the stub approach. Mock objects focus only on the testing aspect of the mediation and leave out the implementation details of the real objects that you will develop later. This is accomplished by creating an interface that both the mock object and the true implementation will inherit.

The mock objects also assist in the testing by providing a convenient way to preload the expected results of the calls to the interface, determining what method was called and not called and if any method was called more times than expected. All of these conveniences will help you narrow down where a bug might be when you have a bug.

The dynamic part of NMock has to do with how the mock objects are created. Most objects in your application will be created by using a class that explicitly defines the object. Using NMock, you will not need to explicitly write a class for each mock object you will employ. Instead, you will create an interface that describes the methods that you want to implement. Then, when you use this interface in conjunction with NMock, an object will be created for you on the fly at runtime. This is the dynamic aspect of NMock.

In this chapter, you will work through an example of creating a mock object to represent an external system. Before you dive into the example though, you will need to install NMock.

■**Note** NMock is a tool developed by a group of ThoughWorks developers that includes Joe Walnes, Chris Stevenson, Owen Rogers, Nat Pryce, and Steve Freeman. For more information about NMock, visit `http://nmock.truemesh.com/index.html` and `http://confluence.public.thoughtworks.org/ display/NMock/Home`.

Installing NMock

Start your installation by downloading the latest version of NMock from `http://nmock.truemesh.com/index.html`. Just click the Download link on the left side of the web page and follow the instructions for downloading.

After you have successfully downloaded NMock, extract the zip file and place the extracted contents anywhere on your local workstation (such as in a `C:\development\tools\` directory).

That is all there is to the installation.

Creating a Mock Object

Let's assume that there is a customer system that is external to the reservation system we worked with in Chapter 7. You will create a mock object for this customer system.

Defining an Interface

You will start by defining an interface for this customer system, as shown in Listing 8-1.

Listing 8-1. *Customer System Interface*

```
using System;
using System.Collections.Generic;
using System.Text;

namespace Reservation
{
  interface ICustomer
  {
    string GetSeatPreference(int frequentFlyerID);
    string GetFlyerClass(int frequentFlyerID);
  }
}
```

Here, you define an interface that has two methods. The first method retrieves the seat preference of a frequent flyer who is identified by a frequent flyer ID. In this case, a seat preference is either a window or an aisle. The second method retrieves the frequent flyer's status level, such as base, elite, or premier.

Notice that this is an ordinary interface. There is nothing here that associates this interface with NMock.

Save this class and all the following files in a folder together. Name this class ICustomer.cs.

Creating the Classes

The part of your reservation application that will need this external customer resource is a reservation class that finds the best seat available on any given flight for a customer, based on that customer's status level and seat preference. To be able to build and test your reservation logic, you also need to enhance the Flight class from the previous chapter and create a new Seats class.

The Reservation Class

Listing 8-2 shows the Reservation class. Save this class with the name Reservation.cs.

Listing 8-2. *The Reservation Class*

```
using System;
using System.Collections;
using System.Collections.Generic;
using System.Text;

namespace Reservation
{
  class Reservation
  {
    private int frequentFlyerID;
    private Flight scheduledFlight;
    private ICustomer customerAccess;
    private ArrayList availableSeats;

    public Reservation(Flight scheduledFlight,
                                  int frequentFlyerID,
                                  ICustomer customer)
    {
      this.frequentFlyerID = frequentFlyerID;
      this.scheduledFlight = scheduledFlight;
      this.customerAccess = customer;
      this.availableSeats = scheduledFlight.AvailableSeats;
    }

    public Seat GetBestAvailableSeat()
    {
      Seat bestSeat = null;
      ArrayList preferredSeats = AvailableSeatsByPosition();

      foreach (Seat availableSeat in preferredSeats)
      {
        if (bestSeat == null)
        {
          bestSeat = availableSeat;
        }
        else
        {
          int rowNumber = availableSeat.RowNumber;

          if (bestSeat.RowNumber > rowNumber)
          {
            bestSeat = availableSeat;
          }
        }
      }
    }
```

```
      return bestSeat;
    }

    private ArrayList AvailableSeatsByPosition()
    {
      ArrayList matchingSeats = new ArrayList();
      string customerSeatPreference =
          this.customerAccess.GetSeatPreference(this.frequentFlyerID);
      string customerFlyerClass =
          this.customerAccess.GetFlyerClass(this.frequentFlyerID);

      foreach (Seat availableSeat in this.availableSeats)
      {
        if (availableSeat.Location.Equals(customerSeatPreference))
        {
          SeatClass seatClass = availableSeat.SeatType;

          if (customerFlyerClass.Equals("BASE") &&
              (int)seatClass < 3)
          {
            continue;
          }
          else
          {
            matchingSeats.Add(availableSeat);
          }
        }
      }

      return matchingSeats;
    }
  }
}
```

The constructor method for this class takes a Flight object, an integer that represents the frequent flyer ID, and the interface in Listing 8-1 as parameters to the constructor.

Once the reservation has been set up, a call to the GetBestAvailableSeat method can be made. This method will try to locate the best available seat on the flight passed in for the customer, represented by the frequent flyer ID also passed in. A private method is also defined to select the subset of seats still available on the flight, based on the customer's seat preference and status level.

The Flight Class

Listing 8-3 shows the Flight.cs file, which is an updated version of the Flight class you created in Chapter 7 (Listing 7-2).

Listing 8-3. *The Flight Class*

```
using System;
using System.Collections;
using System.Collections.Generic;
using System.Text;

namespace Reservation
{
  class Flight
  {
    private int flightNumber;
    private string originatingAirport;
    private string destinationAirport;
    private ArrayList availableSeats;
    private DateTime departure;
    private DateTime arrival;

    static void Main(string[] args)
    {
    }

    public Flight(int flightNumber,
                        string originatingAirport,
                        string destinationAirport,
                        ArrayList availableSeats)
    {
      this.flightNumber = flightNumber;
       this.originatingAirport = originatingAirport;
      this.destinationAirport = destinationAirport;
       this.availableSeats = availableSeats;
    }

    public void ScheduleFlight(DateTime departure, DateTime arrival)
     {
      this.departure = departure;
      this.arrival = arrival;
    }

    public DateTime Departure
    {
      get
      {
        return this.departure;
      }
    }
```

```
    public DateTime Arrival
    {
      get
      {
        return this.arrival;
      }
    }

    public ArrayList AvailableSeats
    {
      get
      {
        return this.availableSeats;
      }
    }

    public void ReserveSeat(Seat reservedSeat)
    {
      if (this.availableSeats.Contains(reservedSeat))
      {
        this.availableSeats.Remove(reservedSeat);
      }
    }
  }
}
```

What has changed here from the previous version is that you have declared a new attribute called availableSeats, which contains a list of available seats for the flight. You have also created property accessors for this attribute. This class also has a new method called ReserveSeat, which, when passed a seat that exists in the availableSeats list, will reserve that seat by removing it from the list of available seats for this flight.

The Seat Class

Listing 8-4 shows the code for the Seat class. Save it in a file called Seat.cs.

Listing 8-4. *The Seat Class*

```
using System;
using System.Collections.Generic;
using System.Text;

namespace Reservation
{
  enum SeatClass
  {
    FirstClass = 1, BusinessClass, EconomyClass
  }
```

```
class Seat
{
  private int rowNumber;
  private char rowLetter;
  private string location;
  private SeatClass seatType;

  public Seat(int rowNumber,
                   char rowLetter,
                   string seatLocation,
                   SeatClass seatClass)
  {
    this.rowNumber = rowNumber;
    this.rowLetter = rowLetter;
    this.location = seatLocation;
    this.seatType = seatClass;
  }

  public int RowNumber
  {
    get
    {
      return this.rowNumber;
    }

    set
    {
      this.rowNumber = value;
    }
  }

  public char RowLetter
  {
    get
    {
      return this.rowLetter;
    }

    set
    {
      this.rowLetter = value;
    }
  }

  public string Location
  {
    get
```

```
    {
      return this.location;
    }

    set
    {
      this.location = value;
    }
  }

  public SeatClass SeatType
  {
    get
    {
      return this.seatType;
    }

    set
    {
      this.seatType = value;
    }
  }
 }
}
```

In the Seat class, you define a seat on an airplane with a row number (1, 2, 3, and so on), seat letter (A, B, D, and so on), a location (window or aisle), and a seat type (first class, business class, or economy class). You have defined an enumeration to make using seat class types a little easier.

Incorporating NMock

This all looks great so far, but you still haven't written any code that uses a mock object. Remember that mock objects come into play when you are unit testing. So, next you are going to expand the unit test class from the previous chapter and incorporate the NMock tool. Update the ReservationTest.cs class (Listing 7-1) from the previous chapter as shown in Listing 8-5.

Listing 8-5. *The ReservationTest Class with a Mock Object*

```
using NUnit.Framework;
using System;
using System.Collections;
using System.Collections.Generic;
using System.Text;
using NMock;
```

```csharp
namespace Reservation
{
  [TestFixture]
  public class ReservationTest
  {
    Flight denverToHouston;
    ArrayList initialSeats;

    [SetUp]
    public void Init()
    {
      initialSeats = new ArrayList();
      Seat seat1A = new Seat(1, 'A', "WINDOW", SeatClass.FirstClass);
      initialSeats.Add(seat1A);
      Seat seat1B = new Seat(1, 'B', "AISLE", SeatClass.FirstClass);
      initialSeats.Add(seat1B);
      Seat seat1D = new Seat(1, 'D', "AISLE", SeatClass.FirstClass);
      initialSeats.Add(seat1D);
      Seat seat1E = new Seat(1, 'E', "WINDOW", SeatClass.FirstClass);
      initialSeats.Add(seat1E);
      Seat seat2A = new Seat(2, 'A', "WINDOW", SeatClass.BusinessClass);
      initialSeats.Add(seat2A);
      Seat seat2B = new Seat(2, 'B', "AISLE", SeatClass.BusinessClass);
      initialSeats.Add(seat2B);
      Seat seat2D = new Seat(2, 'D', "AISLE", SeatClass.BusinessClass);
      initialSeats.Add(seat2D);
      Seat seat2E = new Seat(2, 'E', "WINDOW", SeatClass.BusinessClass);
      initialSeats.Add(seat2E);
      Seat seat3A = new Seat(3, 'A', "WINDOW", SeatClass.EconomyClass);
      initialSeats.Add(seat3A);
      Seat seat3B = new Seat(3, 'B', "AISLE", SeatClass.EconomyClass);
      initialSeats.Add(seat3B);
      Seat seat3D = new Seat(3, 'D', "AISLE", SeatClass.EconomyClass);
      initialSeats.Add(seat3D);
      Seat seat3E = new Seat(3, 'E', "WINDOW", SeatClass.EconomyClass);
      initialSeats.Add(seat3E);
      Seat seat4A = new Seat(4, 'A', "WINDOW", SeatClass.EconomyClass);
      initialSeats.Add(seat4A);
      Seat seat4B = new Seat(4, 'B', "AISLE", SeatClass.EconomyClass);
      initialSeats.Add(seat4B);
      Seat seat4D = new Seat(4, 'D', "AISLE", SeatClass.EconomyClass);
      initialSeats.Add(seat4D);
      Seat seat4E = new Seat(4, 'E', "WINDOW", SeatClass.EconomyClass);
      initialSeats.Add(seat4E);
      denverToHouston = new Flight(4332, "DEN", "IAH", initialSeats);
    }
```

```csharp
[TearDown]
public void Destroy()
{
  denverToHouston = null;
  initialSeats = null;
}

[Test]
public void ScheduleFlight()
{
  DateTime departure = new DateTime(2005, 2, 11, 8, 25, 0, 0);
  DateTime arrival = new DateTime(2005, 2, 11, 11, 25, 0, 0);

  denverToHouston.ScheduleFlight(departure, arrival);
  Assert.AreEqual(departure, denverToHouston.Departure);
  Assert.AreEqual(arrival, denverToHouston.Arrival);
}

[Test]
public void ReserveBestAvailableSeat()
{
  // Set up the mock object for the Customer system
  DynamicMock maryJones = new DynamicMock(typeof(ICustomer));
  maryJones.ExpectAndReturn("GetSeatPreference", "WINDOW", 1001);
  maryJones.ExpectAndReturn("GetFlyerClass", "BASE", 1001);

  // Exercise the test and use the mock object
  Reservation maryJonesReservation =
    new Reservation(denverToHouston, 1001, (ICustomer)maryJones.MockInstance);

  Seat seat = maryJonesReservation.GetBestAvailableSeat();
  denverToHouston.ReserveSeat(seat);

  // Verify assumptions
  Assert.AreEqual(3, seat.RowNumber);
  Assert.AreEqual('A', seat.RowLetter);
  Assert.IsFalse(denverToHouston.AvailableSeats.Contains(seat));

  maryJones.Verify();
  }
 }
}
```

Notice that you are enhancing the setup by creating a list of available seats for the flight. You also have created a new test, ReserveBestAvailableSeat. This test shows NMock in action.

First, you define the mock object using this line:

```csharp
DynamicMock maryJones = new DynamicMock(typeof(ICustomer));
```

This line tells NMock which object needs a mock object. But, before the mock object is actually dynamically created, you need to set up what the return values should be when the methods on the mock object are called later, as follows:

```
maryJones.ExpectAndReturn("GetSeatPreference", "WINDOW", 1001);
maryJones.ExpectAndReturn("GetFlyerClass", "BASE", 1001);
```

The first parameter to the ExpectAndReturn method indicates to which corresponding method in the mock object the return value belongs. The second parameter indicates the actual return value. The last parameter is really an array of parameters that the mock method (GetSeatPreference, for example) takes. Since the GetSeatPreference method expects only one parameter (the frequent flyer ID), you can just pass the value as a shortcut.

By defining expected return values for GetSeatPreference and GetFlyerClass, you are telling NMock that those are the only two methods on the mock object that should be called and that each of those methods should be called only once.

Once you have defined the mock object and its expected return values, you are ready to actually use the mock object. You do that in the next three lines of code:

```
Reservation maryJonesReservation =
    new Reservation(denverToHouston, 1001, (ICustomer)maryJones.MockInstance);

Seat seat = maryJonesReservation.GetBestAvailableSeat();
denverToHouston.ReserveSeat(seat);
```

After you have exercised the code you wanted to test, you need to verify your assumptions. These assumptions include the expected state of the application after the code using the mock object was executed, that only the mock object methods you expected to be called were called, and that those mock object methods were called only the expected number of times. This is accomplished in the next four lines of code:

```
Assert.AreEqual(3, seat.RowNumber);
    Assert.AreEqual('A', seat.RowLetter);
    Assert.IsFalse(denverToHouston.AvailableSeats.Contains(seat));

    maryJones.Verify();
```

Running the Test

To actually run the test, you will use your NAnt tool. The default.build file is updated here to incorporate nmock.dll. There are a few other tweaks made to the build file to make it more efficient. Your default.build file should look like Listing 8-6.

Listing 8-6. *NAnt Build File for Using a Mock Object*

```xml
<?xml version="1.0"?>
<project name="NMock Testing" default="test" basedir=".">
    <property name="build.dir" value="build" />
    <property name="basename" value="ReservationTests" />
    <property name="debug" value="true" />

    <target name="clean">
        <delete dir="${build.dir}"
                    if="${directory::exists(property::get-value('build.dir'))}" />
    </target>

    <target name="compile">
        <csc target="library"
                output="${build.dir}/${basename}.dll"
                debug="${debug}">
            <sources>
                <include name="*.cs" />
            </sources>
            <references>
                <include name="System.dll" />
                <include name="System.Data.dll" />
                <include name="C:\Program Files\NUnit 2.2\bin\nunit.core.dll" />
                <include name=
"C:\Program Files\NUnit 2.2\bin\nunit.framework.dll" />
                <include name=
"C:\Program Files\NUnit 2.2\bin\nunit.extensions.dll" />
                <include name="C:\Program Files\NUnit 2.2\bin\nunit.util.dll" />
                <include name="C:\development\tools\NMock\nmock.dll" />
            </references>
        </csc>
    </target>

    <target name="test" depends="compile">
        <copy file="C:\development\tools\NMock\nmock.dll" todir="${build.dir}" />
        <exec program="nunit-console.exe"
                basedir="C:\Program Files\NUnit 2.2\bin"
                workingdir="${build.dir}" >
            <arg value="${basename}.dll" />
        </exec>
    </target>
</project>
```

After updating the build file, open a command-prompt window and switch to the directory where you saved all your source files for this chapter. Then execute the nant command. If all went as expected, you should see something similar to Figure 8-1.

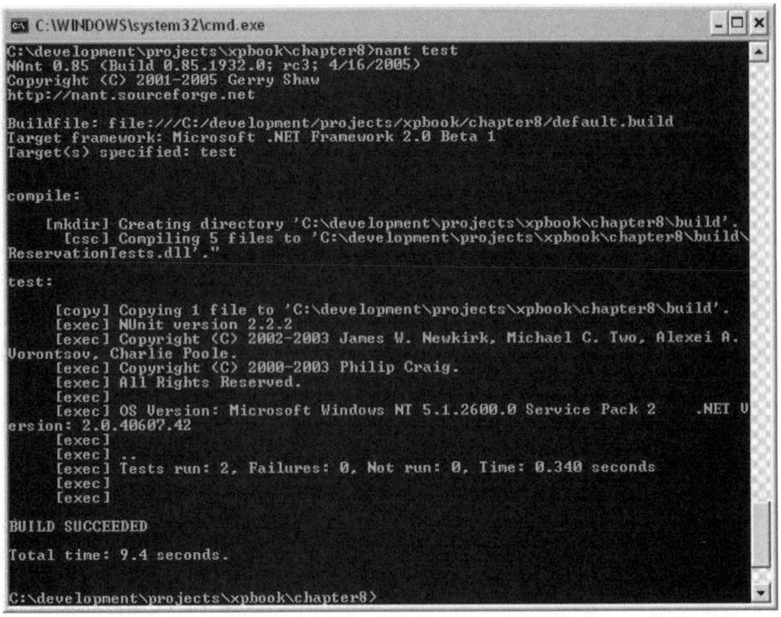

Figure 8-1. *Results of testing with a mock object*

Summary

By expanding your tool set with a mock object tool, you can now test your application without worrying too much about external dependent resources. This will allow you to sustain a better velocity and improve the feedback that your application gives you.

The next tool that you will find valuable is CruiseControl.NET, covered in the next chapter. This tool will allow you to take all the other tools you have acquired and automate their use.

CHAPTER 9

■ ■ ■

Automation Environment Tool: CruiseControl.NET

In this chapter, you will add another essential tool to your XP tool set: CruiseControl.NET (CCNet). But this isn't just another tool—this tool brings all the other tools together to create something greater. CCNet will use NAnt to build the source code in an automated fashion, and it will use NUnit and NMock to automate your tests as well.

This chapter will not take you through the entire CCNet setup and execution processes. However, you will learn how the pieces fit together and the benefits of using this type of tool.

What Is CCNet?

CCNet is often referred to as an *integration server* because it integrates several tools together. You configure CCNet to run automatically at certain intervals, such as once every two hours. This allows you to get automated feedback, at regular intervals, regarding the quality of the code being developed. CCNet provides this feedback by letting you know when the build breaks, which unit tests failed, and when the last successful build was completed.

CCNet is actually a set of tools bundled together:

- CruiseControl.NET Server, the server itself and its associated configuration files

- CCTray, a client system tray application that lets you see the state of the project from the integration server's perspective

- Web Dashboard, an ASP.NET web application that lets you see the state of the project from the integration server's perspective

CCNet works its magic by monitoring a source code repository. When changes occur (new source code is checked in or existing source code is changed or deleted), this tool will check out all of the existing source code, build it using NAnt, and run all your unit tests using NUnit and NMock.

The advantage this tool gives you is that it automates the integration process. You will not need to rely solely on the developers to perform integration testing. This tool is not meant to discourage your developers from performing integration testing on their own, but rather to enhance the overall integration process and quality.

Of course, this also satisfies the fundamental XP practice of continuous integration, as well as the XP value of feedback. It provides rapid feedback regarding the success or failure of the integration build and testing.

In this chapter, you will learn how to install and configure the various CCNet components.

■**Note**   CCNet is another open source tool from the folks at ThoughtWorks. There are more than 15 committers to this project. Visit `http://confluence.public.thoughtworks.org/display/CCNET/Welcome+to+CruiseControl.NET` for more information about CCNet.

Installing CCNet

Start your installation by downloading CCNet from `http://confluence.public.thoughtworks.org/display/CCNET/Download`. When you have successfully downloaded the CCNet file, unzip the file and place the unzipped contents anywhere on your local workstation. We'll refer to this location as `<installDir>`.

After you have installed CCNet, you need to set up its components: the server, tray application, and dashboard.

Setting Up the CCNet Server

In order to use CCNet, you need to start by configuring the server. You accomplish this by creating a configuration file. Then you can start up the server.

Creating the CCNet Configuration File

You create a configuration file named `ccnet.config` and save it in the server directory within the directory where you installed CCNet (`<installDir>\server\ccnet.config`). In this configuration file, you configure CCNet to work with your source control system, as well as with NAnt.

Listing 9-1 shows an example of a `ccnet.config` file.

Listing 9-1. *CCNet Configuration File (ccnet.config)*

```
<cruisecontrol>
  <project name="Chapter9">
    <webURL>http://www.spotteddogsoftware.net/ccnet/xpbook</webURL>
    <triggers>
      <intervalTrigger seconds="60" />
    </triggers>
    <modificationDelaySeconds>10</modificationDelaySeconds>
```

```
<sourcecontrol type="svn">
  <executable>c:\development\tools\subversion\bin\svn.exe</executable>
  <trunkUrl>svn://svn.mycompany.com/xpbookproject/trunk</trunkUrl>
  <workingDirectory>c:\development\projects\book\chapter9</workingDirectory>
</sourcecontrol>

<build type="nant">
  <executable>c:\development\tools\nant-0.85-rc1\bin\nant.exe</executable>
  <baseDirectory>c:\development\projects\book\chapter9</baseDirectory>
  <baseTimeoutSeconds>300</baseTimeoutSeconds>
</build>

<tasks>
  <merge>
    <files>
      <file>
c:\development\projects\book\chapter9\build\test\unit-test-results.xml
      </file>
    </file>
  <merge>
</tasks>

<publishers>
  <xmllogger />
</publishers>

  </project>
</cruisecontrol>
```

The sourcecontrol tag is used to indicate which source control system you are using with CCNet. In this example, the type is set to "svn", which stands for Subversion. Other common types are "cvs" for CVS and "vss" for Visual SourceSafe.

You also need to specify the location of the executable for your specified source control system and the working directory where the source code should be checked out to on the server. You specify these items by using the executable and workingDirectory tags, respectively. Since this example uses Subversion, the configuration file must also specify the trunkUrl tag, which indicates where the source code repository resides within the Subversion system.

The build tag is used to set up the build tool you are using with CCNet. You specify the build tool by indicating it in the type attribute on the build tag. Here, you see that "nant" is used as the type. You also need to specify where NAnt is installed on the server using the executable tag. The baseDirectory tag is specified so that when NAnt is invoked by CCNet, the base directory will be provided to NAnt from CCNet automatically. The buildTimeoutSeconds tag is an optional tag that specifies the number of seconds for CCNet to wait before assuming that the process has hung and should be terminated.

> **Note** At the time of this writing, CCNet supported source code repositories for CVS, Subversion, Visual SourceSafe, Perforce, Rational ClearCase, SourceGear Vault, PVCS, and StarTeam. You can also use various build tools with CCNet. See `http://confluence.public.thoughtworks.org/display/CCNET/Using+CruiseControl.NET+with+other+applications` for a full list of the applications that you can integrate with CCNet and their associated configuration file tags.

Starting the CCNet Server

Once you have a properly defined the CCNet configuration file, you are ready to start the CCNet server. You can execute the CCNet server either as a console application (using the Windows Command Prompt application) or set up CCNet server as a Windows service.

If you choose to run the server as a console application, you will need to start and stop the server yourself. This is okay at first, while you are working out the configuration file setup. But after you have determined that the configuration file is correct for your needs, you should set up the CCNet server as a Windows service, so that you are not left with the task of manually managing the CCNet server.

Running the Server As a Console Application

To start the CCNet server as a console application, launch the Windows Command Prompt application (Start menu ➤ All Programs ➤ Accessories ➤ Command Prompt). In the command-prompt window, change directories to the location where the CCNet server executable resides. This directory is located at `<installDir>\server\`. Then run the server by typing `ccnet.exe` at the command prompt.

Setting Up the Server As a Service

When you set up the CCNet server as a Windows service, you can use the Windows Service Manager to start and stop the CCNet server. This has the added benefit that if Windows is rebooted, the server will be restarted automatically for you.

To set up CCNet server as a service, you need to modify another configuration file located in the same directory as the `ccnet.config` file that you created. The service configuration file is named `ccnet.service.exe.config`. Set the value of the `ccnet.config` setting in this file to point to your `ccnet.config` file.

Once the `ccnet.service.exe.config` file is set up properly, you are ready to install the CCNet server service. Open a command-prompt window and change to the `<installDir>\server\` directory. Then enter `installutil ccservice.exe` at the command prompt.

> **Note** If installing CCNet as a service doesn't go smoothly, consult the CruiseControl.NET website and refer to the detailed information about configuring CCNet server as a service at `http://confluence.public.thoughtworks.org/display/CCNET/The+Server+Service+Application`.

Setting Up CCTray

Once you have the CCNet server up and running, you will want to monitor what the server is doing. One quick way to see the status of the server is to set up the CCTray utility. System tray utilities are those icons that reside to the far right on your Windows task bar (assuming that the Windows task bar is in its default location). You have more than likely used system tray utilities when you have checked on your network status or adjusted your speaker volume.

■**Note** CCTray does not require a special or separate installation step. If you want to have CCTray always running, you can set up `cctray.exe` as a startup item that will start automatically when you log in to your Windows account.

Starting CCTray

To start CCTray, open a command-prompt window and change to the `<installDir>\cctray\` directory. Then enter `cctray.exe` at the command prompt.

This will run the CCTray utility and place the CCTray icon in the system tray.

Configuring CCTray

Next, you need to configure the utility. Right-click the CCTray icon in the system tray and select Settings to open the Settings dialog box. In this dialog box, you can set the following parameters:

- **Poll every *xx* seconds**: CCTray will check with the CCNet server every *xx* seconds to see if the state of the build has changed.

- **Server**: This is the URI to the remote interface of the CCNet server.

- **Project Name**: This indicates which CCNet server project CCTray should monitor, as described in the CCNet server configuration file named `ccnet.config` and stored in `<installDir>\server\`.

- **Show balloon notification**: Enables or disables the balloon notification messages.

- **Show agent**: Enables or disables notification of completed builds using an agent. In order to use agents, you must install some additional software (from `www.microsoft.com/msagent`) and edit the CCTray configuration file (`cctray-settings.xml`) by hand.

- **Hide after announcement**: Enables or disables turning off the agent after the agent delivers the completed build message.

- **Agent**: The agent to use to deliver the completed build message.

- **Audio (Successful/Fixed/Broken/Still failing)**: The location of a WAV audio file that CCTray will play when the build completes.

After you've set the parameters in the Settings dialog box and saved them, an XML-based configuration file will be created (the first time you create settings) or updated (after you have created settings and saved them). This file is named `cctray-settings.xml` and saved in the `<installDir>`\cctray\ directory. Listing 9-2 shows an example of a `cctray-settings.xml` file.

Listing 9-2. *A CCTray Configuration File (cctray-settings.xml)*

```xml
<?xml version="1.0" encoding="utf-8" ?>
<CruiseControlMonitor xmlns:xsd="http://www.w3.org/2001/XMLSchema"
  xmlns:xsi="http://www.w3.org/2001/XMLSchema-instance"
  xmlns="http://www.sf.net/projects/ccnet">
  <PollingIntervalSeconds>10</PollingIntervalSeconds>
  <RemoteServerUrl>tcp://YourHostname:1234/CruiseManager.rem</RemoteServerUrl>
  <ProjectName>YourProjectName</ProjectName>
  <NotificationBalloon ShowBalloon="true" />

  <Sounds>
    <AnotherSuccessfulBuildSound Play="true" FileName="woohoo.wav" />
    <AnotherFailedBuildSound Play="true" FileName="doh.wav" />
    <BrokenBuildSound Play="true" FileName="doh.wav" />
    <FixedBuildSound Play="true" FileName="excellent.wav" />
  </Sounds>

  <Messages>
    <AnotherSuccess>
      <Message>Yet another successful build!</Message>
      <Message>That's what I'm talking about!</Message>
      <Message>I like your style...</Message>
    </AnotherSuccess>
    <AnotherFailure>
      <Message>The build is still broken...</Message>
      <Message>Oh oh, the build is still broken...</Message>
      <Message>That didn't work...</Message>
      <Message>Better luck next time!</Message>
    </AnotherFailure>
    <Fixed>
      <Message>Recent checkins have fixed the build.</Message>
      <Message>Yeeha! woo Woo WOO!!!</Message>
    </Fixed>
    <Broken>
      <Message>Recent checkins have broken the build.</Message>
      <Message>If it ain't broke, don't fix it!</Message>
    </Broken>
  </Messages>
```

```
<Agents CurrentAgentName="Peedy" ShowAgent="false" HideAfterMessage="false">
  <AvailableAgents>
    <Agent Name="Peedy" AcsFileName="Peedy.acs" SpeakOutLoud="false" />
    <Agent Name="Cat"
              AcsFileName="C:\Program Files\Microsoft Office\Office\OFFCAT.ACS"
              SpeakOutLoud="false" />
    <Agent Name="Clippy"
              AcsFileName="C:\Program Files\Microsoft Office\Office\CLIPPIT.ACS"
              SpeakOutLoud="false" />
  </AvailableAgents>
</Agents>

</CruiseControlMonitor>
```

Optionally, you can create and/or update this configuration file manually using any text editor.

Using CCTray

The CCTray utility will display different colored icons in the system tray, as follows:

- Green means the build was successful.

- Red means the build failed.

- Gray indicates the server is unavailable or returned an error status.

- Yellow means the server is currently building the code.

When a build completes, a balloon notification will appear for CCTray, telling you the status of the build.

Right-clicking the CCTray icon in the system tray displays a menu with options for the following functions:

- Launch a web browser and display the CCNet build web page.

- Configure the CCTray settings.

- Force the CCNet server to start a build (only available if CCNet server is not currently running a build).

- Exit the CCTray utility.

Although the CCTray is helpful, to get detailed information about a completed build, especially a failed or broken build, you need to use the Web Dashboard.

USING AGENTS FOR BUILD COMPLETION NOTIFICATION

Agents are technology from Microsoft that, using agent-enabled applications, display animated characters to the user. If you have ever used Microsoft Office, you have more than likely seen the animated paper clip, or dog, or some other character. Those characters are agents and are used to (in theory, anyway) enrich the user's experience within an application that uses the agent.

In order to use agents with CCTray, first download the Microsoft Agent software from www.microsoft.com/msagent. Select the link for Downloads for End-Users.

Once you have installed the Microsoft Agent software, you will need to edit the CCTray configuration file, cctray-settings.xml, by hand. (This file will not exist if you have not already initially saved your CCTray settings at least once or previously created the configuration file by hand.) The configuration file contains a section for specifying agents using their absolute path to their ACS file location. If you have Microsoft Office 2000 or greater installed, you will find some ACS files located in the C:\Program Files\Microsoft Office\Office\ directory. You can also find a host of other agents at www.msagentring.org.

Setting Up the Web Dashboard

The Web Dashboard is where you will get the lowdown on what is really happening with the CCNet builds. This is a web-based tool, hence the *Web* in its name. If you have multiple projects set up for this CCNet server, you will be able to view all of their builds' statuses from this dashboard.

To use the Web Dashboard, you need to have Internet Information Server (IIS), Microsoft's web application server, installed first. Then you can install and configure the Web Dashboard.

■**Note** If IIS is not already installed on your system, install it before proceeding. Consult your Microsoft documentation if you need assistance with IIS installation.

Installing the Web Dashboard

To install the Web Dashboard, you use the IIS Admin tool to map a virtual directory to the Web Dashboard folder you installed when you installed CCNet (<*installDir*>/webdashboard/), and then configure it. Follow these steps.

1. To start the IIS Admin tool, select Start menu ➤ All Programs ➤ Administrative Tools ➤ Internet Information Services, as shown in Figure 9-1.

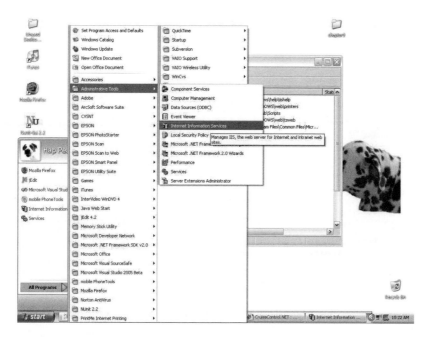

Figure 9-1. *Starting the IIS Admin tool*

2. Select New ➤ Virtual Directory, as shown in Figure 9-2. A wizard guides you through
    the process of mapping the virtual directory. When you have completed the mapping,
    a new entry will appear in the list under the Default Web Site on the left side of the IIS
    Admin window, as shown in Figure 9-3.

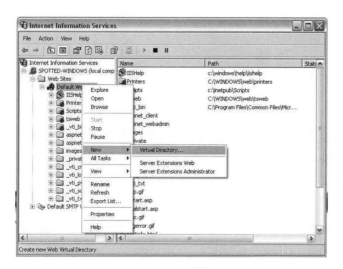

Figure 9-2. *Creating a new virtual directory*

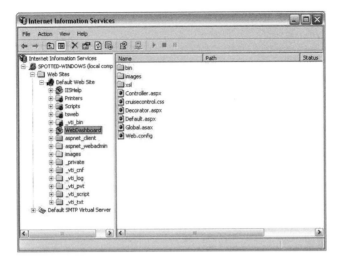

Figure 9-3. *The new WebDashboard site*

3. Right-click the WebDashboard entry in the list and select Properties, as shown in Figure 9-4.

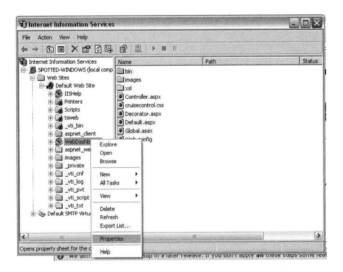

Figure 9-4. *Selecting to set the WebDashboard site properties*

4. Select the Virtual Directory tab in the WebDashboard Properties window and click the Configure button to display the Application Configuration dialog box, as shown in Figure 9-5.

Figure 9-5. *Configuring the WebDashboard virtual directory*

5. Click the Add button in the Application Configuration dialog box to display the Add/Edit Application Extension Mapping dialog box.

6. In the Executable field in the Add/Edit Application Extension Mapping dialog box, enter the location of the `aspnet_isapi.dll` file. (In .NET 2.0, this is usually `C:\WINDOWS\Microsoft.NET\Framework\v2.0.40607\aspnet_isapi.dll`). In the Extension field, enter `.xml`. Make sure the Script Engine check box is checked and that the Check That the File Exists check box is not checked. Your dialog box should look similar to Figure 9-6.

Figure 9-6. *Adding the WebDashboard mapping*

7. Click the OK button on the Add/Edit Application Extension Mapping dialog box, and then click the OK button in the Application Configuration dialog box.

8. In the WebDashboard Properties dialog box, under the Documents tab, make sure that `Default.aspx` is in the list under Enable Default Document, as shown in Figure 9-7. Add it if it is not in the list.

Figure 9-7. *Enabling theWebDashboard default documents*

9. Click the OK button in the WebDashboard Properties dialog box.

As long as you are running the IIS/WebDashboard website on the same server as you are running the CCNet server, and you have not modified any of the CCNet server's remote settings, you do not need to do any further Web Dashboard configuration.

Running the Web Dashboard

If you set up everything correctly, you can now point a web browser at the Web Dashboard website. The URL for the website will be the `webUrl` that you specified in your `ccnet.config` file for the CCNet server. As an example, the `webUrl` used in Listing 9-1 is `http://www.spotteddogsoftware.net/ccnet/xpbook`. Of course, your `webUrl` is based on your own web server installation.

Figure 9-8 shows an example of running the Web Dashboard.

From here, you can navigate through the different projects to see the completed build results. Just click a project link on the left side of the window to view that project. You will see a list of recent builds, and you can click a link to see the most recent build report. Figure 9-9 shows an example of a build report for a project.

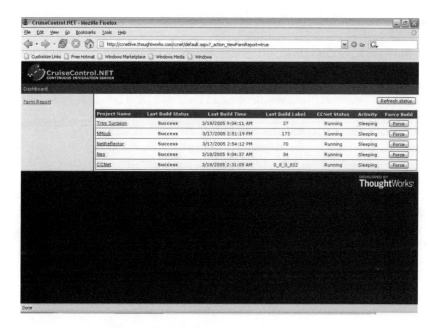

Figure 9-8. *Running the Web Dashboard*

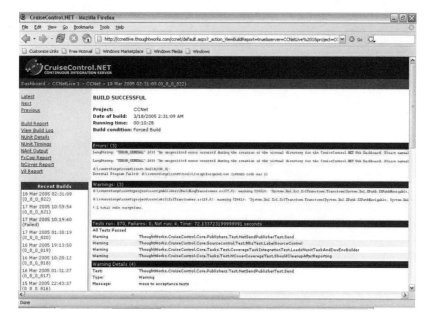

Figure 9-9. *A build report in the Web Dashboard*

Summary

CCNet takes advantage of your other tools—NAnt as a way to build your source code, NUnit for testing, and NMock for mock objects when and where you need them—and wraps them in automation. By doing this, you have put in place a way to receive rapid feedback at steady intervals. You will still want all the developers to run their own local builds and unit tests, and perform their own integration testing before they check in their source code changes. But with the help of CCNet, you have a way of communicating the project's status to everyone all the time. This will also help prevent your developers from getting lazy or sloppy about their source code check-ins, because they know that CCNet will always report the truth. This will also help you produce higher-quality software.

In the next chapter, you will add another valuable tool to your XP tool set: refactoring. It is not a tool that you automate with CCNet, as with NAnt and NMock, but you will use it every day that you write code.

CHAPTER 10

■■■

Refactoring

In this chapter, we are going to cover some of the types of refactoring you can do on the source code you create and manage. Recall from Chapter 1 that Martin Fowler defines refactoring as "the process of changing a software system in such a way that it doesn't alter the external behavior or the code yet improves the internal structure" (in his book, *Refactoring: Improving the Design of Existing Code* [Addison Wesley, 1999]).

Refactoring will be important to you because it will improve your application. It will do this by making your source code easier to maintain. It also has the potential to improve the performance of your application, as your source code becomes leaner with less redundancy. Learn refactoring techniques and always be on the lookout for where you can apply them, and you will be well on your way to being a top-notch developer.

Visual Studio 2005 and Refactoring

Visual Studio 2005 adds a new XP feature directly in the IDE. You now have several refactoring tools at your disposal. The following refactoring tools are available via the Refactor menu on the menu bar and also on the context menu when you right-click a class, interface, method, or variable name in your source code:

- Extract Method

- Rename

- Encapsulate Field

- Extract Interface

- Promote Local Variable to Parameter

- Remove Parameters

- Reorder Parameters

Each of the refactoring tools is described in the following sections.

Extract Method

The Extract Method tool allows you to select a contiguous section of code that is within an existing method, and then have that selection of code extracted from its current location to a method of its own. You will use this tool when you have an existing method that is getting too long (many lines of code) or when the method is doing several different actions.

For example, you might have a method whose purpose is to make a reservation. Looking at the code within the method, you notice that, in addition to actually making a reservation, the method also contains code (functionality) to look up the available seats for the flight. This functionality may be needed in the process of making a reservation, but it is not the primary objective of making a reservation. Also, looking for available seats might be used in more places than just making a reservation. So, you should highlight the section of code that pertains to the functionality of looking for available seats, and then select the Extract Method tool to move that code to its own method.

Listing 10-1 shows the source code in this example before the Extract Method tool is invoked.

Listing 10-1. *Code Before Invoking Extract Method*

```
public void PlaceReservation(int numberOfSeats, string flightNumber,
    DateTime flightDate, ArrayList persons)
{
  // ... Code leading up to this point in the method

  // See if seats are still available
  bool seatsAreAvailable = false;
  string connectionString = DataUtilities.ConnectionString;
  try
  {
    OdbcConnection dataConnection = new OdbcConnection();
    dataConnection.ConnectionString = connectionString;
    dataConnection.Open();
    OdbcCommand dataCommand = new OdbcCommand();
    dataCommand.Connection = dataConnection;
    StringBuilder commandText = new StringBuilder("SELECT * FROM Flight");
    commandText.Append(" WHERE flightNumber = '");
    commandText.Append(flightNumber);
    commandText.Append("' AND flightDate = '");
    commandText.Append(flightDate);
    commandText.Append("' AND availableSeates >= ");
    commandText.Append(numberOfSeats);
    dataCommand.CommandText = commandText.ToString();
    OdbcDataReader dataReader = dataCommand.ExecuteReader();
    if (dataReader.Read())
    {
      seatsAreAvailable = true;
    }
  }
  catch (Exception e)
```

```
  {
    // Handle exception
  }

  if (seatsAreAvailable)
  {
    // Code to make the reservation here...
  }
}
```

Select the code fragment starting just after the // See if seats are still available comment up to and including the end bracket on the catch clause, and then invoke the Extract Method tool. Listing 10-2 shows the source code after Extract Method is invoked.

Listing 10-2. *Code After Invoking Extract Method*

```
public void PlaceReservation(int numOfSeats, String flightNum,
    Date flightDate, ArrayList persons)
{
  // ... Code leading up to this point in the method

  // See if seats are still available
  bool seatsAvailable = AreSeatsAvailable(numOfSeats, flightNum, flightDate);

  if (seatsAvailable)
  {
    // code to make reservation
  }
}

public bool AreSeatsAvailable(int numberOfSeats,
    String flightNumber, Date flightDate)
{
  bool seatsAreAvailable = false;
  string connectionString = DataUtilities.ConnectionString;
  try
  {
    OdbcConnection dataConnection = new OdbcConnection();
    dataConnection.ConnectionString = connectionString;
    dataConnection.Open();
    OdbcCommand dataCommand = new OdbcCommand();
    dataCommand.Connection = dataConnection;
    StringBuilder commandText = new StringBuilder("SELECT * FROM Flight");
    commandText.Append(" WHERE flightNumber = '");
    commandText.Append(flightNumber);
    commandText.Append("' AND flightDate = '");
    commandText.Append(flightDate);
    commandText.Append("' AND availableSeates >= ");
```

```
      commandText.Append(numberOfSeats);
      dataCommand.CommandText = commandText.ToString();
      OdbcDataReader dataReader = dataCommand.ExecuteReader();
      if (dataReader.Read())
      {
        seatsAreAvailable = true;
      }
    }
    catch (Exception e)
    {
      // Handle exception
    }
    return seatsAreAvailable;
}
```

Rename

You will more than likely find times when you need to rename a class, interface, method, or variable. This name is usually used in multiple places throughout your source code, and possibly in multiple source files. If you don't change the name in all the locations it is referenced, errors will occur. Sometimes, these errors will be caught by the compiler, but that is not always the case. The Rename tool ensures the name will be changed to the same value everywhere that it is used.

Listing 10-3 shows some sample source code before the Rename tool is invoked.

Listing 10-3. *Code Before Invoking Rename*

```
class MyClass
{
  public void MyMethod()
  {
  }
}

class MyOtherClass
{
  public void MyOtherMethod()
  {
    MyClass myClass = new MyClass();
    myClass.MyMethod();
  }
}
```

Select the MyClass class name and invoke the Rename tool to rename the class to Examples. Listing 10-4 shows the source code after the Rename tool is invoked.

Listing 10-4. *Code After Invoking Rename*

```
class Examples
{
  public void MyMethod()
  {
  }
}

class MyOtherClass
{
  public void MyOtherMethod()
  {
    Examples myClass = new Examples();
    myClass.MyMethod();
  }
}
```

Note When you rename a class or an interface using the Rename tool, Visual Studio does not rename the file. For example, if the filename was `MyClass.cs` before using the Rename tool, the filename will still be `MyClass.cs` after renaming the class to `Examples`.

Encapsulate Field

You will create properties from class fields often. Properties are also referred to as *getters* and *setters*. The class fields are private, which makes them encapsulated or hidden within the class, which is proper object-oriented development. You use properties when you want to set the value of a class field or get the value of the class field. The values can be specific to an instance of the class or to the class in general.

The Encapsulate Field tool automates the coding for the properties. You create the fields within the class. Then you select the field name and use the Encapsulate Field tool to create the property code. This tool will always create both getter and setter methods.

Listing 10-5 shows an example of some source code before the Encapsulate Field tool is invoked.

Listing 10-5. *Code Before Invoking Encapsulate Field*

```
class Examples
{
  private string firstName;
}
```

Select the `firstName` class field and invoke the Encapsulate Field tool. Listing 10-6 shows the source code after Encapsulate Field is invoked.

Listing 10-6. *Code After Invoking Encapsulate Field*

```
class Examples
{
  private string firstName;

  public string FirstName
  {
    get { return firstName; }
    set { firstName = value; }
  }
}
```

Extract Interface

After creating a class, you might find that several consumers (other classes that call/reference methods of this class) call the same subset of methods. Or, more commonly, you might find that there are one or more classes that share the same set of methods (features or functionality) as that class you created. When you see this happen, it is a good indication that you should create an interface of the common methods.

The reason for creating such an interface is to show the commonality between these classes so other people looking at the class will know that this class shares functionality with other classes that implement the same interface. This also allows the consumer of these classes to more freely choose which class that implements this interface is most appropriate for its use or to allow any class that implements this interface to be used.

Listing 10-7 shows an example of some source code before invoking the Extract Interface tool.

Listing 10-7. *Code Before Invoking Extract Interface*

```
class FullTimeEmployee
{
  private string name;
  private string phoneNumber;
  private int numberOfPaidDaysOff;

  public string Name
  {
    get { return name; }
    set { name = value; }
  }

  public string PhoneNumber
  {
    get { return phoneNumber; }
    set { phoneNumber = value; }
  }
```

```
  public int NumberOfPaidDaysOff
  {
    get { return numberOfPaidDaysOff; }
    set { numberOfPaidDaysOff = value; }
  }
}

class PartTimeEmployee
{
  private string name;
  private string phoneNumber;
  private int maxNumberOfHours;

  public string Name
  {
    get { return name; }
    set { name = value; }
  }

  public string PhoneNumber
  {
    get { return phoneNumber; }
    set { phoneNumber = value; }
  }

  public int MaxNumberOfHours
  {
    get { return maxNumberOfHours; }
    set { maxNumberOfHours = value; }
  }
}
```

Select the class name `FullTimeEmployee`, and then invoke the Extract Interface tool. In the dialog box, enter a name for the interface class—`IEmployee` in this example. You also need to select which methods to be included in the interface—`Name` and `PhoneNumber` in this example. Listing 10- 8 shows the source code after the Extract Interface tool is invoked. Note that the `PartTimeEmployee` class changes had to be made manually.

Listing 10-8. *Code After Invoking Extract Interface*

```
interface IEmployee
{
  string Name { get; set; }
  string PhoneNumber { get; set; }
}
```

```csharp
class FullTimeEmployee : IEmployee
{
  private string name;
  private string phoneNumber;
  private int numberOfPaidDaysOff;

  public string Name
  {
    get { return name; }
    set { name = value; }
  }

  public string PhoneNumber
  {
    get { return phoneNumber; }
    set { phoneNumber = value; }
  }

  public int NumberOfPaidDaysOff
  {
    get { return numberOfPaidDaysOff; }
    set { numberOfPaidDaysOff = value; }
  }
}

class PartTimeEmployee : IEmployee
{
  private string name;
  private string phoneNumber;
  private int maxNumberOfHours;

  public string Name
  {
    get { return name; }
    set { name = value; }
  }

  public string PhoneNumber
  {
    get { return phoneNumber; }
    set { phoneNumber = value; }
  }
}
```

Promote Local Variable to Parameter

After coding a method that has local variables defined, you may decide that it would be better to have the local variable passed in as a parameter to the method. The Promote Local Variable to Parameter tool allows you to select the local variable and make it a parameter to the method. In order to use this tool, the local variable must be initialized, because the initialized value is used as the value passed to this method from all references to this method.

Listing 10-9 shows an example of some source code before the Promote Local Variable to Parameter tool is invoked.

Listing 10-9. *Code Before Invoking Promote Local Variable to Parameter*

```
public ArrayList BuildWidgets(int numberOfWidgets)
{
  ArrayList widgetsBuilt = new ArrayList();
  string widgetType = "Blue Widget";
  // Code to build widgets
  return widgetsBuilt;
}

public void AssembleDohickey()
{
  // Build 2 widgets as a part of the Dohickey
  int numberOfWidgets = 2;
  ArrayList widgetsBuilt = BuildWidgets(numberOfWidgets);
  // Assemble Dohickey
}
```

Select the widgetType local variable name, and then invoke the Promote Local Variable to Parameter tool. Listing 10-10 shows the source code after Promote Local Variable to Parameter is invoked.

Listing 10-10. *Code After Invoking Promote Local Variable to Parameter*

```
public ArrayList BuildWidgets(int numberOfWidgets, string widgetType)
{
  ArrayList widgetsBuilt = new ArrayList();
  // Code to build widgets
  return widgetsBuilt;
}

public void AssembleDohickey()
{
  // Build 2 widgets as a part of the Dohickey
  int numberOfWidgets = 2;
  ArrayList widgetsBuilt = BuildWidgets(numberOfWidgets, "Blue Widget");
  // Assemble Dohickey
}
```

Remove Parameters

Sometimes, after creating a method, you find that one or more parameters of the method signature are not used, but you may already have references to that method passing those parameters. The Remove Parameters tool allows you to remove the unused parameters from the method and everywhere the method is referenced.

Listing 10-11 shows an example of some source code before the Remove Parameters tool is invoked.

Listing 10-11. *Code Before Invoking Remove Parameters*

```
public void ProcessFoo(Boolean isGood, string name)
{
  // Code to process Foo
}

public void Bar()
{
  // Process Foo
  Boolean isGood = new Boolean(true);
  string fooName = "MyFoo";
  ProcessFoo(isGood, fooName);
}
```

Click anywhere in the parameter list, and then invoke the Remove Parameters tool. Select the name parameter from the list in the dialog box, and then click the Remove button. Click the OK button when you're finished. Listing 10-12 shows the source code after Remove Parameters is invoked.

Listing 10-12. *Code After Invoking Remove Parameters*

```
public void ProcessFoo(Boolean isGood)
{
  // Code to process Foo
}

public void Bar()
{
  // Process Foo
  Boolean isGood = new Boolean(true);
  string fooName = "MyFoo";
  ProcessFoo(isGood);
}
```

Reorder Parameters

After creating a method, you might find that the order of the parameters in the method signature needs to be changed to make more logical sense, but you may have already coded references to this method. You need to make sure those references pass the parameters in the new reordered sequence. The Reorder Parameters tool allows you to change the order of the parameters in the method signature and also change the order of the parameters in all the places that method is referenced.

Listing 10-13 shows an example of some source code before the Reorder Parameters tool is invoked.

Listing 10-13. *Code Before Invoking Reorder Parameters*

```
public void SubmitOrder(string customerName,
    string orderID, Address customerAddress)
{
  // Code to submit the order
}

public void CheckOut()
{
  // Submit customer order
  string customerName = "Smith";
  string orderID = "CO1001";
  Address customerAddress =
    new Address("1234 Main Street", "Hometown", "CO", "80123");
  SubmitOrder(customerName, orderID, customerAddress);
}
```

Click anywhere in the parameter list before invoking the Reorder Parameters tool. Move the orderID to the top of the list in the Reorder Parameters dialog box using the arrow buttons on the right side of the dialog box. Listing 10-14 shows the result of using the Reorder Parameters tool.

Listing 10-14. *Code After Invoking Reorder Parameters*

```
public void SubmitOrder(string orderID,
    string customerName, Address customerAddress)
{
  // Code to submit the order
}

public void CheckOut()
{
  // Submit customer order
  string customerName = "Smith";
  string orderID = "CO1001";
  Address customerAddress =
    new Address("1234 Main Street", "Hometown", "CO", "80123");
  SubmitOrder(orderID, customerName, customerAddress);
}
```

Summary

In this chapter, we covered the refactoring tools that are built into Visual Studio 2005. We briefly explained each of the refactoring tools and when or why you might use them. You also saw examples of how the refactoring tools affect the code you develop.

There are numerous other refactoring techniques that are not automated in Visual Studio. We highly recommend reading Martin Fowler's *Refactoring: Improving the Design of Existing Code* (Addison Wesley, 1999) to learn about the additional refactoring that can benefit your projects.

That wraps up the XP tools part of this book. In the next part, we will take you through XP in practice. You will have a chance to become more familiar with some of the tools in your tool set, too. So, sit back, roll up your sleeves, and let's get down to business.

PART 3

XP in Action

■■■

CHAPTER 11

Release Planning— The Journey Begins

In this chapter, we are going to practice what we have been preaching. We will start with the exploration phase of release planning by having the customer introduce his business problem. Then will have the customer create user stories based on the needs he identified in his problem introduction, starting with the highest priority features. When enough user stories have been created (more than will fit into a release), we will assign each user story a value (ideal days) estimate using story points. This will complete the exploration phase of release planning.

Then we will start the planning phase (planning game) portion of release planning. The customer will declare when he would like to have the first release delivered. The tracker will declare the release velocity of the team, based on the number of developers and the release date. The customer will then select a subset of all the user stories. These will be the focus of the release. They should not total more than the team's declared release velocity. The outcome of the entire release plan will be the scope of work that will deliver business value to the customer in the shortest amount of time possible.

Business Problem Introduction

Northwind Inc. is a large, independent reseller of unusual and exotic food and beverage products. To date, on the consumer side of the business, sales of Northwind products have been through direct-mail catalogs. People's orders are taken over the telephone, and then processed through Northwind's corporate systems. Numerous corporate systems process the order from initial input of the order all the way down to shipment and delivery of the order. Figure 11-1 shows the flow of an order through the Northwind corporate system.

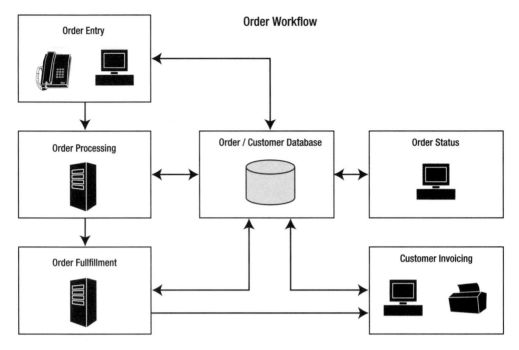

Figure 11-1. *Workflow of a customer order*

The Northwind senior management has defined the following mission statement for this project:

Create a Web presence that allows customers to self-order Northwind products and track the status of their orders all the way through to shipment.

The objectives to be reached by this project over its life span are as follows:

- Put the entire product catalog on the Web with consumer access.

- Provide a secure means of allowing consumers to select and order Northwind products.

- Provide a secure means of allowing consumers to check the status of an order from order creation to order shipment.

Story Writing

Continuing with the exploration phase of our project, it's time for story writing. As you learned in Chapter 3, a user story contains one, and only one, business feature. It is written on an index card, has a title, and includes a few sentences that describe the feature.

■**Note** Some customers may come to the release planning meeting with requirements already written out in one form or another. It is okay to refer to those requirements while creating the user stories, but the customer still needs to break up the requirements into user stories.

When we talked about writing this section, we discussed many different methods of conveying the information. We came to the conclusion that an example of the dialogue between the XP team and customer would best demonstrate the story writing process.

Helping the Customer Write the Stories

As we explained in Part 1 of this book, the customer is responsible for writing the stories. Of course, the customer gets some assistance from the XP team. The dialogue may go something like this:

XP team: Can you begin by providing the top features that you'd like to see in this release of the Northwind project? Try to keep these features simple and autonomous. We'll be writing each of these features down on index cards, where they'll become user stories. Remember, all we need at this point is a title and a few sentences that describe each defined feature.

Customer: The first requirement that must be part of this application is a login. The user must provide a valid user ID and password prior to doing anything else.

XP team: How do customers establish accounts with you?

Customer: They have to contact us, and we'll create an account for them.

XP team: Should we include contact information on the login page?

Customer: Yeah, that's a good idea.

XP team: Okay, so why don't you title your first story something like Login and provide a couple of sentences describing the login functionality, including something about the contact information. Try not to be detailed at this point.

Customer: How does that look?

Login

Uses user id / password required to login.

* Customer contact information for setting up new accounts.

XP team: Great. What's the next feature you're looking for?

Customer: Once they log in, I'd like the user to be able to browse the items in my catalog.

XP team: Do you want to display all of the catalog items at once, or do you want to use some sort of category display?

Customer: I'd like to display my categories, and based on the category selected, display the items in that category.

XP team: Okay, now give this story a title and a brief description.

Customer: Is this descriptive enough?

```
Browse Catalog
    Display categories / sub-categories
    until drill down to an item.

    Display only active items.
```

XP team: That looks really good. I think you're getting the hang of this.

Customer: I just thought of something. My users are going to be browsing our system with Internet Explorer 5 and above. How do I capture this requirement?

XP team: Well, something like this is really not a requirement—it's a constraint. In XP, we capture constraints much like user stories, except that they don't describe a feature, and we call them constraint cards.

▓**Note** A *constraint card* is just an index card that serves as a placeholder for constraint information, so the team and the customer do not forget about the constraint.

Customer: So, do I simply write the constraint on an index card?

XP team: Yes, you just want to make sure that you account for the constraint during the iteration phase of the project.

Customer: Is this good enough?

Constraint

Must work with IE 5x

XP team: That's great. Now, let's move on to your next feature.

Customer: I guess the next thing that I'd like to do is allow the user to perform a text search of the catalog.

XP team: What do you want to search on? Which attributes of the catalog item are you interested in?

Customer: Well, at this point, I want to search on the item's title and description. What do we do if I decide later that I want to search on a different attribute of my item?

XP team: At this point, we'll only focus on your current need, but if you change your mind later, we'll create a new user story, and we may need to balance the release.

Customer: Okay, we can handle that later. For now, I'm only interested in the title and description.

XP team: Great. Go ahead and create your story card for the current search, and we'll move on.

Customer: Okay, here's the current story.

Search for Product

Search the Title / Product Name

Description

XP team: What's your next feature?

Customer: I have a catalog. The user can browse the database. I guess I need a shopping cart. Do I just write down "shopping cart"?

XP team: That's more of an object. It really needs to be an action.

Customer: How about this?

Customers should be able to order product.

XP team: That looks more like a description. We may want to retitle this card. Go ahead and rip up this card and create a new one.

Customer: Okay, on this shopping cart, I'd like to add, remove, display, and update the shopping cart. How does this look?

Shopping Cart

Add

Remove

Display

Update

XP team: That looks better.

Customer: Next, I want to allow the users to order their selected items.

XP team: What do you want to call this story?

Customer: How about Check Out?

XP team: That sounds good. Why don't you provide a brief description?

Customer: What do you think of this?

Check Out

   Convert a shopping cart to an order.

XP team: What does that mean other than transferring items from a shopping cart to an order? Do you need to gather any additional information?

Customer: No, we already have their account information. We may allow them to ship the product to a different address in the future, but for now, they can only use their account's shipping address.

XP team: Do they need an order confirmation?

Customer: That's a good idea. What do you recommend?

XP team: Let's create a new story and call it something like Display Order Confirmation.

Customer: Okay, what kind of confirmation do you think we should use?

XP team: It's very common to provide an immediate order number in the response, and then also send an e-mail confirming the order.

Customer: That's an excellent idea. How does this look?

Display Order Confirmation

   Provide feedback Confirm order with
   an order number.
      – Web-based
      – email

XP team: Excellent. What's next?

Customer: I think the users should be able to look up an existing order's status. They should also be able to look at their order history.

XP team: It sounds like you've described two features—order status and order history. Why don't we break these features into two different stories?

Customer: Okay, I'll start with Display Order Status, and then describe another story named Display Order History.

XP team: Sounds good. What's Display Order Status?

Customer: I think it should display the status of an order given an order number.

XP team: What are the possible statuses?

Customer: At this point, we only have two statuses—processing and shipped.

XP team: Okay, make sure we capture these values.

Customer: What do you think of this?

Display Order Status

    Allow customer to look at order
    status using their order number.

    Status:
        – Processing
        – Shipped

XP team: Fantastic! What about the Display Order History story?

Customer: That one is pretty easy. I just want the customer to be able to display the entire order history on a single page.

Display Order History
    Display all orders for a given
    Customer.

XP team: Outstanding. I think we're making great progress. What's next?

Customer: Let me think. At this point, I can browse, search, shop, create an order, check on an order, and recall all of a customer's orders. I think the next step is to add some administrative features.

XP team: What did you have in mind?

Customer: Well, I need to be able to add and edit customers. Should this be on the same card?

XP team: No, it really sounds like two functions—adding and editing.

Customer: Okay, let's add a new customer first.

XP team: Before we do this, can anyone add a new customer or should they have a particular role?

Customer: No, only designated employees should be able to add new customers.

XP team: So, make sure you record that in your story.

Customer: How about this card, Add New Customer Account?

Add New Customer Account

Add a Customer to database

Only designated employees have
this ability.

XP team: That's good. What about the customer edit?

Customer: That should really be about the same.

XP team: Do you want to give customers the ability to modify their own accounts?

Customer: Yes, the only users allowed to edit a customer account are the customer or one of our employees.

XP team: Does a customer have a status? It might make sense to disable a customer account if he's delinquent. What do you think?

Customer: That makes a lot of sense. Why don't we give the customers a status of active or inactive? Does this capture enough information?

Edit Customer Account

Update Customer account information

Must be either an employee or that
Customer.

Change Customer status active/inactive

XP team: Yeah, that's great.

Customer: I think I have one more feature to add. I want to add some product administration.

XP team: What kind of functionality do you think you'll need?

Customer: At this point, I only want to add and edit products.

XP team: Again, that sounds like two stories. Which feature would you like to begin with?

Customer: Let's begin with adding a new product.

XP team: Okay, can anyone add a new product, or do we need to restrict this feature to a particular role?

Customer: Good catch—only employees can add new products. Do you think this captures enough information?

Add New Product

    Add new product to the products
      database.

   * Must be an employee

XP team: That will do fine. How about editing products?

Customer: It is exactly like Add New Product, except that you're changing the attributes of an existing product.

XP team: Do you want to be able to edit all of a product's attributes?

Customer: I really don't know at this point. I do know that I want to be able to change price and inventory, but I'm not sure about the rest. Can I defer until later in the project?

XP team: Yeah, that's no problem. Just make sure you write down those attributes that you are sure about at this point.

Customer: Okay, I think I have it. What about this?

Edit Product

    Change all product features

    Inventory

    Pricing

    Must be an employee

XP team: That's great for now. We can further qualify it when we get to the iteration.

Customer: I think that's it. Can you think of anything that I may have left out?

XP team: Let's see. You begin with a login, you browse the catalog displaying lists of products for each category. . .wait, what about selecting a product? I don't think we have that defined.

Customer: You're right. We haven't defined that functionality. I guess that would be something as simple as Display Product Detail.

XP team: That sounds good, but what product attributes do you want to display?

Customer: At this point, just the general product information. Can I wait to get descriptive?

XP team: Sure. One thing that we do need to discuss is the inventory. Do we want to display the number of items in stock?

Customer: No, I think we should show the product as available if there is more than one item in stock, or show it as back-ordered if the product has a negative or zero inventory.

```
Display Product Detail
    General Information
    Availability
        → If greater than Ø available
        → If less than Ø back-ordered
```

XP team: Can you think of anything else?

Customer: Not at this point. I think we have a pretty good first pass. What happens if I come up with new functionality?

XP team: That's no big deal. We'll create a new story card and adjust the release, if necessary.

Creating a High-Level Design

The XP team members then talk among themselves and do a very quick high-level design. They first talk about the flow of processing when a user orders a product. Then they walk through the administrative features of the system and the account management features. The result is some high-level diagrams that show screen flow through the system, as illustrated in Figures 11-2, 11-3, and 11-4.

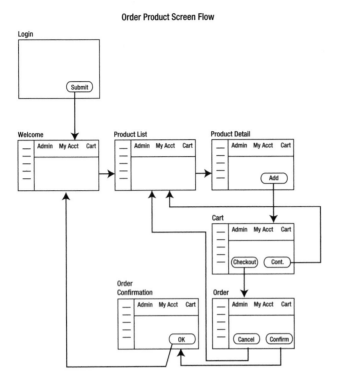

Figure 11-2. *A high-level design of ordering a product*

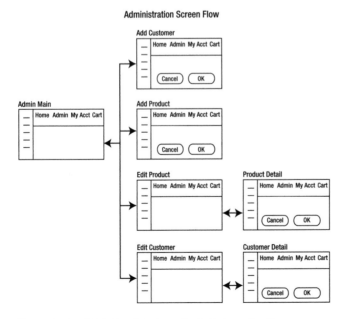

Figure 11-3. *A high-level design of administrative features*

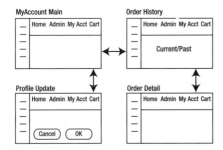

Figure 11-4. *A high-level design of account management features*

Comparing the Stories with the Mission

Now that we have a first pass at our user stories, we need to make sure that our stories match our previously defined mission statement, repeated here:

> *Create a Web presence that allows customers to self-order Northwind products and track the status of their orders all the way through to shipment.*

The conversation may go something like this:

XP team: Do you think that we've sufficiently covered all of the requirements defined by our mission statement?

Customer: Yes, I think we have. We can browse and search the catalog, we can order products, and we can track those products through shipping. I feel like that about covers it.

XP team: Great. Let's move on.

Story Estimating

The next stage in the exploration phase is to begin estimating the level of effort required to complete the user stories. We will review each user story for this purpose. In the process, the testers are going to be asking themselves and the customer if the user story is testable.

If we don't know how to estimate a story, we will spike it. Recall from Chapter 3 that a spike is when the team needs to gain more understanding about the technology or implementation of the story before the story can be estimated.

All estimates are in story points, which are ideal days in length. As a general rule, we recommend that you don't go smaller than a quarter of a story point on any given user story.

Story estimating starts by having the customer read each story again. The developers discuss at a high level what they think they will need to do in order to complete the story. The testers discuss what the acceptance test will be at a high level. If anyone starts diving too deep into the details of a user story, as is often the case, the XP coach will steer the conversation back on track by refocusing the team to the higher-level details. The goal here is to get just enough of an idea as to what each feature (user story) will cost, so the customer can decide if the feature is worth keeping without spending too much time and money arriving at the answer.

Reviewing Each Story

Let's go through each story and estimate its story points.

Login: This user story is very straightforward. The development team and the testers have designed this type of feature many times in the past. The team knows it will need to enhance the existing database a little, and that the login screen will be very simple. Authentication will be the biggest amount of work in this user story. After a brief discussion, we assign an estimate of 1.0 story points.

Add New Customer Account: This user story is also a very common feature. There will be very little database work here, and the entry screen is straightforward, too. We give this story an estimate of 3.0 story points.

Edit Customer Account: This user story is much like the Add New Customer Account user story. Initially, the team talks about leveraging the work from the Add New Customer Account user story, but the XP coach reminds them that it will be the order in which the user stories will be completed is the customer's decision. The estimate should be based on doing the user story all by itself. If it turns out later that the team can leverage work already completed for, say, the Add New Customer Account feature, then the team will finish this Edit Customer Account story earlier than estimated, and they will go back to the customer and ask for more work. Also, there is a difference here, where the user as well as someone with administrative rights can execute this feature. The administrator can edit any customer's data, but the users can edit only their own data. This will add to the complexity of the feature. So, the team talks some more and arrives at an estimate of 3.5 story points.

Add New Product: For this user story, the team members discuss that they estimated the Add New Customer Account user story as 3.0 story points and that this feature is about the same degree of difficulty and effort. Therefore, we give this user story an estimate of 3.0 story points also.

Edit Product: Only users of the application with administrative rights can execute this feature. This will make the processing of this feature simpler than the Edit Customer Account feature. However, a product is more complicated than a customer record. We give this feature an estimate of 3.5 story points.

Search for Product: This user story is considered more difficult and complex than the previous user stories. There is concern that a given search result could return a significant amount of data that will need to be managed correctly so that the application is scalable, as the product data increases over time. The team feels that the level of effort and difficulty is more than twice as hard as the edit features previously discussed. We agree on an estimate of 7.0 story points.

Browse Catalog: This user story also presents some difficulty, as page geometry can get tricky when creating a balanced presentation. The team estimates this feature at 4.0 story points.

Display Product Detail: This user story is easier than the Browse Catalog user story. The team gives this feature an estimate of 2.0 story points.

When the customer reads the next user story, Shopping Cart, the team members confer and decide that the story is really four features in one. They ask the customer if the user story could be split into four cards: Add Product to Shopping Cart, Remove Product from Shopping Cart, Update Shopping Cart Contents, and Display Shopping Cart Contents. The customer agrees, creates the new user story cards, and tears up the originals so they will not be confused with the existing valid user stories.

Add Product to Shopping Cart

From product detail page, allow
user to add product to shopping
cart.

Remove Product from Shopping Cart

From display shopping cart page,
allow the user to remove a product
from the shopping cart.

Update Shopping Cart Contents

From display shopping cart page,
allow the user to modify the quantity
of any product in their cart.
If the user sets the quantity to Ø,
remove the item from their cart
immediately.

Display Shopping Cart Contents
    Display all products in the
    shopping cart.

    If there are no products in the
    shopping cart, display empty
    shopping cart.

Add Product to Shopping Cart: This user story looks simple, but the processing that needs to happen behind the scenes for updating the cart's contents will require some more database work. Also, the customer overhears the developers' and testers' conversation and realizes that he will need a visual update to indicate to the user that the selected product was successfully added to the cart. For now, this is just added to the user story. The estimate is 2.0 story points.

Remove Product from Shopping Cart: This user story is fairly simple. There isn't much discussion here. The team estimates 1.5 story points.

Update Shopping Cart Contents: This user story gets a little tricky, because if the user enters a quantity of zero, the same action taken for the Remove Product from Shopping Cart needs to happen. The estimate the team gives is 2.5 story points.

Display Shopping Cart Contents: This user story is very simple. The team estimates 1.0 story points.

After the customer rereads the Check Out user story, the developers and testers start to talk and decide that the intent of the user story is really to display to the users their new order and ask the users to confirm their order before processing the order. The customer overhears their conversation and chimes in, agreeing with their conclusion. The customer rewrites the user story with the title Display Checkout Confirmation.

Display Checkout Confirmation
    Display Shopping cart contents
    with a confirmation button.

Display Checkout Confirmation: The team comes to the agreement that the estimate on this new story is 1.0 story point.

Display Order Confirmation: This user story sounds like a lot of processing. The team members have not done a feature like this before, but they know someone else outside the team who has. They give a quick call to that person and start to get a feel for how big this feature really is. With the knowledge the team gained by talking with the person outside the group about this feature, the team gives an estimate of 5.5 story points.

Display Order Status: This user story looks like there might be a bit of back-end processing and verification going on. So, the team estimates this feature at 2.0 story points.

Display Order History: This user story appears to be about half the degree of difficulty and effort as the Display Order Status story. Therefore, the team uses the estimate of 1.0 story points.

Getting the Big Picture

The user stories have all been estimated, so that the customer now understands what the cost of implementing each feature will be. These are intentionally high-level estimates, to allow everyone to start to understand the size of this project and determine if the project is worth the investment. We are making this determination as soon and as quickly as possible to minimize the upfront costs of the project as much as possible.

Table 11-1 summarizes all of our stories and their associated estimates. Note that we are listing the user stories in a table simply for clarity in the book. In reality, you will write the estimates on the cards and lay the user stories out on a table or wall to get the "big picture" view.

Table 11-1. *Estimated User Stories*

User Story	Estimated Story Points
Login	1.0
Add New Customer Account	3.0
Edit Customer Account	3.5
Add New Product	3.0
Edit Product	3.5
Search for Product	7.0
Browse Catalog	4.0
Display Product Detail	2.0
Add Product to Shopping Cart	2.0
Remove Product from Shopping Cart	1.5
Update Shopping Cart	2.5
Display Shopping Cart Contents	1.0
Display Checkout Confirmation	1.0
Display Order Confirmation	5.5
Display Order Status	2.0
Display Order History	1.0
Story Point Total	43.50

Declared Velocity

Now the planning game phase begins. The developers and testers talk to the customer about how often the customer would like to see progress during development. They tell the customer that they can deliver new functionality in as little time as every week and as long as every three weeks, but every two weeks is ideal. The customer agrees that delivery of new features every two weeks is good for him.

Next, the customer asks when all the features described can be delivered. Because this is a new development team, without any XP team history, the team's tracker does a quick *one-time* calculation. There are four developers on the team and it was just decided that the team will deliver in two-week iterations. The calculation shows that this team will deliver all the requested features in four iterations or two months, as follows:

1. Calculate the velocity of a single iteration:

    (4/3 × 10) (Truncate) = 13

2. Divide the total number of user story points by the number of story points in a single iteration, and then round up, because the team does full iterations:

    (44.5/13) (Round Up) = 4

The customer states that the projects must be delivered in four weeks, or two iterations, because of market demands and pressure from the executive management groups. The customer asks the developers and testers to please work harder and get all the work done in four weeks. The developers and testers tell the customer that they will, of course, work as hard as they can. If they finish early, they will come back and ask for more work, but if they overcommit now, the team will be setting themselves up for failure from the start.

The developers and testers ask the customer to please select a subset of the user stories that will not exceed the number of story points they can complete in two iterations, which, in this case, is 26 story points.

Story Selection

At this point, we have our user stories, we know our velocity, and we know how long our release is going to be. We get down to business and select the features that will be in our first release.

According to the calculations from the previous section, our velocity provides us with 26 ideal days to accomplish our first release, but we have 43.5 ideal days of work to do, so something is going to be pushed to the next release. It is now the job of the customer to prioritize the user stories and select the ones that provide the most business value for this release.

Prioritizing the Stories

The first round of story prioritization might begin like this:

Coach: The first thing you need to do is prioritize your stories.

Customer: Okay, give me a few minutes. I'm going to rearrange my story cards into the priority that will provide me the most value. . . . I believe I have it. The main thing is that my users must have the ability to browse and submit orders.

The customer comes up with the priorities shown in Table 11-2.

Table 11-2. *Prioritized User Stories*

Story	Story Points
Login	1.0
Browse Catalog	4.0
Display Product Detail	2.0
Search for Product	7.0
Add Product to Shopping Cart	2.0
Remove Product from Shopping Cart	1.5
Update Shopping Cart	2.5
Display Shopping Cart Contents	1.0
Display Checkout Confirmation	1.0
Display Order Confirmation	5.5
Display Order Status	2.0
Display Order History	1.0
Add New Customer Account	3.0
Edit Customer Account	3.5
Add New Product	3.0
Edit Product	3.5
Story Point Total	43.50

Selecting a Subset of Stories

Next, the customer selects the subset of stories that the team should complete in the first release.

Coach: Okay, now select a subset of your defined user stories that doesn't total more than 26 story points.

Customer: Okay, I have removed as many user stories as possible, but I am still over my point total by 4.5 points.

Table 11-3 shows the customer's dilemma.

Table 11-3. *First Subset Cut*

Story	Story Points
Login	1.0
Browse Catalog	4.0
Display Product Detail	2.0
Search for Product	7.0
Add Product to Shopping Cart	2.0
Display Shopping Cart Contents	1.0
Remove Product from Shopping Cart	1.5
Update Shopping Cart	2.5

continued

Table 11-3. *Continued*

Story	Story Points
Display Checkout Confirmation	1.0
Display Order Confirmation	5.5
Display Order Status	2.0
Display Order History	1.0
Story Point Total	30.50

Refining the Subset Selection

Now we need to help the customer arrive at the best solution.

Customer: What can I do?

Coach: You have a few options here. You can juggle your priorities so that you have exactly 26 points. You can just remove a user story that totals 4.5 points or more. Or you can try to simplify one of your existing user stories.

Customer: I really don't want to change my priorities, and I don't want to remove any items. What do you suggest?

Coach: Well, I think I would try to pare down the Search for Product story. It is your largest user story. We can probably keep the basic functionality, while reducing the level of effort. Let's ask the developers what they think. Developers?

Developers: The largest effort involved in this story is handling multiple pages of search results. If we can display all of the search results on a single page and restrict the search to the Product Name field, then I think we can reduce this story to 1.5 ideal days.

Coach: How does that sound?

Customer: Great. I can work with this. I'll rewrite the story card.

Search for Product

Given some text, search for the
existence of that text in the
description of each product.

List all results on the same page.

Coach: Okay, we are at exactly 25 ideal days. This leaves us 1 story point short. Is there any outstanding user story that equals exactly 1 point?

Customer: No, I can't find anything. I don't even see a story that I can simplify. What happens to my extra point?

Coach: If we finish either iteration early, we'll look at adding some additional work.

Table 11-4 shows the complete list of user stories selected for this release.

Table 11-4. *User Stories for the First Release*

Story	Story Points
Login	1.0
Browse Catalog	4.0
Display Product Detail	2.0
Add Product to Shopping Cart	2.0
Remove Product from Shopping Cart	1.5
Update Shopping Cart	2.5
Display Shopping Cart Contents	1.0
Display Checkout Confirmation	1.0
Display Order Confirmation	5.5
Display Order Status	2.0
Search for Product	1.5
Display Order History	1.0
Story Point Total	25

Coach's Journal

We started our project. We had our customer, developers, and testers together in one room to go through the release plan. They were all a little leery about being together. After introductions and an overview of the project's mission and objective, they all started to relax a little.

When we started story writing, the customer looked really nervous. Fortunately, the customer seemed to get the hang of story writing quickly, and the developers and testers were good about giving suggestions. Sometimes, the developers got down too much into the weeds, and I had to pull them out of the details. They reacted well though and were good about not getting wrapped up in too many details before giving high-level estimates.

■**Note** In reality, everyone on the team should keep a journal and write in it every day. In order to keep this book as simple as possible, we will journal from only the development coach's perspective, and we will include only one journal entry per chapter.

Summary

In this chapter, we began the journey that will take us through the rest of the book. We started with an introduction to the business problem. We explored the business problem and created user stories along the way. Then we assigned a cost to each of the user stories.

We then started the planning game portion of the release plan. The team's tracker declared the amount of work the team could sign up for, without overcommitting the team's time. Harnessed with this information, the customer was able to prioritize the user stories based on business need and cost, and then select the subset of user stories that can be completed by the release date. This subset of stories makes up the release that we will develop over the rest of the book.

All of these activities were accomplished as a team—customer, developer, tester, and so forth. This creates a highly collaborative environment that allows the team to work smarter and faster. Release planning will normally occur over the course of three to five days instead of the traditional weeks and months needed for analysis.

CHAPTER 12

∎∎∎

Iteration Planning for the First Iteration

In this chapter, we will continue with the example introduced in Chapter 11. In that chapter, we went through the release planning step for a sample project. Now we are going to create an iteration plan for the first iteration.

We will start with the story selection process, where we will be prioritizing and selecting the user stories that will be accomplished in the first iteration. We will then move on to the process of tasking the selected stories. This process will involve breaking down each story into a group of tasks. Next, we will walk through the developers selecting tasks and providing an ideal estimate for those tasks. Finally, we will complete our iteration plan by balancing the iteration. This process focuses on aligning the story and task estimates.

Story Selection

The first step in creating the iteration plan is to select the user stories that will be part of this iteration. Recall from the previous chapter that we have 26 story points (ideal days) in our entire release and we have two equal iterations of two weeks. This tells us that our customer can select up to 13 points per iteration.

Selecting the stories is the responsibility of the customer, but he is assisted by the entire team. Here's how it might go (with the coach interacting with the customer in this example):

Coach: We said during release planning that we can accomplish 13 story points' worth of work in a single iteration. So, first, we'd like you to prioritize your user stories and select a set of stories that don't total more than 13 story points.

Customer: Okay, I have them prioritized, so let's begin.

Table 12-1 shows the prioritized stories for our entire release.

Table 12-1. *Prioritized User Stories for the Entire Release*

Story	Story Points
Login	1.0
Browse Catalog	4.0
Display Product Detail	2.0
Add Product to Shopping Cart	2.0
Remove Product from Shopping Cart	1.5
Update Shopping Cart	2.5
Display Shopping Cart Contents	1.0
Display Checkout Confirmation	1.0
Display Order Confirmation	5.5
Display Order Status	2.0
Search for Product	1.5
Display Order History	1.0
Story Point Total	25

Coach: Now, starting with your highest priority, select a group of stories that's as close to 13 points as possible.

Customer: All right, I have the stories I'd like to see in my first iteration.

Table 12-2 shows the current stories for the first iteration.

Table 12-2. *Current Stories for the First Iteration*

Story	Story Points
Login	2.0
Browse Catalog	4.0
Display Product Detail	2.0
Add Product to Shopping Cart	2.0
Remove Product from Shopping Cart	1.5
Update Shopping Cart	2.5
Story Point Total	14

Coach: You've selected stories that total 14 story points, which puts you 1 story point over the allotted 13.

Customer: Can't we squeeze in an extra point?

Coach: If we were to agree to that much work, we'd more than likely fail to complete the iteration on time. So, we need you to remove 1 point from the stories selected.

Customer: But, my last story, Update Shopping Cart, is 2.5 points. I thought we couldn't break stories between iterations.

Coach: You're correct, but you do have other options for dealing with this extra point. One is to simplify the Update Shopping Cart user story and have the developers reestimate the split stories. Or, you could remove the Update Shopping Cart user story and select other user stories that don't total more than 1.5 story points.

Customer: Okay, let me look at my stories. I have a story Search for Product that is exactly 1.5 points. I guess I could move it up in the priority list and push Update Shopping Cart to the next iteration. So, now I have a story list for this iteration.

Table 12-3 shows the prioritized stories for this iteration.

Table 12-3. *Prioritized User Stories for the First Iteration*

Story	Story Points
Login	2.0
Browse Catalog	4.0
Display Product Detail	2.0
Add Product to Shopping Cart	2.0
Remove Product from Shopping Cart	1.5
Search for Product	1.5
Story Point Total	13

Customer: This will give me exactly 13 points. But what would have happened if I didn't have a story with the exact amount of remaining points?

Coach: That's a good question. You could either simplify a user story so that the story points on it didn't exceed the number of story points or you could remove the last story and leave the iteration short. In that case, the team would most likely finish the iteration early. If they did finish early enough, the team might go back and select additional stories, which could result in actually completing more stories than originally allocated for the iteration. This is just one way the team's velocity can go up.

Customer: Good enough. I have my stories for this iteration. What's next?

Coach: Now the developers will task out the stories for this iteration. At the end of their tasking, we'll check to see if the iteration is still balanced (that we haven't overcommitted ourselves from the beginning).

Story Tasking and Assignment

Now we start breaking up the user stories into tasks. We are going to estimate the tasks in ideal hours, as opposed to the ideal days used when estimating user stories. Each developer gets 26 ideal task points.

The developers brainstorm the tasks as a group. This way, every developer understands what each task means. When a developer later signs up for a task, the developer will be able to estimate it.

Breaking Up the Stories into Tasks

We will go through each story (in their priority order) and do the task breakdown. We will write the tasks for each user story on the back of its index card.

Login

Our first user story is Login. The developers know they will need a screen to capture the user ID and password. Also, the developers know that the current database schema does not support a user ID and password combination, so that will have to be updated. Lastly, there will need to be an intermediate page to determine if the login failed or succeeded. The developers will use the intermediate page as the manager to decide if the application goes back to the login page or moves forward to the main screen. Figure 12-1 shows these tasks.

Tasks	Owner	Est.	Act.
Create Login Screen.			
Create text entry fields for username and password.			
Build query to database to validate username and password.			
Determine login request success or failure.			

Figure 12-1. *Login story tasks*

Browse Catalog

The Browse Catalog user story will require the developers to create a main page for the application. The developers discuss what it will take to display a list of product categories and decide that they will need to build a query to the database that will return a dataset. Then the application will need to display the results of the dataset on the main page. Figure 12-2 shows the Browse Catalog story tasks.

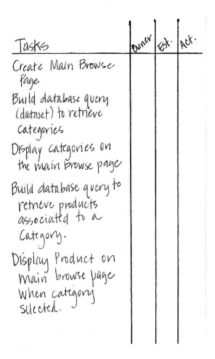

Figure 12-2. *Browse Catalog story tasks*

Display Product Detail

The Display Product Detail user story involves creating yet another page. When the user selects a specific product from a list of available products, the detail information about that selected product needs to be retrieved from the database, again in the form of a dataset. Also, the availability of the product (number of product units currently available in inventory) needs to be determined. All of this information must be displayed on the page. Figure 12-3 shows the Display Product Detail story tasks.

Task	Owner	Est.	Act.
Create Product Detail Page			
Build database query (dataset) to retrieve all specific information on a given product			
Set Availability of product			
Display product detail on page			

Figure 12-3. *Display Product Detail story tasks*

Add Product to Shopping Cart

For the Add Product to Shopping Cart user story, the developers decide that the best solution is to add a button to the product detail page (developed for the Display Product Detail user story). When the user clicks the Add Product button, a shopping cart icon located at the top of the page should be updated to show one more item in the user's shopping cart. In addition, a new shopping cart object will need to be created if one does not already exist for this user. Then a new product item object will need to be created and added to the shopping cart object. Finally, the shopping cart object needs to be added to the HTTP session so that the shopping cart will be available to other actions and pages that the user invokes. Figure 12-4 shows the Add Product to Shopping Cart story tasks.

Task	Owner	Est.	Act.
Create "Add Product" button on Product Detail page			
Update Shopping Cart items total icon.			
Add item to Shopping Cart in session			
Create shopping cart Object			
Create product line item object			

Figure 12-4. *Add Product to Shopping Cart story tasks*

Remove Product from Shopping Cart

When the developers get to the Remove Product from Shopping Cart user story, they see that they need to add a button to the Display Shopping Cart page, which does not exist yet. The customer has not selected the Display Shopping Cart Contents user story for this release. There is a clear dependency here that can be handled a couple different ways:

- Create a fake Display Shopping Cart page that will display the contents of a static shopping cart. Then they could add the Remove Product button to this fake page, which would remove the product from the prebuilt static shopping cart and handle the appropriate updates to the page to show that the product was removed. If the developers take this approach, it will increase the complexity of the tasks, but it serves to keep the user story autonomous.

- Try to task out the Display Shopping Cart page and see if the total of all the tasks are still within the team's allowable story and task points for the iteration. This is the approach that our development team will take, as you will see later in this chapter when we balance the iteration.

Figure 12-5 shows the tasks for the Remove Product from Shopping Cart story.

Task	Owner	Est.	Act.
Create "Remove Product" button on Display shopping Cart page			
Update product quantity from Shopping Cart when button clicked			
Update Shopping Cart items total Icon			

Figure 12-5. *Remove Product from Shopping Cart story tasks*

Search for Product

To figure out the tasks necessary for the Search for Product story, the developers need to ask the customer for more information about how and when the customer wants to search for products. This is an example of when a user story is "a promise for a future conversation."

After this conversation, the developers know that they need to add a text field with an associated Search button to the main toolbar that displays across the top of all pages. The text field will be used to capture the search criteria. When the user clicks the Search button, a query using the search criteria will be sent to the database, and a result will be returned in the form of another dataset. Then the dataset will be used to display the results to the user in a Search Result page. Figure 12-6 shows the tasks for the Search for Product story.

Task	Owner	Est.	Act.
Create text entry field to search on with button			
Execute search on product data that contains search criteria and build dataset			
Display result dataset in Search for Product screen			

Figure 12-6. *Search for Product story tasks*

Signing Up for Tasks

After all of the user stories are tasked, the developers must sign up for the tasks they want to take. Each developer is estimating in task points (ideal hours), and each developer owns his estimate. In our example, each developer currently has a total of 26 task points to use. In order to reduce the dependencies of developers and the user stories they are working on, it is best if one developer signs up for as many of the tasks on a single story as he possibly can.

There are several approaches to accomplishing signing up for tasks, such as the following:

- Copy all of the tasks from the back of the user story cards (where we created them in the previous section) to something bigger, like flip chart paper that sticks to a wall. Then have all the developers make a mad dash up to the list of tasks and sign up, all at the same time. As noted in Chapter 4, such an approach can be great entertainment, but can also get a little aggressive.

- Have each developer sign up for one task at a time and repeat this for the entire team round-robin style. When the development team has used up all the task points or all the tasks have been assigned, you stop. This is the approach that our XP coach chose to take. Figures 12-7 through 12-12 shows the results.

Tasks	Owner	Est.	Act.
Create Login Screen	HM	.50	
Create Text entry fields for username and password	HM	.25	
Build query to database to validate username and password	HP	2	
Determine login request success or failure.	HM	4	

Figure 12-7. *Login story tasks, with owners and estimates*

Tasks	Owner	Est.	Act.
Create Main Browse Page	JG	2	
Build database query (dataset) to retrieve categories	JG	12	
Display categories on the main browse page	JG	12	
Build database query to retrieve products associated to a category	MF	0.5	
Display product on main browse page when category selected	MF	1.0	

Figure 12-8. *Browse Catalog story tasks, with owners and estimates*

Task	Owner	Est.	Act.
Create Product Detail Page	HP	8	
Build database query (data set) to retrieve all specific information on a given product	HP	8	
Set Availability of product	HP	4	
Display product detail on page	HP	4	

Figure 12-9. *Display Product Detail story tasks, with owners and estimates*

Task	Owner	Est.	Act.
Create "Add Product" button on Product Detail page	HM	.25	
Update Shopping Cart items total icon.	HM	4	
Add item to Shopping Cart in session	HM	.50	
Create shopping cart object	MF	8	
Create product line item object	MF	6	

Figure 12-10. *Add Product to Shopping Cart story tasks, with owners and estimates*

Task	Owner	Est.	Act.
Create "Remove Product" button on Display shopping Cart page	HM	1	
Update product quantity from Shopping Cart when button clicked	HM	4.5	
Update Shopping Cart items total Icon	HM	4	

Figure 12-11. *Remove Product from Shopping Cart story tasks, with owners and estimates*

Task	Owner	Est.	Act.
Create text entry field to search on with button	MF	.50	
Execute search on product data that contains search criteria and build data set	MF	6	
Display result dataset in Search for Product screen	MF	4	

Figure 12-12. *Search for Product story tasks, with owners and estimates*

Iteration Balancing

Regardless of the approach you take for task sign-up, it is very likely that the developers will have task points left over or some tasks will remain unassigned. If developers still have task points, you need to look at possibly taking on more work in the iteration. If you have tasks left unassigned, you need to either simplify the user story to the point where those tasks can be eliminated or remove the entire user story and select a simpler user story to include in the iteration.

In our example, it turned out that the tasks for all the user stories in this iteration were assigned. All of the developers used up their task points, except for one. The developer with the initials HM did not use all of her task points; she has 7 task points left over. Here's how the coach might present the situation to the customer:

Coach: It looks like we have 7 extra points to spend. Is there anything else that you'd like to move into this iteration?

Customer: Well, I'd like to move the Display Shopping Cart Contents story into the iteration, but it's 1 story point, which equals 8 task points. This would put me over by 1 task point.

Coach: Why don't we task that story out and see if we can get a more granular estimate?

Customer: Great. Let's give it to the developers.

Coach: Well, what do you know? The developers estimated the story's tasks to total exactly 7 task points.

Figure 12-13 shows the Display Shopping Cart Contents story tasks and assignments.

Task	Owner	Est.	Act.
Create Shopping Cart screen	HM	1	
Display Shopping Cart product line items	HM	6	

Figure 12-13. *Display Shopping Cart Contents story tasks, with owners and estimates*

Here are our finalized stories for the first iteration:

- Login

- Browse Catalog

- Display Product Detail

- Add Product to Shopping Cart

- Remove Product from Shopping Cart

- Search for Product

- Display Shopping Cart Contents

When we added the Display Shopping Cart Contents Story to our current iteration, you might have expected our team velocity to increase by the number of story points assigned to this story, but this is not the case. When we get into story tasking, we are assigning more granular estimates (in the form of task points) to each of our stories. When we have tasked out all of the stories in our iteration, we total the task points and add/remove stories to/from the iteration accordingly. This is exactly what happened when we balanced our current iteration. We had 7 extra task points, which allowed us to add the Display Shopping Cart Contents story.

Coach's Journal

We learned a lot more about the project when we started looking at the details of the stories in the first iteration. I think that keeping the focus to just the user stories in the first iteration helped us see the details better, without getting caught up in the specifics of the project as a whole. The customer seemed to appreciate the gaps we were finding early. It would be better if we had discovered the gaps up front, but I guess nobody is perfect.

The developers are a little leery about all this estimating. They estimate at the story level, then again at the task level, and the estimate keeps getting adjusted. I had to remind them that refining their estimates is a good thing. The story estimates helped us all get an idea of just how big this project really is quickly, and the task estimates helped us rethink the size of a given story based on more detailed information. They still aren't too sure about all this estimating, but they are willing to keep trying it.

Summary

As you saw from this chapter and the previous chapter, XP is loaded with planning. Who needs complicated project plans and Gantt charts? Keeping those up to date is a task in itself. In XP, we manage project change with course corrections during each iteration.

In this chapter, we took the entire release plan created in Chapter 11 and had the customer select a portion for the team to focus on for the first iteration. This portion of stories from the release plan was made up of the customer's highest priority features. This helps ensure that the customer will get the features he needs the most first.

By tasking out the user stories selected for the iteration, the team was able to focus on the details that are important to this iteration. That kept the discussion as brief as possible and focused on a smaller set of details. This helped uncover new information and details about features that would not have necessarily been discovered in a broader conversation.

Lastly, we made sure that all the developers had signed up for as much work as possible without overcommitting themselves. Who knows what will happen during the iteration? An unexpected technical problem could occur, or some other details not yet thought about could be brought to light during the iteration. If the team had signed up for more work at the beginning of the iteration than was reasonable for the members to complete, there would be a big possibility that they would not complete the iteration in the allotted time.

■ ■ ■

CHAPTER 13

First Iteration

In the previous chapter, we developed an iteration plan for our sample project. Now we're ready to work on the first iteration.

This chapter will be mainly from a developer's perspective of the iteration. We will take a quick look at what other XP team members are doing, but the actual output of those roles will not be demonstrated. The goal of this chapter is to demonstrate the developer's XP practices in action.

To get your environment prepared for this chapter, you need to walk through the steps outlined in Appendix A. In Appendix A, you will be guided through how to set up a Visual Studio solution with multiple projects. This type of solution/project configuration works well for development projects that have multiple team members.

Daily Stand-Ups

Each day of the iteration, the team will have a stand-up meeting at a standard time. The coach is responsible for moderating the stand-up. The attendees all stand up during the meeting to encourage the participants to keep the meeting brief. The attendees will identify any issues or concerns they currently have. These issues and concerns will be acknowledged, and someone will take ownership of them, but resolutions will not occur during the stand-up.

One of the issues that came up during the course of this iteration was the connection string used for connection to the database. One of the developer's Microsoft SQL Server Database Engine (MSDE) was set up to use her machine name instead of localhost. This was an issue because the developer needed to change the connection string in several locations, which was time-consuming, not to mention begging for refactoring. One of the other developers on the team agreed to take ownership of the issue and propose a solution by the time the second iteration was ready to begin.

Design Meeting

After the daily stand-up, any design issues are addressed as needed. Some or all of the developers and testers meet briefly (no more than two hours) to discuss the design and resolve any issues. They stay focused on what needs to be designed for this iteration. Remember that XP is making the bet that it will cost less to develop what is needed today and change when needed, versus developing today what you think you might be needed in the future (but you don't actually end up using).

More design meetings occur at the start of the iteration than at the end. If you find you are still having a lot of design meetings at the end of your iteration, that may be a sign that your high-level design is still weak.

The design for the first iteration in our example is shown in Figure 13-1.

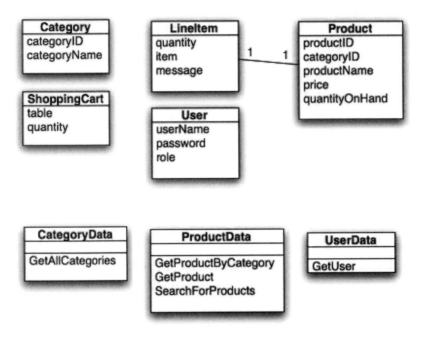

Figure 13-1. *The design for the first iteration*

Developers' Duties: Pair Up and Test, Code, and Refactor

After the daily stand-up and/or design meeting, the teams pair up. They switch their pair at least once a day. Remember that no one can refuse to pair with someone else, but you can ask for a little time before you get together with the other person.

■**Note** Don't forget that pairing is for the entire team. This includes developers with developers, testers with testers, developers with customers, testers with customers and developers with testers.

With your pair in tow, you are ready to get down to developing solutions to the stories selected for this iteration. You are working on one of the tasks you have signed up for or working with someone else on one of the tasks that developer chose. Make a note of the time you started working on the task, so you can keep track of your actual time spent on the task for the tracker. Only track the time for your own tasks.

Developing the Login User Story

The first user story that we are going to develop is Login. In iteration planning (Chapter 12), this story was broken down into the following tasks:

- Create login screen

- Create text entry fields for username and password

- Build query to database to validate username and password

- Determine login request success or failure

Before you begin, you need to clean up the Northwind solution you created in Appendix A. Delete any empty (default) classes that were autogenerated by the IDE (Class1.cs) or web pages (WebPage1.aspx or Default.aspx) and any test classes you created (CategoryTests.cs and the associated Category.cs class). If you did not create the Northwind solution in Appendix A, do that now.

The first task that you are going to work on is the one to validate the username and password against the database.

■Note The source code presented here is not meant to necessarily show the best way to code a .NET web application. The source code is intentionally kept as basic and simple as possible, so that you can focus on the XP technique of developing software in a .NET environment. Apress has many great books on C# and the .NET Framework that you can refer to for thorough coverage of those topics.

Build Query to Database to Validate Username and Password Task

The Login user story has one business class (User.cs) and one data class (UserData.cs) that need unit tests. You are going to code iteratively, so you will start with the smallest unit test possible.

Using the test-driven development approach, you start with the UserTests.cs file shown in Listing 13-1, which you need to add to the TestLayer project. You will need to add a reference to the BusinessLayer and DataLayer projects on the TestLayer project, if you have not done so already.

Listing 13-1. *UserTests.cs File*

```
#region Using directives
using System;
using System.Collections.Generic;
using System.Text;
using NUnit.Framework;
using BusinessLayer;
using DataLayer;
#endregion
```

```
namespace TestLayer
{
  [TestFixture]
  public class UserTests
  {
    public UserTests()
    {
    }

    [SetUp]
    public void Init()
    {
    }

    [TearDown]
    public void Destroy()
    {
    }

    [Test]
    public void TestGetUser()
    {
      UserData userData = new UserData();
      Assert.IsNotNull(userData.GetUser("bogususer", "password"),
        "GetUser returned a null value, gasp!");
    }
  }
}
```

If you build the solution now, you will get several errors because your web application does not have a concept of a UserData class. To address that issue, you will need to define a minimal UserData class so you can successfully build but not pass the test. Listing 13-2 shows the minimal UserData.cs file that needs to be added to the DataLayer project. You will need to add a reference to the BusinessLayer project on the DataLayer project, if you have not done so already.

Listing 13-2. *Minimal UserData.cs File*

```
#region Using directives
using System;
using System.Collections.Generic;
using System.Text;
using BusinessLayer;
#endregion
```

```
namespace DataLayer
{
  public class UserData
  {
    public UserData()
    {
    }

    public User GetUser(string username, string password)
    {
      User user = null;

      return user;
    }
  }
}
```

Set the TestLayer project as the startup project and build the solution. You still get compiler errors—although the UserData class is now defined, you introduced another class (User) that is yet to be defined

Listing 13-3 shows the minimal source for the User.cs class that needs to be added to the BusinessLayer project.

Listing 13-3. *Minimal User.cs File*

```
#region Using directive
using System;
using Sytem.Collections.Generic;
using System.Text;
#endregion

namespace BusinessLayer
{
  public class User
  {
    public User()
    {
    }
  }
}
```

USING A MOCK OBJECT

If the database had not been ready when you started coding this portion of the user story, you could have used a mock object here instead. To do that, you would first add a reference to the NMock DLL (nmock.dll) to the TestLayer project. Next, you would create an interface class called IUserData.cs that looks like the following.

```
#region Using directives
using System;
using System.Collections.Generic;
using System.Text;
using BusinessLayer;
#endregion

namespace DataLayer
{
  interface IuserData
  {
    User GetUser(string username, string password);
  }
}
```

Then you would make the UserTests.cs class look like the following.

```
#region Using directives
using System;
using System.Collections.Generic;
using System.Text;
using NUnit.Framework;
using NMock;
using BusinessLayer;
using DataLayer;
#endregion

namespace TestLayer
{
  [TestFixture]
  public class UserTests
  {
    public UserTests()
    {
    }

    [SetUp]
    public void Init()
    {
    }
```

```
    [TearDown]
    public void Destroy()
    {
    }

    [Test]
    public void TestGetUser()
    {
      DynamicMock userData = new DynamicMock (typeof(IUserData));
      Assert.IsNotNull(userData.GetUser("bogususer", "password"),
        "GetUser returned a null value, gasp!");
    }
  }
}
```

When the database became available, you would implement the UserData.cs class as shown in Listing 13-2 and have the UserData class inherit (implement) the IUserData interface. At that time, you would also update the UserTests.cs class to use the UserData.cs class instead of the mock object you implemented.

Now rebuild and run the solution. You will not get any compiler errors, but when the test executes, the test fails. That's because you are simply returning a null value for the user. Let's fix that first. Start by modifying the UserData.cs file as shown in Listing 13-4.

Listing 13-4. *Modified UserData.cs File*

```
#region Using directives
using System;
using System.Collections.Generic;
using System.Text;
using BusinessLayer;
#endregion

namespace DataLayer
{
  public class UserData
  {
    public UserData()
    {
    }
```

```
    public User GetUser(string username, string password)
    {
      User user = null;
      user = new User();
      return user;
    }
  }
}
```

Notice that you just wrote a test, coded a little, and then refactored. This is the coding habit you want to develop. Once you have adopted this style of coding, you will find that you will produce fewer bugs and have a greater sense that the quality of the code you are creating is continually getting better.

Now when you rebuild the solution, it builds just fine and your test passes, but nothing of any significance is really happening. To take the next step, you need to modify your UserData class to connect to the Northwind database to get the user's role, along with the username and password, using the username and password passed to the UserData class from the UserTests class. Listing 13-5 shows the UserData.cs file with these changes.

Listing 13-5. *UserData.cs File Modified to Connect to the Database*

```
#region Using directives
using System;
using System.Collections.Generic;
using System.Data;
using System.Data.Odbc;
using System.Text;
using BusinessLayer;
#endregion

namespace DataLayer
{
  public class UserData
  {
    private static string connectionString =
      "Driver={Microsoft Access Driver (*.mdb)};" +
      "DBQ=c:\\xpnet\\database\\Northwind.mdb";

    public UserData()
    {
    }

    public User GetUser(string username, string password)
    {
      User user = null;
```

```
    try
    {
      OdbcConnection dataConnection = new OdbcConnection();
      dataConnection.ConnectionString = connectionString;
      dataConnection.Open();
      OdbcCommand dataCommand = new OdbcCommand();
      dataCommand.Connection = dataConnection;

      // Build command string
      StringBuilder commandText =
        new StringBuilder("SELECT * FROM Users WHERE UserName='");
      commandText.Append(username);
      commandText.Append("' AND Password='");
      commandText.Append(password);
      commandText.Append("'");

      dataCommand.CommandText = commandText.ToString();

      OdbcDataReader dataReader = dataCommand.ExecuteReader();

      // Make sure that we found our user
      if ( dataReader.Read() )
      {
        user = new User(dataReader.GetString(0),
          dataReader.GetString(1));
      }

      dataConnection.Close();
    }
    catch(Exception e)
    {
      Console.WriteLine("Error: " + e.Message);
    }

    return user;
  }
 }
}
```

When you rebuild the solution now, you have a compile error because you don't have a
User class that has a constructor that takes arguments. Listing 13-6 shows the change to the
User class.

Listing 13-6. *Modified User.cs File*

```
#region Using directives
using System;
using System.Collections.Generic;
using System.Text;
#endregion

namespace BusinessLayer
{
  public class User
  {
    private string userName;
    private string password;

    public User()
    {
    }

    public User(string userName, string password)
    {
      this.userName = userName;
      this.password = password;
    }
  }
}
```

Lastly, you need to enhance the UserTests class to pass a username and password to the UserData class. Since this is a test, you need to create test data that you feel confident will not exist in the database. That way, you can set up the data and remove it when your test has completed safely. You will refactor the database connections better later, but for now, you will take the simplest approach possible. Listing 13-7 shows the modifications to the UserTests.cs file.

Listing 13-7. *Modified UserTests.cs File*

```
#region Using directives
using System;
using System.Collections.Generic;
using System.Data;
using System.Data.Odbc;
using System.Text;
using NUnit.Framework;
using BusinessLayer;
using DataLayer;
#endregion
```

```csharp
namespace TestLayer
{
  [TestFixture]
  public class UserTests
  {
    private StringBuilder connectionString;

    public UserTests()
    {
      // Build connection string
      connectionString =
        new StringBuilder("Driver={Microsoft Access Driver (*.mdb)}");
      connectionString.Append(";DBQ=c:\\xpnet\\database\Northwind.mdb");
    }

    [SetUp]
    public void Init()
    {
      try
      {
        OdbcConnection dataConnection = new OdbcConnection();
        dataConnection.ConnectionString = connectionString.ToString();
        dataConnection.Open();

        OdbcCommand dataCommand = new OdbcCommand();
        dataCommand.Connection = dataConnection;

        // Build command string
        StringBuilder commandText =
          new StringBuilder("INSERT INTO Users (UserName, Password");
        commandText.Append(" VALUES ('bogususer', 'password')");

        dataCommand.CommandText = commandText.ToString();

        int rows = dataCommand.ExecuteNonQuery();

        // Make sure that the INSERT worked
        Assert.AreEqual(1, rows, "Unexpected row count returned.");

        dataConnection.Close();
      }
      catch(Exception e)
      {
        Assert.Fail("Error: " + e.Message);
      }
    }
```

```
    [TearDown]
    public void Destroy()
    {
      try
      {
        OdbcConnection dataConnection = new OdbcConnection();
        dataConnection.ConnectionString = connectionString.ToString();
        dataConnection.Open();

        OdbcCommand dataCommand = new OdbcCommand();
        dataCommand.Connection = dataConnection;

        // Build command string
        StringBuilder commandText =
          new StringBuilder("DELETE FROM Users WHERE username='bogususer'");

        dataCommand.CommandText = commandText.ToString();

        int rows = dataCommand.ExecuteNonQuery();

        // Make sure that the DELETE worked
        Assert.AreEqual(1, rows, "Unexpected row count returned");

        dataConnection.Close();
      }
      catch(Exception e)
      {
          Assert.Fail("Error: " + e.Message);
      }
    }


    [Test]
    public void TestGetUser()
    {
      UserData userData = new UserData();

      Assert.IsNotNull(userData.GetUser("bogususer", "password"),
        "GetUser returned a null value, gasp!");
    }
  }
}
```

Rebuild the solution again and run your tests. If you get any errors, look at the build or runtime output to see where the error occurred.

Don't forget that testing is not just all "happy day" scenarios. Add a negative test where you pass in a bad username and password, as shown in Listing 13-8. In this test, you should expect to get a null user back, since the user should not exist in the database.

Listing 13-8. *Negative Test for UserTests.cs*

```
#region Using directives
using System;
using System.Collections.Generic;
using System.Data;
using System.Data.OdbcClient;
using System.Text;
using NUnit.Framework;
using BusinessLayer;
using DataLayer;
#endregion

namespace TestLayer
{
  [TestFixture]
  public class UserTests
  {
    private StringBuilder connectionString;

    public UserTests()
    {
      // Build connection string
      connectionString =
        new StringBuilder("Driver={Microsoft Access Driver (*.mdb)}");
      connectionString.Append(";DBQ=c:\\xpnet\\database\Northwind.mdb");
    }

    [SetUp]
    public void Init()
    {
      try
      {
        OdbcConnection dataConnection = new OdbcConnection();
        dataConnection.ConnectionString = connectionString.ToString();
        dataConnection.Open();

        OdbcCommand dataCommand = new OdbcCommand();
        dataCommand.Connection = dataConnection;

        // Build command string
        StringBuilder commandText =
          new StringBuilder("INSERT INTO Users (UserName, Password");
        commandText.Append(" VALUES ('bogususer', 'password')");

        dataCommand.CommandText = commandText.ToString();
```

```
    int rows = dataCommand.ExecuteNonQuery();

    // Make sure that the INSERT worked
    Assert.AreEqual(1, rows, "Unexpected row count returned.");

    dataConnection.Close();
  }
  catch(Exception e)
  {
    Assert.Fail("Error: " + e.Message);
  }
}

[TearDown]
public void Destroy()
{
  try
  {
    OdbcConnection dataConnection = new OdbcConnection();
    dataConnection.ConnectionString = connectionString.ToString();
    dataConnection.Open();

    OdbcCommand dataCommand = new OdbcCommand();
    dataCommand.Connection = dataConnection;

    // Build command string
    StringBuilder commandText =
      new StringBuilder("DELETE FROM Users WHERE username='bogususer'");

    dataCommand.CommandText = commandText.ToString();

    int rows = dataCommand.ExecuteNonQuery();

    // Make sure that the DELETE worked
    Assert.AreEqual(1, rows, "Unexpected row count returned");

    dataConnection.Close();
  }
  catch(Exception e)
  {
    Assert.Fail("Error: " + e.Message);
  }
}
```

```
  [Test]
  public void TestGetUser()
  {
    UserData userData = new UserData();

    Assert.IsNotNull(userData.GetUser("bogususer", "password"),
      "GetUser returned a null value, gasp!");
  }

  [Test]
  public void NegativeTestGetUser()
  {
    UserData userData = new UserData();

    Assert.IsNull(userData.GetUser("", ""),
      "GetUser did not return a null value, gasp!");
  }
 }
}
```

Rebuild the solution and run the test again. This time two tests should run, and both should pass successfully.

Let's move on to the Create Login Screen task for the Login user story.

Create Login Screen Task

For the Create Login Screen task, you are going to add a new web form (.aspx) to the NorthwindWeb project. Name that web page Login.aspx. Switch to the Source view of the file and make it look like the code in Listing 13-9.

Listing 13-9. *Login.aspx File*

```
<%@ Page language="C#" CodeFile="login.aspx.cs" Inherits="Login_aspx %>
<!DOCTYPE html PUBLIC "-//W3C//DTD XHTML 1.1//EN"
                    "http://www.w3.org/TR/xhtml11/DTD/xhtml11.dtd">
<html xmlns="http://www.w3.org/1999/xhtml">
  <head runat="server">
    <title>Login</title>
  </head>
  <body>
    <form id="login" method="post" runat="server">
      <div>
        <asp:Label ID="titleLabel" style="z-index: 104;
          left: 427px; position: absolute; top: 56px"
          Runat="server">Northwind Login</asp:Label>
```

```
        <asp:Button ID="submitButton" OnClick="SubmitButton_Click"
         style="z-index: 105;
           left: 576px; position: absolute; top: 231px"TabIndex="3"
           Runat="server" Text="Login">
        </asp:Button>
      </div>
    </form>
  </body>
</html>
```

Then select the View ➤ Code menu item and make the Login.aspx.cs file look like Listing 13-10.

Listing 13-10. *Login.aspx.cs File*

```csharp
using System;

public partial class Login_aspx : System.Web.UI.Page
{
  private void SubmitButton_Click(object sender, System.EventArgs e)
  {
  }
}
```

Next, let's tackle creating the text-entry fields for the login screen.

Create Text Entry Fields for Username and Password Task

Now you need to add the data-entry fields to the login screen. You will pass the entered user-name and password to the UserData.cs class for validation. To accomplish this, you need to make the Login.aspx file (Source view) look like Listing 13-11.

Listing 13-11. *Modified Login.aspx File*

```
<%@ Page language="C#" CodeFile="login.aspx.cs" Inherits="Login_aspx %>
<!DOCTYPE html PUBLIC "-//W3C//DTD XHTML 1.1//EN"
                    "http://www.w3.org/TR/xhtml11/DTD/xhtml11.dtd">
<html xmlns="http://www.w3.org/1999/xhtml">
  <head runat="server">
    <title>Login</title>
  </head>
  <body>
    <form id="login" method="post" runat="server">
      <div>
        <asp:Label ID="titleLabel" style="z-index: 104;
          left: 427px; position: absolute; top: 56px"
          Runat="server">Northwind Login</asp:Label>
```

```
        <asp:Label ID="usernameLabel" style="z-index: 101;
          left: 362px; position: absolute; top: 126px"
          Runat="server">Username:</asp:Label>
        <asp:Label ID="passwordLabel" style="z-index: 102;
          left: 364px; position: absolute; top: 184px"
          Runat="server">Password:</asp:Label>
        <asp:TextBox ID="usernameTextBox" style="z-index: 103;
          left: 452px; position: absolute; top: 121px" TabIndex="1"
          Runat="server" Width="145px" Height="22px">
        </asp:TextBox>
        <input style="z-index: 106; left: 451px; width: 145px;
          position: absolute; top: 181px; height: 22px" tabindex="2"
          type="password" name="passwordTextBox" id="passwordTextBox" />
        <asp:Button ID="submitButton" OnClick="SubmitButton_Click"
         style="z-index: 105;
          left: 576px; position: absolute; top: 231px"TabIndex="3"
          Runat="server" Text="Login">
        </asp:Button>
      </div>
    </form>
  </body>
</html>
```

Then enhance the Login.aspx.cs file as shown in Listing 13-12.

Listing 13-12. *Modified Login.aspx.cs File*

```
using System;
using BusinessLayer;
using DataLayer;

public partial class Login_aspx : System.Web.UI.Page
{
  private void SubmitButton_Click(object sender, System.EventArgs e)
  {
    string passwordText = Request.Params["passwordTextBox"];
    UserData userData = new UserData();
    User user = userData.GetUser(usernameTextBox.Text, passwordText);
  }
}
```

That's it for this task. Let's move to the last one for this user story.

Determine Login Request Success or Failure Task

Lastly, you need to give the users an indication of whether or not they successfully logged in. First, enhance the Login.aspx file as shown in Listing 13-13.

Listing 13-13. *Further Modifications to Login.aspx*

```
<%@ Page language="C#" CodeFile="login.aspx.cs" Inherits="Login_aspx %>
<!DOCTYPE html PUBLIC "-//W3C//DTD XHTML 1.1//EN"
                      "http://www.w3.org/TR/xhtml11/DTD/xhtml11.dtd">
<html xmlns="http://www.w3.org/1999/xhtml">
  <head runat="server">
    <title>Login</title>
  </head>
  <body>
    <form id="login" method="post" runat="server">
      <div>
        <asp:Label ID="titleLabel" style="z-index: 104;
          left: 427px; position: absolute; top: 56px"
          Runat="server">Northwind Login</asp:Label>
        <asp:Label id="usernameLabel" style="z-index: 101;
          left: 362px; position: absolute; top: 126px"
          Runat="server">Username:</asp:Label>
        <asp:Label ID="passwordLabel" style="z-index: 102;
          left: 364px; position: absolute; top: 184px"
          Runat="server">Password:</asp:Label>
        <asp:TextBox ID="usernameTextBox" style="z-index: 103;
          left: 452px; position: absolute; top: 121px" TabIndex="1"
          Runat="server" Width="145px" Height="22px">
        </asp:TextBox>
        <input style="z-index: 106; left: 451px; width: 145px;
          position: absolute; top: 181px; height: 22px" tabindex="2"
          type="password" name="passwordTextBox" id="passwordTextBox" />
        <asp:Button ID="submitButton" OnClick="SubmitButton_Click"
          style="z-index: 105;
          left: 576px; position: absolute; top: 231px"TabIndex="3"
          Runat="server" Text="Login">
        </asp:Button>
        <asp:Label ID="successLabel" style="z-index: 107;
          left: 332px; position: absolute; top: 311px"
          Runat="server" Width="389px" Visible="False">
        </asp:Label>
      </div>
    </form>
  </body>
</html>
```

Then you need to enhance the Login.aspx.cs class to check the returned value from the database query and set the success label as appropriate, as shown in Listing 13-14.

Listing 13-14. *Further Modifications to Login.aspx.cs*

```
using System;
using BusinessLayer;
using DataLayer;

public partial class Login_aspx
{
  private void SubmitButton_Click(object sender, System.EventArgs e)
  {
    string passwordText = Request.Params["passwordTextBox"];
    UserData userData = new UserData();
    User user = userData.GetUser(usernameTextBox.Text, passwordText);

    successLabel.Visible = true;

    if (user != null)
    {
      // Go to main NorthwindWeb page eventually
      // But for now, just display a success message
      successLabel.Text = "User login succeeded, woohoo!";
    }
    else
    {
      // Go back to this page to let the user try again
      successLabel.Text = "User login failed, gasp!";
    }
  }
}
```

Now run your unit test to see if everything is passing. Make sure that the TestLayer project is set as the startup project. Then rebuild the solution. If everything built correctly, start the TestLayer project by selecting Build ➤ Start (or by pressing F5). Then click the Run button to execute the unit tests. You should get a green bar.

Next, set the startup project to the NorthwindWeb project and Login.aspx as the start page. This will allow you to see your code in action, as a user would. If all goes well, your web browser should pop up and display the login web page.

So, you have completed all the defined tasks for the Login user story. You created a login screen with text-entry fields for the username and password, and you processed the login request by verifying the username and password against the database. You then determined if the user successfully logged in and displayed either a success or failure message. You also created both positive and negative tests against the business layer of the web application. You have successfully completed your part of the user story as far as you know, but the user story is not completed until the user story has been accepted by the customer. For acceptance of the user story, the customer must define the acceptance criteria with the help of the acceptance tester, as discussed in the "Other Team Members' Duties" section later in the chapter.

Now let's work on another user story.

Developing the Browse Catalog User Story

The next user story you are going to develop is Browse Catalog. This user story has the following tasks:

- Create main browse page

- Build database query (dataset) to retrieve categories

- Display categories on the main browse page

- Build database query to retrieve products associated with a category

- Display product on main browse page when category selected

In this user story, you have two business layer classes (Category and Product) with corresponding data layer classes (CategoryData and ProductData).

As with the Login user story, you'll start with a database query.

Build Database Query (Dataset) to Retrieve Categories Task

You will start again with a minimal test class for just the categories (CategoryTests.cs) that you will add to the TestLayer project, as shown in Listing 13-15.

Listing 13-15. *Minimal CategoryTests.cs File*

```
#region Using directives
using System;
using System.Collections;
using System.Collections.Generic;
using System.Text;
using NUnit.Framework;
using DataLayer;
#endregion

namespace TestLayer
{
  [TestFixture]
  public class CategoryTests
  {
    public CategoryTests()
    {
    }

    [SetUp]
    public void Init()
    {
    }
```

```
    [TearDown]
    public void Destroy()
    {
    }

    [Test]
    public void TestFindAllCategories()
    {
      ArrayList categories = CategoryData.GetAllCategories();
      Assert.IsNotNull(categories, "GetAllCategories returned a null value, gasp!");
      Assert.IsTrue(categories.Count > 0, "Bad category count, gasp!");
    }
  }
}
```

Now rebuild the solution and verify that you cannot compile successfully. If you did compile successfully, you have an issue, because the CategoryData class should not be defined yet.

Listing 13-16 shows the source for the CategoryData class that you should add to the DataLayer project.

Listing 13-16. *CategoryData.cs File*

```
#region Using directives
using System;
using System.Collections;
using System.Collections.Generic;
using System.Text;
#endregion

namespace DataLayer
{
  public class CategoryData
  {
    public CategoryData()
    {
    }

    public static ArrayList GetAllCategories()
    {
      ArrayList categories = null;

      return categories;
    }
  }
}
```

Set the TestLayer project as the default project. Rebuild and run the solution. This time, everything compiled successfully, but the test for the CategoryTests class failed because the collection of categories being returned is null. Fix the test by retrieving the categories from the database and populating those categories into the collection you are returning in the GetAllCategories method call in the CategoryData class. Listing 13-17 shows the updated source of the CategoryData class.

Listing 13-17. *Modified CategoryData.cs File*

```
#region Using directives
using System;
using System.Collections;
using System.Collections.Generic;
using System.Data;
using System.Data.Odbc;
using System.Text;
using BusinessLayer;
#endregion

namespace DataLayer
{
  public class CategoryData
  {
    private static string connectionString =
      "Driver={Microsoft Access Driver (*.mdb)};" +
      "DBQ=c:\\xpnet\\database\\Northwind.mdb";

    public CategoryData()
    {
    }

    public static ArrayList GetAllCategories()
    {
      ArrayList categories = new ArrayList();

      try
      {
        OdbcConnection dataConnection = new OdbcConnection();
        dataConnection.ConnectionString = connectionString;
        dataConnection.Open();

        OdbcCommand dataCommand = new OdbcCommand();
        dataCommand.Connection = dataConnection;
```

```
        // Build command string
        string commandText = "SELECT * FROM Categories";
        dataCommand.CommandText = commandText;
        OdbcDataReader dataReader = dataCommand.ExecuteReader();

        // Iterate over the query results
        while ( dataReader.Read() )
        {
          Category category = new Category(dataReader.GetInt32(0),
            dataReader.GetString(1));

          categories.Add(category);
        }

        dataConnection.Close();
      }
      catch(Exception e)
      {
        Console.WriteLine("Error: " + e.Message);
      }

      return categories;
    }
  }
}
```

If you try to build the solution now, it will fail because the Category class is undefined. To fix that, you need to add a new class called Category.cs to the BusinessLayer project. Listing 13-18 shows the source code for the Category class.

Listing 13-18. *Category.cs File*

```
#region Using directives
using System;
using System.Collections.Generic;
using System.Tesxt;
#endregion

namespace BusinessLayer
{
  public class Category
  {
    private int categoryID;
    private string categoryName;
```

```
    public Category()
    {
    }

    public Category(int categoryID, string categoryName)
    {
      this.categoryID = categoryID;
      this.categoryName = categoryName;
    }
  }
}
```

Lastly, you want to update the source for the CategoryTests.cs file as shown in Listing 13-19.

Listing 13-19. *Modified CategoryTests.cs File*

```
#region Using directives
using System;
using System.Collections;
using System.Collections.Generic;
using System.Data;
using System.Data.Odbc;
using System.Text;
using NUnit.Framework;
using DataLayer;
#endregion

namespace TestLayer
{
  [TestFixture]
  public class CategoryTests
  {
    private StringBuilder connectionString;
    private int categoryID;

    public CategoryTests()
    {
      // Build connection string
      connectionString =
        new StringBuilder("Driver={Microsoft Access Driver (*.mdb)};");
      connectionString.Append("DBQ=c:\\xpnet\\database\\Northwind.mdb ");
    }
```

```
[SetUp]
public void Init()
{
  try
  {
    OdbcConnection dataConnection = new OdbcConnection();
    dataConnection.ConnectionString = connectionString.ToString();
    dataConnection.Open();

    OdbcCommand dataCommand = new OdbcCommand();
    dataCommand.Connection = dataConnection;

    // Build command string
    StringBuilder commandText =
      new StringBuilder("INSERT INTO Categories");
    commandText.Append(" (CategoryName) VALUES ('Bogus Category')");

    dataCommand.CommandText = commandText.ToString();

    int rows = dataCommand.ExecuteNonQuery();

    // Make sure that the INSERT worked
    Assert.AreEqual(1, rows, "Unexpected row count, gasp!");

    // Get the ID of the category we just inserted
    // This will be used to remove the category in the TearDown
    commandText =
      new StringBuilder("SELECT CategoryID FROM Categories ");
    commandText.Append("WHERE CategoryName =");
    commandText.Append("'Bogus Category'");

    dataCommand.CommandText = commandText.ToString();

    OdbcDataReader dataReader = dataCommand.ExecuteReader();

    // Make sure that we found our bogus category
    if (dataReader.Read())
    {
      categoryID = dataReader.GetInt32(0);
    }
```

```
      dataConnection.Close();
    }
    catch(Exception e)
    {
      Assert.Fail("Error: " + e.Message);
    }
  }

  [TearDown]
  public void Destroy()
  {
    try
    {
      OdbcConnection dataConnection = new OdbcConnection();
      dataConnection.ConnectionString = connectionString.ToString();
      dataConnection.Open();

      OdbcCommand dataCommand = new OdbcCommand();
      dataCommand.Connection = dataConnection;

      // Build command string
      StringBuilder commandText =
        new StringBuilder("DELETE FROM Categories ");
      commandText.Append("WHERE CategoryID = ");
      commandText.Append(categoryID);

      dataCommand.CommandText = commandText.ToString();

      int rows = dataCommand.ExecuteNonQuery();

      // Make sure that the DELETE worked
      Assert.AreEqual(1, rows, "Unexpected row count, gasp!");

      dataConnection.Close();
    }
    catch(Exception e)
    {
      Assert.Fail("Error: " + e.Message);
    }
  }
```

```
    [Test]
    public void TestFindAllCategories()
    {
      ArrayList categories = CategoryData.GetAllCategories();
      Assert.IsNotNull(categories, "GetAllCategories returned a null value, gasp!");
      Assert.IsTrue(categories.Count > 0, "Bad category count, gasp!");
    }
  }
}
```

This time, when you rebuild and run the solution, everything should compile and all your tests should pass. If they didn't, you need to look at the output for the build or the tests to see what went wrong.

Build Database Query to Retrieve Products Associated with a Category Task

The categories are mapped to multiple products. In order to retrieve the list of products associated with the categories, you need to get them from the database using the category selected. Start by adding a new test class (ProductTests.cs) to the TestLayer project. Listing 13-20 shows the minimal source for the ProductTests.cs class.

Listing 13-20. *Minimal ProductTests.cs File*

```
#region Using directives
using System;
using System.Collections;
using System.Collections.Generic;
using System.Text;
using NUnit.Framework;
using DataLayer;
#endregion

namespace TestLayer
{
  [TestFixture]
  public class ProductTests
  {
    private int categoryID;

    public ProductTests()
    {
    }

    [SetUp]
    public void Init()
    {
    }
```

```
    [TearDown]
    public void Destroy()
    {
    }

    [Test]
    public void TestGetProductsByCategory()
    {
      ArrayList products = ProductData.GetProductsByCategory(categoryID);
      Assert.IsNotNull(products, "GetProductsByCategory returned a null value,
gasp!");
      Assert.IsTrue(products.Count > 0, "Bad Products count, gasp!");
    }
  }
}
```

Build the solution and verify that it does not build correctly. Then add the minimal
ProductData.cs class file shown in Listing 13-21 to the DataLayer project.

Listing 13-21. *Minimal ProductData.cs File*

```
#region Using directives
using System;
using System.Collections;
using System.Collections.Generic;
using System.Text;
#endregion

namespace DataLayer
{
  public class ProductData
  {
    public ProductData()
    {
    }

    public static ArrayList GetProductsByCategory(int categoryID)
    {
      ArrayList products = null;

      return products;
    }
  }
}
```

As with the Login user story, you should be able to build and run the solution for this story (assuming you have set the TestLayer project as the startup project). The ProductTests GetProductsByCategory test case will fail because you are returning a null ArrayList at this time. Fix this by first enhancing the ProductData.cs class as shown in Listing 13-22.

Listing 13-22. *Modified ProductData.cs Class*

```
#region Using directives
using System;
using System.Collections;
using System.Collections.Generic;
using System.Data;
using System.Data.Odbc;
using System.Text;
using BusinessLayer;
#endregion

namespace DataLayer
{
  public class ProductData
  {
    private static string connectionString =
      "Driver={Microsoft Access Driver (*.mdb)};" +
      "DBQ=c:\\xpnet\\database\\Northwind.mdb";

    public ProductData()
    {
    }

    public static ArrayList GetProductsByCategory(int categoryID)
    {
      ArrayList products = new ArrayList();

      try
      {
        OdbcConnection dataConnection = new OdbcConnection();
        dataConnection.ConnectionString = connectionString;
        dataConnection.Open();

        OdbcCommand dataCommand = new OdbcCommand();
        dataCommand.Connection = dataConnection;

        // Build command string
        StringBuilder commandText =
          new StringBuilder("SELECT * FROM Products WHERE CategoryID=");
        commandText.Append(categoryID);
        commandText.Append(" AND UnitsInStock > 0");
```

```
            dataCommand.CommandText = commandText.ToString();

            OdbcDataReader dataReader = dataCommand.ExecuteReader();

            while (dataReader.Read())
            {
              Product product = new Product();
              product.ProductID = dataReader.GetInt32(0);
              product.ProductName = dataReader.GetString(1);
              product.CategoryID = dataReader.GetInt32(3);
              product.Price = dataReader.GetDecimal(5);
              product.Quantity = dataReader.GetInt16(6);

              products.Add(product);
            }

            dataConnection.Close();
        }
        catch(Exception e)
        {
          Console.WriteLine("Error: " + e.Message);
        }

        return products;
      }
    }
}
```

Next, create the Product.cs class shown in Listing 13-23 in the BusinessLayer project.

Listing 13-23. *Product.cs File*

```
#region Using directives
using System;
using System.Collections.Generic;
using System.Text;
#endregion

namespace BusinessLayer
{
  public class Product
  {
    private int productID;
    private int categoryID;
    private string productName;
    private decimal price;
    private int quantity;
```

```csharp
public Product()
{
}

public Product(int productID,
  int categoryID,
  string productName,
  decimal price,
  int quantity)
{

  this.productID = productID;
  this.categoryID = categoryID;
  this.productName = productName;
  this.price = price;
  this.quantity = quantity;
}

public int ProductID
{
  get
  {
    return this.productID;
  }
  set
  {
    this.productID = value;
  }
}

public int CategoryID
{
  get
  {
    return this.categoryID;
  }
  set
  {
    this.categoryID = value;
  }
}
```

```
    public string ProductName
    {
      get
      {
        return this.productName;
      }
      set
      {
        this.productName = value;
      }
    }

    public decimal Price
    {
      get
      {
        return this.price;
      }
      set
      {
        this.price = value;
      }
    }

    public int Quantity
    {
      get
      {
        return this.quantity;
      }
      set
      {
        this.quantity = value;
      }
    }
  }
}
```

Next, update the ProductTests.cs file to set up and tear down a category for testing. Make the changes shown in Listing 13-24.

Listing 13-24. *Modified ProductTests.cs File*

```csharp
#region Using directives
using System;
using System.Collections;
using System.Collections.Generic;
using System.Data;
using System.Data.Odbc;
using System.Text;
using NUnit.Framework;
using DataLayer;
#endregion

namespace TestLayer
{
  [TestFixture]
  public class ProductTests
  {
    private StringBuilder connectionString;
    private int productID;
    private int categoryID;
    private string productName;
    private decimal price;
    private int quantity;

    public ProductTests()
    {
      productName = "Bogus Product";
      price = 10.00M;
      quantity = 10;
      categoryID = 4;

      // Build connection string
      connectionString =
        new StringBuilder("Driver={Microsoft Access Driver (*.mdb)};");
      connectionString.Append("DBQ=c:\\xpnet\\database\\Northwind.mdb");
    }

    [SetUp]
    public void Init()
    {
      try
      {
        OdbcConnection dataConnection = new OdbcConnection();
        dataConnection.ConnectionString = connectionString.ToString();
        dataConnection.Open();
```

```
OdbcCommand dataCommand = new OdbcCommand();
dataCommand.Connection = dataConnection;

// Build command string
StringBuilder commandText =
  new StringBuilder("INSERT INTO Products (ProductName, ");
commandText.Append("CategoryID, UnitPrice, ");
commandText.Append("UnitsInStock) VALUES ('");
commandText.Append(productName );
commandText.Append("', ");
commandText.Append(categoryID);
commandText.Append(", ");
commandText.Append(price);
commandText.Append(", ");
commandText.Append(quantity );
commandText.Append(")");

dataCommand.CommandText = commandText.ToString();

int rows = dataCommand.ExecuteNonQuery();

// Make sure that the INSERT worked
Assert.AreEqual(1, rows, "Unexpected row count, gasp!");

// Get the ID of the category we just inserted
// This will be used to remove the category in the TearDown
commandText =
  new StringBuilder("SELECT ProductID FROM");
commandText.Append(" Products WHERE ProductName = ");
commandText.Append("'Bogus Product'");

dataCommand.CommandText = commandText.ToString();

OdbcDataReader dataReader = dataCommand.ExecuteReader();

// Make sure that we found our product
if (dataReader.Read())
{
  productID = dataReader.GetInt32(0);
}
```

```
      dataConnection.Close();
    }
    catch(Exception e)
    {
      Assert.Fail("Error: " + e.Message);
    }
}

[TearDown]
public void Destroy()
{
    try
    {
      OdbcConnection dataConnection = new OdbcConnection();
      dataConnection.ConnectionString = connectionString.ToString();
      dataConnection.Open();

      OdbcCommand dataCommand = new OdbcCommand();
      dataCommand.Connection = dataConnection;

      // Build command string
      StringBuilder commandText =
        new StringBuilder("DELETE FROM Products WHERE ProductID = ");
      commandText.Append(productID);

      dataCommand.CommandText = commandText.ToString();

      int rows = dataCommand.ExecuteNonQuery();

      // Make sure that the DELETE worked
      Assert.AreEqual(1, rows, "Unexpected row count, gasp!");

      dataConnection.Close();
    }
    catch(Exception e)
    {
      Assert.Fail("Error: " + e.Message);
    }
}
```

```
    [Test]
    public void TestGetProductsByCategory()
    {
      ArrayList products = ProductData.GetProductsByCategory(categoryID);
      Assert.IsNotNull(products, "GetProductsByCategory returned a null value,
gasp!");
      Assert.IsTrue(products.Count > 0, "Bad Products count, gasp!");
    }
  }
}
```

Now everything should build and run successfully. You should add some more tests (both positive and negative) to the ProductTests.cs class, as shown in Listing 13-25.

Listing 13-25. *More Tests for ProductTests.cs*

```
#region Using directives
using System;
using System.Collections;
using System.Collections.Generic;
using System.Data;
using System.Data.Odbc;
using System.Text;
using NUnit.Framework;
using DataLayer;
using BusinessLayer;
#endregion

namespace TestLayer
{
  [TestFixture]
  public class ProductTests
  {
    private StringBuilder connectionString;
    private int productID;
    private int categoryID;
    private string productName;
    private decimal price;
    private int quantity;

    public ProductTests()
    {
      productName = "Bogus Product";
      price = 10.00M;
      quantity = 10;
      categoryID = 4;
```

```
    // Build connection string
    connectionString =
      new StringBuilder("Driver={Microsoft Access Driver (*.mdb)};");
    connectionString.Append("DBQ=c:\\xpnet\\database\\Northwind.mdb");
}

[SetUp]
public void Init()
{
  try
  {
    OdbcConnection dataConnection = new OdbcConnection();
    dataConnection.ConnectionString = connectionString.ToString();
    dataConnection.Open();

    OdbcCommand dataCommand = new OdbcCommand();
    dataCommand.Connection = dataConnection;

    // Build command string
    StringBuilder commandText =
      new StringBuilder("INSERT INTO Products (ProductName, ");
    commandText.Append("CategoryID, UnitPrice, ");
    commandText.Append("UnitsInStock) VALUES ('");
    commandText.Append(productName );
    commandText.Append("', ");
    commandText.Append(categoryID);
    commandText.Append(", ");
    commandText.Append(price);
    commandText.Append(", ");
    commandText.Append(quantity );
    commandText.Append(")");

    dataCommand.CommandText = commandText.ToString();

    int rows = dataCommand.ExecuteNonQuery();

    // Make sure that the INSERT worked
    Assert.AreEqual(1, rows, "Unexpected row count, gasp!");

    // Get the ID of the category we just inserted
    // This will be used to remove the category in the TearDown
    commandText =
      new StringBuilder("SELECT ProductID FROM");
    commandText.Append(" Products WHERE ProductName = ");
    commandText.Append("'Bogus Product'");
```

```
      dataCommand.CommandText = commandText.ToString();

      OdbcDataReader dataReader = dataCommand.ExecuteReader();

      // Make sure that we found our product
      if (dataReader.Read())
      {
        productID = dataReader.GetInt32(0);
      }

      dataConnection.Close();
    }
    catch(Exception e)
    {
      Assert.Fail("Error: " + e.Message);
    }
}

[TearDown]
public void Destroy()
{
  try
  {
    OdbcConnection dataConnection = new OdbcConnection();
    dataConnection.ConnectionString = connectionString.ToString();
    dataConnection.Open();

    OdbcCommand dataCommand = new OdbcCommand();
    dataCommand.Connection = dataConnection;

    // Build command string
    StringBuilder commandText =
      new StringBuilder("DELETE FROM Products WHERE ProductID = ");
    commandText.Append(productID);

    dataCommand.CommandText = commandText.ToString();

    int rows = dataCommand.ExecuteNonQuery();

    // Make sure that the DELETE worked
    Assert.AreEqual(1, rows, "Unexpected row count, gasp!");
```

```
    dataConnection.Close();
  }
  catch(Exception e)
  {
    Assert.Fail("Error: " + e.Message);
  }
}

[Test]
public void TestGetProductsByCategory()
{
  ArrayList products = ProductData.GetProductsByCategory(categoryID);
  Assert.IsNotNull(products,
    "GetProductsByCategory returned a null value, gasp!");
  Assert.IsTrue(products.Count > 0, "Bad Products count, gasp!");
}
[Test]
public void NegativeTestGetProductsByCategory()
{
  ArrayList products = ProductData.GetProductsByCategory(555555);
  Assert.AreEqual(0, products.Count, "Products list was not empty, gasp!");
}

[Test]
public void TestGetProduct()
{
  Product product = ProductData.GetProduct(productID);
  Assert.IsNotNull(product, "Product was null, gasp!");
  Assert.AreEqual(productID, product.ProductID, "Incorrect Product ID, gasp!");
}

[Test]
public void NegativeTestGetProduct()
{
  Product product = ProductData.GetProduct(55555);
  Assert.IsNull(product "Product was not null, gasp!");
}

[Test]
public void TestSearchForProducts()
{
  ArrayList products = ProductData.SearchForProducts(productName);
  Assert.IsNotNull(products, "Product list was null, gasp!");
  Assert.IsTrue(products.Count > 0, "Incorrect product count, gasp!");
}
```

```
    [Test]
    public void NegativeTestSearchForProducts()
    {
      ArrayList products = ProductData.SearchForProducts("Negative Search String");
      Assert.AreEqual(0, product.Count, "Products list was not empty, gasp!");
    }
  }
}
```

Now you will need to enhance the ProductData.cs class to support these additional tests, as shown in Listing 13-26.

Listing 13-26. *Modified ProductData.cs File*

```
#region Using directives
using System;
using System.Collections;
using System.Collections.Generic;
using System.Data;
using System.Data.Odbc;
using System.Text;
using BusinessLayer;
#endregion

namespace DataLayer
{
  public class ProductData
  {
    private static string connectionString =
      "Driver={Microsoft Access Driver (*.mdb)};" +
      "DBQ=c:\\xpnet\\database\\Northwind.mdb";

    public ProductData()
    {
    }

    public static ArrayList GetProductsByCategory(int categoryID)
    {
      ArrayList products = new ArrayList();

      try
      {
        OdbcConnection dataConnection = new OdbcConnection();
        dataConnection.ConnectionString = connectionString;
        dataConnection.Open();
```

```csharp
      OdbcCommand dataCommand = new OdbcCommand();
      dataCommand.Connection = dataConnection;

      // Build command string
      StringBuilder commandText =
        new StringBuilder("SELECT * FROM Products WHERE CategoryID=");
      commandText.Append(categoryID);
      commandText.Append(" AND UnitsInStock > 0");

      dataCommand.CommandText = commandText.ToString();

      OdbcDataReader dataReader = dataCommand.ExecuteReader();

      while (dataReader.Read())
      {
        Product product = new Product();
        product.ProductID = dataReader.GetInt32(0);
        product.ProductName = dataReader.GetString(1);
        product.CategoryID = dataReader.GetInt32(3);
        product.Price = dataReader.GetDecimal(5);
        product.Quantity = dataReader.GetInt16(6);

        products.Add(product);
      }

      dataConnection.Close();
    }
    catch(Exception e)
    {
      Console.WriteLine("Error: " + e.Message);
    }

    return products;
  }

public static Product GetProduct(int productID)
{
  Product product = null;

  try
  {
    OdbcConnection dataConnection = new OdbcConnection();
    dataConnection.ConnectionString = connectionString;
    dataConnection.Open();
```

```
    OdbcCommand dataCommand = new OdbcCommand();
    dataCommand.Connection = dataConnection;

    // Build command string
    StringBuilder commandText =
      new StringBuilder("SELECT * FROM Products WHERE ProductID=");
    commandText.Append(productID);

    dataCommand.CommandText = commandText.ToString();

    OdbcDataReader dataReader = dataCommand.ExecuteReader();

    if (dataReader.Read())
    {
      product = new Product();
      product.ProductID = dataReader.GetInt32(0);
      product.ProductName = dataReader.GetString(1);
      product.CategoryID = dataReader.GetInt32(3);
      product.Price = dataReader.GetDecimal(5);
      product.Quantity = dataReader.GetInt16(6);
    }

    dataConnection.Close();
  }
  catch(Exception e)
  {
    Console.WriteLine("Error: " + e.Message);
  }

  return product;
}

public static ArrayList SearchForProducts(string searchString)
{
  ArrayList products = new ArrayList();

  try
  {
    OdbcConnection dataConnection = new OdbcConnection();
    dataConnection.ConnectionString = connectionString;
    dataConnection.Open();

    OdbcCommand dataCommand = new OdbcCommand();
    dataCommand.Connection = dataConnection;
```

```
      // Build command string
      StringBuilder commandText =
        new StringBuilder("SELECT * FROM Products WHERE ProductName LIKE '%");
      commandText.Append(searchString);
      commandText.Append("%'");

      dataCommand.CommandText = commandText.ToString();

      OdbcDataReader dataReader = dataCommand.ExecuteReader();

      while (dataReader.Read())
      {
        Product product = new Product();
        product.ProductID = dataReader.GetInt32(0);
        product.CategoryID = dataReader.GetInt32(3);
        product.ProductName = dataReader.GetString(1);
        product.Price = dataReader.GetDecimal(5);
        product.Quantity = dataReader.GetInt16(6);
        products.Add(product);
      }

      dataConnection.Close();
    }
    catch(Exception e)
    {
      Console.WriteLine("Error: " + e.Message);
    }

    return products;
  }
 }
}
```

Rebuild and run the solution again to verify you have not introduced any new bugs. Next, you will add the presentation layer features of this user story.

Create Main Browse Page Task

You will start with a basic web page. Listing 13-27 shows the code for BrowseCatalog.aspx, which needs to be added as a new web form to the NorthwindWeb project.

Listing 13-27. *BrowseCatalog.aspx File*

```
<%@ Page language="C#" CodeFile="BrowseCatalog.aspx.cs"
  Inherits="BrowseCatalog_aspx" %>
<%@ Import Namespace="System.Collections" %>
<%@ Import Namespace="DataLayer" %>
<%@ Import Namespace="BusinessLayer" %>

<!DOCTYPE html PUBLIC "-//W3C//DTD XHTML 1.1 //EN"
  "http://www.w3.org/TR/xhtml11/DTD/xhtml11.dtd">
<html xmlns="http://www.w3.org/1999/xhtml">
  <head>
    <title>Browse Catalog</title>
  </head>
  <body>
    <table id="Table1" cellSpacing="1" cellPadding="1" width="100%" border="0">
      <tr>
        <td></td>
      </tr>
      <tr>
        <td></td>
      </tr>
    </table>
  </body>
<html>
```

Select the View ➤ Code menu item again and set the BrowseCatalog.aspx.cs file source to match Listing 13-28.

Listing 13-28. *BrowseCatalog.aspx.cs File*

```
using System;
using System.Collections;
using DataLayer;
using BusinessLayer;

public partial class BrowseCatalog_aspx : System.Web.UI.Page
{
}
```

Display Categories on the Main Browse Page Task

Now you need to build the navigation control for displaying categories on the Browse Catalog page. You will use a web user control to do that.

Create a new web user control called Categories.ascx with the source code shown in Listing 13-29.

Listing 13-29. *Categories.ascx File*

```
<%@ Import Namespace="BusinessLayer" %>
<%@ Import Namespace="DataLayer" %>
<%@ Import Namespace="System.Collections" %>
<%@ Control Language="c#"
  CodeFile="Categories.ascx.cs"
  Inherits="Categories_ascx"
  AutoEventWireup="true">

<table width="100">
  <%
    if (categories != null)
    {
      for (int i = 0; i < categories.Count; i++)
      {
        Category category = (Category)categories[i];
  %>
  <tr>
    <td>
      <a href="BrowseCatalog.aspx?categoryID=<%
        Response.Write(category.CategoryID.ToString()); %>">
        <% Response.Write(category.CategoryName); %>
      </a>
    </td>
  </tr>
  <%
      }
    }
  %>
</table>
```

Then select the View ➤ Code menu item and make the Categories.ascx.cs file match the source code shown in Listing 13-30.

Listing 13-30. *Categories.ascx.cs File*

```
using System;
using System.Collections;
using System.Drawing;
using BusinessLayer;
using DataLayer;

public partial class Categories_ascx : System.Web.UI.Page
{
  protected ArrayList categories;
```

```
   private void Page_Load(object sender, System.EventArgs e)
   {
     categories = CategoryData.GetAllCategories();
   }
}
```

Next, enhance BrowseCatalog.aspx to display the categories web user control that you just created, as shown in Listing 13-31.

Listing 13-31. *Modified BrowseCatalog.aspx File*

```
<%@ Page language="C#" CodeFile="BrowseCatalog.aspx.cs"
  Inherits="BrowseCatalog_aspx" %>
<%@ Register TagPrefix="Categories" TagName="LeftNav" Src="Categories.ascx" %>
<%@ Import Namespace="System.Collections" %>
<%@ Import Namespace="DataLayer" %>
<%@ Import Namespace="BusinessLayer" %>

<!DOCTYPE html PUBLIC "-//W3C//DTD XHTML 1.1 //EN"
  "http://www.w3.org/TR/xhtml11/DTD/xhtml11.dtd">
<html xmlns="http://www.w3.org/1999/xhtml">
  <head>
    <title>Browse Catalog</title>
  </head>
  <body>
    <table id="Table1" cellSpacing="1" cellPadding="1" width="100%" border="0">
      <tr>
        <td></td>
      </tr>
      <tr>
        <td width="20%" valign="top" align="left">
          <Categories:LeftNav ID="leftnav" Runat="server" />
        </td>
      </tr>
    </table>
  </body>
<html>
```

Finally, enhance the BrowseCatalog.aspx.cs as shown in Listing 13-32.

Listing 13-32. *Modified BrowseCatalog.aspx.cs File*

```
using System;
using System.Collections;
using System.ComponentModel;
using DataLayer;
using BusinessLayer;
```

```
public partial class BrowseCatalog_aspx : System.Web.UI.Page
{
  private void Page_Load(object sender, System.EventArgs e)
  {
    string categoryID = Request.Params.Get("categoryID");
    if (categoryID != null)
    {
      int id = Convert.ToInt32(categoryID);
    }
  }
}
```

Display Product on Main Browse Page When Category Selected Task

Now you need to display a list of products associated with a category, when a category is selected from the navigation control. To do that, enhance BrowseCatalog.aspx as shown in Listing 13-33.

Listing 13-33. *Further Modifications to BrowseCatalog.aspx*

```
<%@ Page language="C#" CodeFile="BrowseCatalog.aspx.cs"
  Inherits="BrowseCatalog_aspx" %>
<%@ Register TagPrefix="Categories" TagName="LeftNav" Src="Categories.ascx" %>
<%@ Import Namespace="System.Collections" %>
<%@ Import Namespace="DataLayer" %>
<%@ Import Namespace="BusinessLayer" %>

<!DOCTYPE html PUBLIC "-//W3C//DTD XHTML 1.1 //EN"
  "http://www.w3.org/TR/xhtml11/DTD/xhtml11.dtd">
<html xmlns="http://www.w3.org/1999/xhtml">
  <head>
    <title>Browse Catalog</title>
  </head>
  <body>
    <table id="Table1" cellSpacing="1" cellPadding="1" width="100%" border="0">
      <tr>
        <td></td>
        <td></td>
      </tr>
      <tr>
        <td width="20%" valign="top" align="left">
          <Categories:LeftNav ID="leftnav" Runat="server" />
        </td>
```

```
        <td>
          <table width="80%">
            <%
              if ( products != null )
              {
                for ( int i = 0; i < products.Count; i++ )
                {
                  product = (Product)products[i];

            %>
            <tr>
              <td>
                <a href="ProductDetail.aspx?productID=<%
                  Response.Write(product.ProductID.ToString()); %>">
                  <% Response.Write(product.ProductName); %>
                </a>
              </td>
            </tr>
            <%
                }
              }
            %>
          </table>
        </td>
      </tr>
    </table>
  </body>
<html>
```

Don't worry about the fact you have not created a ProductDetail.aspx web form yet. Next, enhance BrowseCatalog.aspx.cs as shown in Listing 13-34.

Listing 13-34. *Further Modifications for BrowseCatalog.aspx.cs*

```
using System;
using System.Collections;
using System.ComponentModel;
using DataLayer;
using BusinessLayer;

public partial class BrowseCatalog_aspx : System.Web.UI.Page
{
  protected ArrayList products;
  protected Product product;
```

```
  private void Page_Load(object sender, System.EventArgs e)
 {
    string categoryID = Request.Params.Get("categoryID");
    if (categoryID != null)
    {
      int id = Convert.ToInt32(categoryID);
      products = ProductData.GetProductsByCategory(id);
    }
  }
}
```

Now you need to enhance the Category.cs file to have properties for categoryID and categoryName. Make Category.cs look like Listing 13-35.

Listing 13-35. *Modified Category.cs Class*

```
#region Using directives
using System;
using System.Collections.Generic;
using System.Text;
#endregion

namespace BusinessLayer
{
  public class Category
  {
    private int categoryID;
    private string categoryName;

    public Category()
    {
    }

    public Category(int categoryID, string categoryName)
    {
      this.categoryID = categoryID;
      this.categoryName = categoryName;
    }

    public int CategoryID
    {
      get
      {
        return this.categoryID;
      }
```

```
      set
      {
        this.categoryID = value;
      }
    }

    public string CategoryName
    {
      get
      {
        return this.categoryName;
      }

      set
      {
        this.categoryName = value;
      }
    }
  }
}
```

This completes all the tasks for this user story. Rebuild the solution and run all of the unit tests again to make sure all tests are still passing. Then set the web application as the default project and set `BrowseCatalog.aspx` as the start page. Select the Debug ➤ Start menu item to launch the web server, and then verify that the categories are displaying along the left side of the page and their associated products appear on the right side when a category is selected. If you select a product from the right side, you will see a server error page, because the `ProductDetail.aspx` page doesn't exist yet. That is okay, because that web page was not part of this user story.

Developing the Remaining User Stories

We still have five other user stories outstanding. These user stories are being developed in parallel with the Login and Browse Catalog user stories. The developers should be switching their pairs frequently during the iteration and working on each other's tasks. The developers are free to work on tasks in any order, as long as all of the user stories and their associated tasks are completed by the end of the iteration.

You can download the source for this iteration, as well as the second iteration, from the Source Code area of the Apress website (`www.apress.com`).

Other Team Members' Duties

As we noted at the beginning of the chapter, we focused on the activities of the developers during the first iteration. Now we will take a quick look at what the other team members have been doing.

Everyone on the team journaled at the end of each day. This information will be used later after the release to review what worked well and what didn't. This helps the team decide how and if they need to tailor XP for their purposes and why.

Acceptance Tester

The acceptance tester started the iteration by working with the customer to develop the acceptance criteria for each user story. After the acceptance tests were identified, the acceptance tester started automating or writing out the acceptance tests. This work happened in parallel with the development effort. In some cases, the acceptance tests were completed (but not tested) even before the development of the user story was complete.

In the case of the Login user story, for example, the acceptance test defined by the customer was to see a success or failure message after supplying a valid or invalid username and password. To begin this acceptance testing process, you would type in a valid username and password (`afuller` and `password`, respectively), and you would see a successful login message at the bottom of the login page. Then you would try a bad username and password (such as `bogususer` and `badpassword`), and you would get a failed password message at the bottom of the login page.

Once the tester feels that the story meets the defined acceptance criteria, he demonstrates the acceptance test to the customer. If the customer is pleased, the story can be marked as complete. If the customer identifies discrepancies in the acceptance of this story, the developers must make the appropriate changes (that satisfy the acceptance test) prior to marking the story as complete.

Tracker

As you are coding on your tasks, don't forget to track your actual time spent coding and testing. Do this by keeping a piece of paper by your development workstation and writing down your actual times as you go, so you won't forget.

The tracker will be coming around at least twice a week to inquire about your progress. The tracker will be asking you how much actual time you have spent working on just the tasks you signed up for and how much ideal time you have left on those tasks. This information is used only to help the coach and customer determine the team's progress.

The tracker will also be posting graphs on the walls in the "bullpen" to show everyone where the team is (stories completed, stories developed but not tested, stories not started, and so forth). This helps the team members get a feel for how they are doing and how much work is left.

Customer

During the iteration, the customer starts by sitting down with the acceptance testers to write out the acceptance tests. The customer also answers questions that the developers have when they start writing unit tests.

As stories are developed and acceptance tests are created, the customer starts accepting or rejecting stories. Also, as developers design interface pieces of the system, they sit with the customer to decide the location, color, size, and so on of the interface components.

Coach

During the iteration, the coach is paying close attention to the daily activities of the team. When the coach notices any member of the team straying from the XP practices (not pairing or switching pairs, not testing first, and so on), he intervenes and corrects the action. Sometimes, when there is a difficult problem or a shortage of pairs, the coach needs to jump in and pair with a developer.

Coach's Journal

During this iteration, I noticed that some of the developers were more comfortable driving and some were more comfortable taking a back seat. We want to have a balance, so I had to remind them not only to switch their pairs periodically (a least once a day), but also to switch who is driving about every hour or two.

I spoke with the customer frequently to make sure he was comfortable with what was going on. One concern that the customer had was getting the acceptance tests written in such a way that he understood what outcome was expected. I sat the customer down with the testers, and we all worked through a couple of acceptance tests together to make sure our customer was comfortable with the process.

Summary

In this first iteration, the team members successfully delivered all the included user stories. There was neither an increase nor a decrease in velocity for the team. Therefore, next iteration, the team will sign up for the same amount of work.

As the source code evolved, there were areas that were identified as needing refactoring (like the connection string). We will address those areas in the next iteration (Chapter 15), but we could have handled them in this iteration as well.

Next, you will start the second iteration by iteration planning again. This will allow you to make any adjustments to the plan based on what you learned from this iteration.

CHAPTER 14

Iteration Planning for the Second Iteration

In this chapter, we will plan our second (and final) iteration. We will begin by examining our previous iteration to determine if we need to change our team velocity. We will then move on to the story selection process, followed by the process of tasking these stories. Once we have completed both the story selection and tasking steps, we will complete our iteration plan by balancing the iteration, if necessary.

Velocity Adjustment

Before you begin any iteration (excluding the first), you must assess the amount of work that you accomplished in the previous iteration. The easiest way to do this is to look at the number of task points completed by each developer.

In our example, each of the four developers completed 26 task points of work (ideal hours). This means that, as a team, they can sign up for exactly 13 story points (ideal days); as individuals, they can sign up for 26 task points. Here is the formula:

(26 task points × 4 developers) / 8 task points for each ideal day = 13 story points

But what if one of the developers had not successfully finished all of the tasks he signed up for? Then that developer would receive credit only for the tasks he did successfully complete. For example, if a developer successfully completed tasks with a total estimate of 20 task points, while the other developers successfully completed all of their tasks that totaled 26 estimated task points, the calculation would look like this:

(26 task points + 26 task points + 26 task points + 20 task points) / 8 task points for each ideal day = 12.25 story points

---

Note If you are following XP to the letter of the law, so to speak, you could say that since some tasks for a story were not completed, and therefore, the story was not accepted, none of the developers with tasks on that story get credit. In other words, even though some of the tasks on a story were completed, because the story was not accepted, no tasks points are given. We are not taking this approach with our teams.

On the other hand, what if one or more of the developers had finished all their tasks early and signed up for and completed tasks on an additional user story (selected by the customer) that was not in the iteration? In that scenario, the developers' velocity would go up. As an example, let's say one of our developers completed tasks that totaled up to 30 task points in the previous iteration, while the remaining developers completed tasks that totaled 26 task points in the iteration. The calculation would be as follows:

(26 task points + 26 task points + 26 task points + 30 task points) / 8 task points for each ideal day = 13.5 story points

Story Selection

It is now time to select the stories for the second iteration. Before we begin, we must look at which stories were completed in the first iteration and make sure that we remove those stories from the remaining collection of stories. In the previous iteration, we completed the following user stories:

- Login

- Browse Catalog

- Display Product Detail

- Add Product to Shopping Cart

- Remove Product from Shopping Cart/Update Shopping Cart Contents (combined)

- Search for Product

- Display Shopping Cart Contents

■**Note** You may have noticed that we picked up an additional story, Update Shopping Cart Contents, in the previous iteration. We actually combined the Remove Product from Shopping Cart and Update Shopping Cart Contents stories into a single story. This additional story did not change our velocity because it was accomplished for free. This is because we were able to complete both of these stories, while implementing the Remove Product from Shopping Cart story. Therefore, the only change created by the completion of the Update Shopping Cart Contents story is that it is complete and will not be selected for a future iteration.

After removing the previously completed stories, the stories listed in Table 14-1 remain.

Table 14-1. *Remaining User Stories for the First Release*

Story	Story Points
Display Checkout Confirmation	1.0
Display Order Confirmation	5.5
Display Order History	1.0
Display Order Status	2.0
Story Point Total	9.5

As we determined in the previous section, we have a team velocity of 13 story points (ideal days) for our current iteration. When we examine the list of remaining stories, we find that it is obviously short of our available velocity. At this point, the customer might ask the coach for input.

Coach: How many story points does the team have available for this iteration?

Customer: The tracker says that the team has 13 total story points for this iteration. After all of the user stories I picked for this release, that leaves me with 3.5 story points left over. What should I do?

Coach: Well, you have a couple of options here. You can just call the release complete and finish early, or you can go back to the original stories from the planning game phase and select a story that adds some additional business value and fits into the current iteration.

Customer: If I can get more work done, then that's what I'd rather do. I'll go back and look at the stories from the planning game.

Table 14-2 shows all of the stories from the planning game phase that were not selected for this release.

Table 14-2. *Remaining Stories from the Planning Game*

Story	Story Points
Add New Customer Account	3.0
Edit Customer Account	3.5
Add New Product	3.0
Edit Product	3.5

Coach: So, do you see anything you'd like to add from the planning game list?

Customer: Well, I have 3.5 story points available. I'd like to move Add New Customer Account into this iteration.

Coach: Great, but that still leaves you with 0.5 story points.

Customer: Yes, but there's really nothing that fits that level of effort. I'm happy with what I have so far. Let's get started.

Table 14-3 shows the current stories for the second iteration.

Table 14-3. *Current Stories for the Second Iteration*

Story	Story Points
Display Checkout Confirmation	1.0
Display Order Confirmation	5.5
Display Order History	1.0
Display Order Status	2.0
Add New Customer Account	3.0
Story Point Total	12.5

Story Tasking and Assignment

The next steps are to divide each story into tasks and then have the developers sign up for tasks.

Breaking Up the Stories into Tasks

The developers begin brainstorming each set of tasks as a group. They task out each story (again, writing the tasks on the back of the user story index card), as described in the following sections.

Display Checkout Confirmation

The first user story is Display Checkout Confirmation. The results of this story should be a page that displays the contents of the shopping cart with a Complete Order button. The developers know that they need to first add a Checkout button to the Shopping Cart page. They also know they will need a screen to actually show the checkout confirmation. Additionally, they will need the ability to cancel a checkout. The page should display the current items in the shopping cart and a subtotal of the item prices. Lastly, the page will need a button that begins the process of placing the order request. That process will result in new Customer, Order, and OrderDetail classes. Figure 14-1 shows the complete list of tasks for this story.

Task	Owner	Est.	Act.
Create Checkout Confirmation Page			
Add button to checkout the Shopping cart contents			
Add button to cancel the Checkout			
Display shopping cart Contents in Checkout Confirmation Page			
Subtotal shopping cart line items and display results			
Add button to process the order request			
Build Customer			
Build Order			
Build Order Detail			

Figure 14-1. *Display Checkout Confirmation story tasks*

Display Order Confirmation

The next user story is Display Order Confirmation. The results of this story should be a page that provides feedback to a user when an order is complete. The developers must first decrement the quantity of each item on the order. They must create a new order in the database. Then they need to add the contents of the shopping cart to the newly created order as line items. While discussing the story, they also realize that they must add a filter to restrict employees from placing orders. The developers know that they need to add an Order Confirmation page, and this page should display a number identifying the new order. Figure 14-2 shows these tasks.

Task	OWNER	EST.	ACT.
Decrement product availabe amount			
Insert order record			
Insert order detail record per line item			
Add filters to remove cart and buy if user is an employee.			
Create Order Confirmation Page			
Display Confirmation message with order number			

Figure 14-2. *Display Order Confirmation story tasks*

Display Order History

For the Display Order History story, the result should be a page that displays a customer's complete history of orders. The developers can immediately recognize four tasks necessary to complete this story: adding a My Account button to a customer's top navigation bar, creating a My Account page with a left-side navigation bar with an Order History link, retrieving all of the customer's previous orders, and displaying those orders. Figure 14-3 shows these tasks.

Task	Owner	Est.	Act.
Add My Account To Nav. bAR			
Create My Account page with Left Hand Nav. bAR			
Display History Information			
Get Customer Order History from database			

Figure 14-3. *Display Order History story tasks*

Display Order Status

The result of the Display Order Status story should be a page that displays the detail of a selected order. The developers talk about this story and come up with three tasks: getting the order detail from the database, creating an order status page, and displaying this order on the Order Status page. Figure 14-4 shows the list of tasks for this story.

TASK	OWNER	EST.	ACT.
Get order/order detail from database			
Create order status page			
Display order status information			

Figure 14-4. *Display Order Status story tasks*

Add New Customer Account

The final user story for this iteration plan is Add New Customer Account. The result of this story should be a page that allows an employee to add a new customer account to the database. After discussing this story, the developers come up with three tasks: adding an Admin button to the top navigation bar (if the user is an employee), creating a customer account page with a form to gather the new customer information, and storing the entered information into the database. Figure 14-5 shows these tasks.

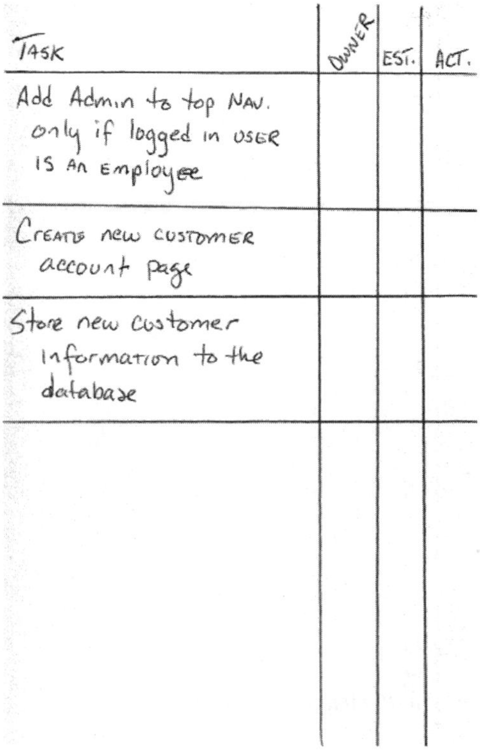

Task	Owner	Est.	Act.
Add Admin to top Nav. only if logged in user is an employee			
Create new customer account page			
Store new customer Information to the database			

Figure 14-5. *Add New Customer Account story tasks*

Signing Up for Tasks

Now that all the user stories are tasked out, the developers must sign up for the tasks that they are going to complete. Remember that in order to reduce the dependencies between user stories, it is often best if one developer signs up for as many of the tasks on a single story as possible.

As we stated in Chapter 12, we estimate tasks in ideal hours, as opposed to ideal days. Using the previously determined calculation, each developer can sign up for 26 ideal task points.

Using the same round-robin approach we used in the first iteration, each developer will estimate and sign up for the defined tasks until he runs out of task points. Figures 14-6 through 14-10 show the results of this effort.

Task	Owner	Est.	Act.
Create Checkout Confirmation Page	HP	0.5	
Add button to checkout the shopping cart contents	HP	0.5	
Add button to cancel the checkout	HP	0.5	
Display shopping cart contents in Checkout Confirmation Page	HP	0.75	
Subtotal shopping cart line items and display results	HP	0.75	
Add button to process the order request	HP	0.5	
Build Customer	HP	1.5	
Build Order	HP	1.5	
Build Order Detail	HP	1.5	

Figure 14-6. *Display Checkout Confirmation story tasks, with owners and estimates*

Task	Owner	Est.	Act.
Decrement product available amount	HP	4.0	
Insert order record	HP	10	
Insert order detail record per line item	HM	10	
Add filters to remove Cart and Buy if user is an employee.	HM	9.5	
Create Order Confirmation Page	HP	0.5	
Display Confirmation message with order number	HP	2.0	

Figure 14-7. *Display Order Confirmation story tasks, with owners and estimates*

Task	Owner	Est.	Act.
Add My Account To Nav. bar	JM	1.5	
Create My Account page with Left Hand Nav. bar	JM	1.0	
Display History Information	JM	2.0	
Get customer order History from database	JM	5.0	

Figure 14-8. *Display Order History story tasks, with owners and estimates*

Task	Owner	Est.	Act.
Get order/order detail from database	JM	12.5	
Create order status page	JM	0.5	
Display order status information	JM	2.0	

Figure 14-9. *Display Order Status story tasks, with owners and estimates*

TASK	OWNER	EST.	ACT.
Add Admin to top NAV. only if logged in USER is An Employee	MF	12.0	
CREATE new CUSTOMER account page	MF	6.0	
Store new customer information to the database	HM	6.0	

Figure 14-10. *Add New Customer Account story tasks, with owners and estimates*

Iteration Balancing

Once the developers have selected and estimated their tasks, we look at the totals and determine if the iteration needs to be balanced.

After totaling each of the estimated tasks, we see that each developer signed up for exactly 26 task points' worth of work. So, in this case, the iteration does not need to be balanced. Of course, this will not always be the situation.

If there had been tasks remaining (not signed up for), we would have needed to reduce functionality within the iteration. This reduction in functionality would have been accomplished either by simplifying user stories or by removing user stories entirely. If all the selected tasks had been signed up for and there were developers with significant unused task points, we would have asked the customer to select additional work for this iteration.

Coach's Journal

The customer was really happy about the extra work we picked up. The developers are starting to get more comfortable about estimating in front of everyone, but they are still concerned that when they go over or under their estimate, it reflects badly on them.

I reinforced the notion that the team and individual velocities would not be used for anything else but a tool to keep them from overcommitting their time to the customer. It will probably take a few more iterations before they start to believe this.

The acceptance testers are concerned about the fact that their time is not being taken into account. They also are worried that the developers may be delivering new functionality to them at the very end of the iteration. I told the team that all new development needs to be completed by the last Wednesday of each iteration, and only bug fixes should be handled the last two days. If there aren't any bug fixes, the team could decide to either take on some very small stories or spike future stories scheduled for the release.

As for accounting for the acceptance testers' times, this isn't defined well in XP. I said I would check the Web to see what other XP folks are doing. It looks like we might have to define our own process to handle this better.

Summary

In this iteration planning phase, we started with the remaining user stories in the release. Because their story points did not add up to the team's velocity for the iteration, the customer was able to pull more functionality into the iteration and the release. In this case, we went all the way back to the stories that were originally outside the release plan. Lastly, we made sure that all the developers had signed up for as much work as possible without overcommitting themselves.

CHAPTER 15

Second Iteration

In the previous chapter, we developed an iteration plan for the second iteration of our sample project. Now we will work on this iteration.

Again, we will demonstrate the XP practices that occur during an iteration from a developer's perspective. We won't cover all the activities that occur during an iteration; refer to Chapters 5 and 13 if you need that information.

This chapter builds on the source code presented in Chapter 13, so make sure you have completed that chapter's coding before proceeding.

Refactoring

As mentioned in Chapter 13, during the first iteration, an issue was brought up in one of the daily stand-ups with regard to the connection string to the database. Different developers used different connection strings based on their local machine's configuration of Open Database Connectivity (ODBC). This needed to be refactored. One of the developers accepted ownership of this issue and promised to provide a solution to be implemented in the second iteration.

The solution that the developer came up with was to refactor the connection string to a DataUtilities.cs class, as shown in Listing 15-1. Now, when the connection string needs to be changed, that must be done in only one location. The entire team acknowledged that eventually, the connection string will need to be placed in some type of configuration file, so that nothing will have to be recompiled when the connection string needs to be changed.

Listing 15-1. *DataUtilities.cs File*

```
#region Using directives
using System;
using System.Collections.Generic;
using System.Text;
#endregion

namespace DataLayer
{
  public class DataUtilities
  {
    private static string connectionString =
      "Driver={Microsoft Access Driver (*.mdb)};DBQ=C:\\xpnet\\database\\Northwind";
```

```
    public DataUtilities()
    {
    }

    public static string ConnectionString
    {
      get
      {
        return connectionString;
      }

      set
      {
        DataUtilities.connectionString = value;
      }
    }
  }
}
```

Then every other place where a connection string is used will be replaced with a property getter call to the DataUtilities class. One example is the ProductData class in the DataLayer project. That class will now look like Listing 15-2.

Listing 15-2. *ProductData.cs with Call to DataUtilities.cs*

```csharp
#region Using directives
using System;
using System.Collections;
using System.Collections.Generic;
using System.Data;
using System.Data.Odbc;
using System.Text;
using BusinessLayer;
#endregion

namespace DataLayer
{
  public class ProductData
  {
    public ProductData()
    {
    }

    public static ArrayList GetProductsByCategory(int categoryID)
    {
      ArrayList products = new ArrayList();
```

```
  try
  {
    OdbcConnection dataConnection = new OdbcConnection();
    dataConnection.ConnectionString = DataUtilities.ConnectionString;
    dataConnection.Open();

    OdbcCommand dataCommand = new OdbcCommand();
    dataCommand.Connection = dataConnection;

    // Build command string
    StringBuilder commandText =
      new StringBuilder("SELECT * FROM Products WHERE CategoryID=");
    commandText.Append(categoryID);
    commandText.Append(" AND UnitsInStock > 0");

    dataCommand.CommandText = commandText.ToString();

    OdbcDataReader dataReader = dataCommand.ExecuteReader();

    while (dataReader.Read())
    {
      Product product = new Product();
      product.ProductID = dataReader.GetInt32(0);
      product.ProductName = dataReader.GetString(1);
      product.CategoryID = dataReader.GetInt32(3);
      product.Price = dataReader.GetDecimal(5);
      product.Quantity = dataReader.GetInt16(6);

      products.Add(product);
    }

    dataConnection.Close();
  }
  catch(Exception e)
  {
    Console.WriteLine("Error: " + e.Message);
  }

  return products;
}

public static Product GetProduct(int ProductID)
{
  Product product = null;
```

```
try
{
  OdbcConnection dataConnection = new OdbcConnection();
  dataConnection.ConnectionString = DataUtilities.ConnectionString;
  dataConnection.Open();

  OdbcCommand dataCommand = new OdbcCommand();
  dataCommand.Connection = dataConnection;

  // Build command string
  StringBuilder commandText =
    new StringBuilder("SELECT * FROM Products WHERE ProductID = ");
  commandText.Append(productID);

  dataCommand.CommandText = commandText.ToString();

  OdbcDataReader dataReader = dataCommand.ExecuteReader();

  if (dataReader.Read())
  {
    product = new Product();
    product.ProductID = dataReader.GetInt32(0);
    product.ProductName = dataReader.GetString(1);
    product.CategoryID = dataReader.GetInt32(3);
    product.Price = dataReader.GetDecimal(5);
    product.Quantity = dataReader.GetInt16(6);
  }

  dataCommand.Close();
}
catch (Exception e)
{
  Console.WriteLine("Error: " + e.Message);
}

return product;
}

public static ArrayList SearchForProducts(string searchString)
{
  ArrayList products = new ArrayList();
```

```
try
{
  OdbcConnection dataConnection = new OdbcConnection();
  dataConnection.ConnectionString = DataUtilities.ConnectionString;
  dataConnection.Open();

  OdbcCommand dataCommand = new OdbcCommand();
  dataCommand.Connection = dataConnection;

  // Build command string
  StringBuilder commandText =
    new StringBuilder("SELECT * FROM Products WHERE ProductName LIKE '%');
  commandText.Append(searchString);
  commandText.Append("%'");

  dataCommand.CommandText = commandText.ToString();

  OdbcDataReader dataReader = dataCommand.ExecuteReader();

  while (dataReader.Read())
  {
    product = new Product();
    product.ProductID = dataReader.GetInt32(0);
    product.ProductName = dataReader.GetString(1);
    product.CategoryID = dataReader.GetInt32(3);
    product.Price = dataReader.GetDecimal(5);
    product.Quantity = dataReader.GetInt16(6);
    products.Add(product);
  }

  dataConnection.Close();
}
catch (Exception e)
{
  Console.WriteLine("Error: " + e.Message);
}

return products;
    }
  }
}
```

You should do the same for the UserData and CategoryData classes in the DataLayer project, as well as for the CategoryTests, ProductTests, ShoppingCartTests, and UserTests classes in the TestLayer. Then rerun all your unit tests to make sure that you have not introduced any errors.

Design Meeting

As in the previous iteration, design meetings occur on a daily basis. The design for this iteration is shown in Figure 15-1.

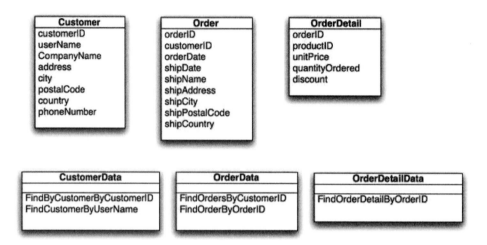

Figure 15-1. *The design for the second iteration*

Developers' Duties

Again, the teams pair up and develop the user stories they have chosen to work on for this iteration. Here, we will focus on one of the five stories in the second iteration: Display Checkout Confirmation.

Developing the Display Checkout Confirmation User Story

The following tasks were identified for the Display Checkout Confirmation story during iteration planning (see Chapter 14):

- Create Checkout Confirmation page
- Add button to check out the shopping cart contents
- Add button to cancel the checkout
- Display shopping cart contents in Checkout Confirmation page
- Subtotal shopping cart line items and display results
- Add button to process the order request
- Build Customer
- Build Order
- Build Order Detail

Build Customer, Build Order, and Build Order Detail are the only tasks that will have business and data classes. The remaining tasks will be at the web layer. We will start out with these three tasks, and then wrap up with the web layer.

As with the tasks in the first iteration, the Build Customer, Build Order, and Build Order Detail tasks use four layers of your solution: the test layer, data layer, web layer, and business layer. Remember that you are taking a test-driven approach. Using that approach, you start with a basic test, add a data class to support the test, and then add a business class to support the data class. Then, as the test evolves, you iteratively enhance the data and business classes as needed. For brevity, we will show only the completed outcome of these tasks in this chapter.

Build Customer Task

The Build Customer task involves building a representation of a customer within your application. A customer is someone who has placed an order. Don't confuse a customer with a user. A user is someone who has access to your website but may not have placed an order. Listings 15-3, 15-4, and 15-5 show the test, data, and business classes for a customer, respectively.

Listing 15-3. *CustomerTests.cs File*

```
#region  Using directives
using System;
using System.Collections.Generic;
using System.Data;
using System.Data.Odbc;
using System.Text;
using NUnit.Framework;
using BusinessLayer;
using DataLayer;
#endregion

namespace TestLayer
{
  [TestFixture]
  public class CustomerTests
  {
    private string  userName;
    private string  userPassword;
    private string  userRole;
    private string  customerID;
    private string  companyName;
    private string  address;
    private string  city;
    private string  postalCode;
    private string  country;
    private string  phoneNumber;
```

```
public CustomerTests()
{
  userName = "bogus user";
  userPassword = "bogus";
  userRole = "customer";
  customerID = "Z1Z1Z";
  companyName = "Bogus Company";
  address = "1234 Main Street";
  city = "Hometown";
  postalCode = "10001";
  country = "United States";
  phoneNumber = "303-555-1234";
}

[SetUp]
public void Init()
{
  CreateUser();
  CreateCustomer();
}

[Test]
public void TestFindCustomerByUserName()
{
  Customer  foundCustomer = CustomerData.FindCustomerByUserName(userName);

  Assert.IsNotNull(foundCustomer, "Found customer object was null, gasp!");
  AssertiAreEqual(customerID, foundCustomer.CustomerID,
    "Customer ID don't match, gasp!");
  Assert.AreEqual(userName, foundCustomer.UserName,
    "Customer user names don't match, gasp!");
  Assert.AreEqual(companyName, foundCustomer.CompanyName,
    "Customer company names don't match, gasp!");
  Assert.AreEqual(address, foundCustomer.Address,
    "Customer addresses don't match, gasp!");
  Assert.AreEqual(city, foundCustomer.City,
    "Customer cities don't match, gasp!");
  Assert.AreEqual(postalCode, foundCustomer.PostalCode,
    "Customer postal codes don't match, gasp!");
  Assert.AreEqual(country, foundCustomer.Country,
    "Customer countries don't match, gasp!");
  Assert.AreEqual(phoneNumber, foundCustomer.PhoneNumber,
    "Customer phone numbers don't match, gasp!");
}
```

```
[TearDown]
public void Destroy()
{
  RemoveCustomer();
  RemoveUser();
}

private void CreateUser()
{
  try
  {
    OdbcConnection dataConnection = new OdbcConnection();
    dataConnection.ConnectionString = DataUtilities.ConnectionString;

    dataConnection.Open();

    OdbcCommand dataCommand = new OdbcCommand();
    dataCommand.Connection = dataConnection;

    // Build command string
    StringBuilder commandText =
      new StringBuilder("INSERT INTO Users (");

    commandText.Append("UserName, ");
    commandText.Append("Password, ");
    commandText.Append("Role) VALUES ('");
    commandText.Append(userName);
    commandText.Append("', '");
    commandText.Append(userPassword);
    commandText.Append("', '");
    commandText.Append(userRole);
    commandText.Append("')");

    dataCommand.CommandText = commandText.ToString();

    int rows = dataCommand.ExecuteNonQuery();

    // Make sure that the INSERT worked
    Assert.AreEqual(1, rows, "Unexpected Users row count ");

    dataConnection.Close();
  }
  catch(Exception e)
  {
    Assert.Fail("Users database error: " + e.Message);
  }
}
```

```csharp
private void RemoveUser()
{
  try
  {
    OdbcConnection dataConnection = new OdbcConnection();
    dataConnection.ConnectionString = DataUtilities.ConnectionString;
    dataConnection.Open();

    OdbcCommand dataCommand = new OdbcCommand();
    dataCommand.Connection = dataConnection;

    // Build command string
    StringBuilder commandText =
      new StringBuilder("DELETE FROM Users WHERE UserName = '");
    commandText.Append(userName);
    commandText.Append("'");

    dataCommand.CommandText = commandText.ToString();

    int rows = dataCommand.ExecuteNonQuery();

    // Make sure that the DELETE worked
    Assert.AreEqual(1, rows"Unexpected Users row count, gasp!");

    dataConnection.Close();
  }
  catch(Exception e)
  {
    Asser.Fail("Users database error: " + e.Message);
  }
}

private void CreateCustomer()
{
  try
  {
    OdbcConnection dataConnection = new OdbcConnection();
    dataConnection.ConnectionString = DataUtilities.ConnectionString;

    dataConnection.Open();

    OdbcCommand dataCommand = new OdbcCommand();
    dataCommand.Connection = dataConnection;
```

```
    // Build command string
    StringBuilder commandText =
      new StringBuilder("INSERT INTO Customers (");
    commandText.Append("CustomerID, ");
    commandText.Append("UserName, ");
    commandText.Append("CompanyName, ");
    commandText.Append("Address, ");
    commandText.Append("City, ");
    commandText.Append("PostalCode, ");
    commandText.Append("Country, ");
    commandText.Append("Phone) VALUES ('");
    commandText.Append(customerID);
    commandText.Append("', '");
    commandText.Append(userName);
    commandText.Append("', '");
    commandText.Append(companyName);
    commandText.Append("', '");
    commandText.Append(address);
    commandText.Append("', '");
    commandText.Append(city);
    commandText.Append("', '");
    commandText.Append(postalCode);
    commandText.Append("', '");
    commandText.Append(country);
    commandText.Append("', '");
    commandText.Append(phoneNumber);
    commandText.Append("')");

    dataCommand.CommandText = commandText.ToString();

    int rows = dataCommand.ExecuteNonQuery();

    // Make sure that the INSERT worked
    Assert.AreEqual(1, rows, "Unexpected Customers row count, gasp!");

    dataConnection.Close();
  }
  catch(Exception e)
  {
    Assert.Fail("Customers database error: " + e.Message);
  }
}
```

```csharp
    private void RemoveCustomer()
    {
      try
      {
        OdbcConnection dataConnection = new OdbcConnection();
        dataConnection.ConnectionString = DataUtilities.ConnectionString;
        dataConnection.Open();

        OdbcCommand dataCommand = new OdbcCommand();
        dataCommand.Connection = dataConnection;

        // Build command string
        StringBuilder commandText =
          new StringBuilder("DELETE FROM Customers WHERE CustomerID = '");
        commandText.Append(customerID);
        commandText.Append("'");

        dataCommand.CommandText = commandText.ToString();

        int rows = dataCommand.ExecuteNonQuery();

        // Make sure that the DELETE worked
        Assert.AreEqual(1, rows, "Unexpected Customers row count, gasp!");

        dataConnection.Close();
      }
      catch(Exception e)
      {
        Assertion.Assert("Customers database error: " +
          e.Message, e.Message.Equals(""));
      }
    }
  }
}
```

Listing 15-4. *CustomerData.cs File*

```csharp
#region Using directive
using System;
using System.Collections.Generic;
using System.Data;
using System.Data.Odbc;
using System.Text;
using BusinessLayer;
#endregion
```

```csharp
namespace DataLayer
{
  public class CustomerData
  {
    public CustomerData()
    {
    }

    public static Customer FindCustomerByUserName(string userName)
    {
      Customer  customer = null;

      try
      {
        OdbcConnection dataConnection = new OdbcConnection();
        dataConnection.ConnectionString = DataUtilities.ConnectionString;
        dataConnection.Open();

        OdbcCommand dataCommand = new OdbcCommand();
        dataCommand.Connection = dataConnection;

        // Build command string
        StringBuilder commandText =
          new StringBuilder("SELECT * FROM Customers WHERE UserName = '");
        commandText.Append(userName);
        commandText.Append("'");

        dataCommand.CommandText = commandText.ToString();

        OdbcDataReader dataReader = dataCommand.ExecuteReader();

        // Make sure that we found our user
        if (dataReader.Read())
        {
          customer = new Customer(dataReader.GetString(0),  // CustomerID
            dataReader.GetString(1),                        // UserName
            dataReader.GetString(2),                        // CompanyName
            dataReader.GetString(5),                        // Address
            dataReader.GetString(6),                        // City
            dataReader.GetString(8),                        // PostalCode
            dataReader.GetString(9),                        // Country
            dataReader.GetString(10)                        // Phone
            );
        }
```

```
          dataConnection.Close();
      }
      catch(Exception e)
      {
        Console.WriteLine("error: " + e.Message);
      }

      return customer;
    }
  }
}
```

Listing 15-5. *Customer.cs File*

```
#region Using directives
using System;
using System.Collections.Generic;
using System.Text;
#endregion

namespace BusinessLayer
{
  public class Customer
  {
    private string  customerID;
    private string  userName;
    private string  companyName;
    private string  address;
    private string  city;
    private string  postalCode;
    private string  country;
    private string  phoneNumber;

    public Customer()
    {
    }

    public Customer(string customerID,
                    string userName,
                    string companyName,
                    string address,
                    string city,
                    string postalCode,
                    string country,
                    string phoneNumber)
```

```
{
  this.customerID = customerID;
  this.userName = userName;
  this.companyName = companyName;
  this.address = address;
  this.city = city;
  this.postalCode = postalCode;
  this.country = country;
  this.phoneNumber = phoneNumber;
}

public string CustomerID
{
  get
  {
    return this.customerID;
  }
  set
  {
    this.customerID = value;
  }
}

public string UserName
{
  get
  {
    return this.userName;
  }
  set
  {
    this.userName = value;
  }
}

public string CompanyName
{
  get
  {
    return this.companyName;
  }
  set
  {
    this.companyName = value;
  }
}
```

```csharp
public string Address
{
  get
  {
    return this.address;
  }
  set
  {
    this.address = value;
  }
}

public string City
{
  get
  {
    return this.city;
  }
  set
  {
    this.city = value;
  }
}

public string PostalCode
{
  get
  {
    return this.postalCode;
  }
  set
  {
    this.postalCode = value;
  }
}

public string Country
{
  get
  {
    return this.country;
  }
  set
  {
    this.country = value;
  }
}
```

```
    public string PhoneNumber
    {
      get
      {
        return this.phoneNumber;
      }
      set
      {
        this.phoneNumber = value;
      }
    }
  }
}
```

Build Order Task

Next comes the Build Order task. The Order class represents an entire order that is associated with a customer. Listings 15-6, 15-7, and 15-8 show the test, data, and business classes for an order, respectively.

■**Note** In the final source code for this iteration, TestInsertOrder is refactored into a CreateOrder private method and used in the setup method for subsequent use by other Order test cases.

Listing 15-6. *OrderTests.cs File*

```csharp
#region Using directives
using System;
using System.Collections.Generic;
using System.Data;
using System.Data.Odbc;
using System.Text;
using NUnit.Framework;
using BusinessLayer;
using DataLayer;
#endregion

namespace TestLayer
{
  [TestFixture]
  public class OrderTests
  {
    private string    userName;
    private string    userPassword;
    private string    userRole;
```

```csharp
  private Customer customer;
  private string    customerID;
  private string    companyName;
  private string    address;
  private string    city;
  private string    postalCode;
  private string    country;
  private string    phoneNumber;
  private int       orderID;
  private DateTime  orderDate;
  private DateTime  shipDate;

  public OrderTests()
  {
    userName = "bogus user";
    userPassword = "bogus";
    userRole = "customer";
    customer = null;
    customerID = "Z1Z1Z";
    companyName = "Bogus Company";
    address = "1234 Main Street";
    city = "Hometown";
    postalCode = "10001";
    country = "United States";
    phoneNumber = "303-555-1234";
    orderDate = new System.DateTime(2999, 1, 1);
    shipDate = new System.DateTime(2999, 1, 2);
    orderID = -1;
  }

  [SetUp]
  public void Init()
  {
    CreateUser();
    CreateCustomer();
  }

  [Test]
  public void TestInsertOrder()
  {
    orderID = OrderData.InsertOrder(customer);

      Assert.IsTrue(orderID > 0, "Order ID was invalid, gasp!");
  }
```

```csharp
[TearDown]
public void Destroy()
{
  RemoveOrder();
  RemoveCustomer();
  RemoveUser();
}

private void CreateUser()
{
  try
  {
    OdbcConnection dataConnection = new OdbcConnection();
    dataConnection.ConnectionString = DataUtilities.ConnectionString;
    dataConnection.Open();

    OdbcCommand dataCommand = new OdbcCommand();
    dataCommand.Connection = dataConnection;

    // Build command string
    StringBuilder commandText =
      new StringBuilder("INSERT INTO Users (");

    commandText.Append("UserName, ");
    commandText.Append("Password, ");
    commandText.Append("Role) VALUES ('");
    commandText.Append(userName);
    commandText.Append("', '");
    commandText.Append(userPassword);
    commandText.Append("', '");
    commandText.Append(userRole);
    commandText.Append("')");

    dataCommand.CommandText = commandText.ToString();

    int rows = dataCommand.ExecuteNonQuery();

    // Make sure that the INSERT worked
    Assert.AreEqual(1, rows, "Unexpected Users row count ");

    dataConnection.Close();
  }
  catch(Exception e)
  {
    Assert.Fail("Users database error: " + e.Message);
  }
}
```

```
private void RemoveUser()
{
  try
  {
    OdbcConnection dataConnection = new OdbcConnection();
    dataConnection.ConnectionString = DataUtilities.ConnectionString;
    dataConnection.Open();

    OdbcCommand dataCommand = new OdbcCommand();
    dataCommand.Connection = dataConnection;

    // Build command string
    StringBuilder commandText =
      new StringBuilder("DELETE FROM Users WHERE UserName = '");
    commandText.Append(userName);
    commandText.Append("'");

    dataCommand.CommandText = commandText.ToString();

    int rows = dataCommand.ExecuteNonQuery();

    // Make sure that the DELETE worked
    Assert.AreEqual(1, rows, "Unexpected Users row count ");

    dataConnection.Close();
  }
  catch(Exception e)
  {
    Assert.fail("Users database error: " + e.Message);
  }
}

private void CreateCustomer()
{
  try
  {
    OdbcConnection dataConnection = new OdbcConnection();
    dataConnection.ConnectionString = DataUtilities.ConnectionString;
    dataConnection.Open();

    OdbcCommand dataCommand = new OdbcCommand();
    dataCommand.Connection = dataConnection;

    // Build command string
    StringBuilder commandText =
      new StringBuilder("INSERT INTO Customers (");
```

```
    commandText.Append("CustomerID, ");
    commandText.Append("UserName, ");
    commandText.Append("CompanyName, ");
    commandText.Append("Address, ");
    commandText.Append("City, ");
    commandText.Append("PostalCode, ");
    commandText.Append("Country, ");
    commandText.Append("Phone) VALUES ('");
    commandText.Append(customerID);
    commandText.Append("', '");
    commandText.Append(userName);
    commandText.Append("', '");
    commandText.Append(companyName);
    commandText.Append("', '");
    commandText.Append(address);
    commandText.Append("', '");
    commandText.Append(city);
    commandText.Append("', '");
    commandText.Append(postalCode);
    commandText.Append("', '");
    commandText.Append(country);
    commandText.Append("', '");
    commandText.Append(phoneNumber);
    commandText.Append("')");

    dataCommand.CommandText = commandText.ToString();

    int rows = dataCommand.ExecuteNonQuery();

    // Make sure that the INSERT worked
    Assert.AreEqual(1, rows, "Unexpected Customers row count ");

    dataConnection.Close();

    // Initialize new Customer
    customer = new Customer(customerID, userName, companyName,
      address, city, postalCode, country, phoneNumber);
    Assert.IsNotNull(customer, "Newly created  customer is null, gasp!");
  }
  catch(Exception e)
  {
    Assert.Fail("Customers database error: " + e.Message,);
  }
}
```

```
private void RemoveCustomer()
{
  try
  {
    OdbcConnection dataConnection = new OdbcConnection();
    dataConnection.ConnectionString = DataUtilities.ConnectionString;
    dataConnection.Open();

    OdbcCommand dataCommand = new OdbcCommand();
    dataCommand.Connection = dataConnection;

    // Build command string
    StringBuilder commandText =
      new StringBuilder("DELETE FROM Customers WHERE CustomerID = '");
    commandText.Append(customerID);
    commandText.Append("'");

    dataCommand.CommandText = commandText.ToString();

    int rows = dataCommand.ExecuteNonQuery();

    // Make sure that the DELETE worked
    AssertAreEqual(1, rows, "Unexpected Customers row count, gasp!");

    dataConnection.Close();

    // Free up our customer object
    customer = null;
  }
  catch(Exception e)
  {
    Assert.Fail("Customers database error: " + e.Message,);
  }
}

private void RemoveOrder()
{
  try
  {
    OdbcConnection dataConnection = new OdbcConnection();
    dataConnection.ConnectionString = DataUtilities.ConnectionString;
    dataConnection.Open();

    OdbcCommand dataCommand = new OdbcCommand();
    dataCommand.Connection = dataConnection;
```

```
      // Build command string
      StringBuilder commandText =
        new StringBuilder("DELETE FROM Orders WHERE OrdersID = ");
      commandText.Append(orderID);

      dataCommand.CommandText = commandText.ToString();

      int rows = dataCommand.ExecuteNonQuery();

      // Make sure that the DELETE worked
      Assert.AreEqual(1, rows, "Unexpected Orders row count, gasp!");

      dataConnection.Close();
    }
    catch(Exception e)
    {
      Assert.Fail("Orders database error: " + e.Message);
    }
  }
 }
}
```

Listing 15-7. *OrderData.cs File*

```
#region Using directives
using System;
using System.Collections.Generic;
using System.Data;
using System.Data.Odbc;
using System.Text;
using BusinessLayer;
#endregion

namespace DataLayer
{
  public class OrderData
  {
    public OrderData()
    {
    }

    public static int InsertOrder(Customer customer)
    {
      DateTime date = DateTime.Now;
      int orderID = -1;
```

```
try
{
  OdbcConnection dataConnection = new OdbcConnection();
  dataConnection.ConnectionString = DataUtilities.ConnectionString;
  dataConnection.Open();

  OdbcCommand dataCommand = new OdbcCommand();
  dataCommand.Connection = dataConnection;

  // Build command string
  StringBuilder commandText =
    new StringBuilder("INSERT INTO Orders (");

  commandText.Append("CustomerID, ");
  commandText.Append("OrdersDate, ");
  commandText.Append("ShippedDate, ");
  commandText.Append("ShipName, ");
  commandText.Append("ShipAddress, ");
  commandText.Append("ShipCity, ");
  commandText.Append("ShipPostalCode, ");
  commandText.Append("ShipCountry) VALUES ('");
  commandText.Append(customer.CustomerID);
  commandText.Append("', '");
  commandText.Append(date.ToString());
  commandText.Append("', '");
  commandText.Append(date.AddDays(3).ToString());
  commandText.Append("', '");
  commandText.Append(customer.UserName);
  commandText.Append("', '");
  commandText.Append(customer.Address);
  commandText.Append("', '");
  commandText.Append(customer.City);
  commandText.Append("', '");
  commandText.Append(customer.PostalCode);
  commandText.Append("', '");
  commandText.Append(customer.Country);
  commandText.Append("')");

  dataCommand.CommandText = commandText.ToString();

  int rows = dataCommand.ExecuteNonQuery();

  // Get the ID of the order we just inserted
  // This will be used to remove the order in the test TearDown
  commandText =
    new StringBuilder("SELECT Max(OrdersID) FROM Orders");
```

```
        dataCommand.CommandText = commandText.ToString();

        OdbcDataReader dataReader = dataCommand.ExecuteReader();

        // Make sure that you found the user
        if (dataReader.Read())
        {
          orderID = dataReader.GetInt32(0);
        }

        dataConnection.Close();
      }
      catch(Exception e)
      {
        Console.WriteLine("error: " + e.Message);
      }
      return orderID;
    }
  }
}
```

Listing 15-8. *Order.cs File*

```
#region Using directives
using System;
using System.Collections.Generic;
using System.Text;
#endregion

namespace BusinessLayer
{
  public class Order
  {
    private int      orderID;
    private string   customerID;
    private DateTime orderDate;
    private DateTime shipDate;
    private string   shipName;
    private string   shipAddress;
    private string   shipCity;
    private string   shipPostalCode;
    private string   shipCountry;

    public Order()
    {
    }
```

```csharp
public Order(int orderID,
  string customerID,
  DateTime orderDate,
  DateTime shipDate,
  string shipName,
  string shipAddress,
  string shipCity,
  string shipPostalCode,
  string shipCountry)
{
  this.orderID = orderID;
  this.customerID = customerID;
  this.orderDate = orderDate;
  this.shipDate = shipDate;
  this.shipName = shipName;
  this.shipAddress = shipAddress;
  this.shipCity = shipCity;
  this.shipPostalCode = shipPostalCode;
  this.shipCountry = shipCountry;
}

public int OrderID
{
  get
  {
    return this.orderID;
  }
  set
  {
    this.orderID = value;
  }
}

public string CustomerID
{
  get
  {
    return this.customerID;
  }
  set
  {
    this.customerID = value;
  }
}
```

```
public DateTime OrderDate
{
  get
  {
    return this.orderDate;
  }
  set
  {
    this.orderDate = value;
  }
}

public DateTime ShipDate
{
  get
  {
    return this.shipDate;
  }
  set
  {
    this.shipDate = value;
  }
}

public string ShipName
{
  get
  {
    return this.shipName;
  }
  set
  {
    this.shipName = value;
  }
}

public string ShipAddress
{
  get
  {
    return this.shipAddress;
  }
  set
  {
    this.shipAddress = value;
  }
}
```

```csharp
    public string ShipCity
    {
      get
      {
        return this.shipCity;
      }
      set
      {
        this.shipCity = value;
      }
    }

    public string ShipPostalCode
    {
      get
      {
        return this.shipPostalCode;
      }
      set
      {
        this.shipPostalCode = value;
      }
    }

    public string ShipCountry
    {
      get
      {
        return this.shipCountry;
      }
      set
      {
        this.shipCountry = value;
      }
    }
  }
}
```

Build Order Detail Task

The order detail represents the line items on the order. This is analogous to the line items of the shopping cart. Listings 15-9, 15-10, and 15-11 show the test, data, and business classes for the order detail, respectively.

Note In the final source code for this iteration, the TestInsertLineItem is refactored into a
CreateOrderLineItem private method and used in the setup method for subsequent use by other
OrderDetail test cases.

Listing 15-9. *OrderDetailTests.cs File*

```
#region Using directive
using System;
using System.Collections.Generic;
using System.Data;
using System.Data.Odbc;
using System.Text;
using NUnit.Framework;
using BusinessLayer;
using DataLayer;
#endregion

namespace TestLayer
{
  [TestFixture]
  public class OrderDetailTests
  {
    private string     userName;
    private string     userPassword;
    private string     userRole;
    private string     customerID;
    private string     companyName;
    private string     address;
    private string     city;
    private string     postalCode;
    private string     country;
    private string     phoneNumber;
    private int        orderID;
    private DateTime    orderDate;
    private DateTime    shipDate;
    private int        productID;
    private string     productName;
    private decimal    unitPrice;
    private int        quantityOrdered;
    private int        stockQuantity;
    private int     categoryID;
    private LineItem     lineItem;
    private Product     product;
```

```csharp
public OrderDetailTests()
{
  userName = "bogus user";
  userPassword = "bogus";
  userRole = "customer";
  customerID = "Z1Z1Z";
  companyName = "Bogus Company";
  address = "1234 Main Street";
  city = "Hometown";
  postalCode = "10001";
  country = "United States";
  phoneNumber = "303-555-1234";
  orderDate = new System.DateTime(2999, 1, 1);
  shipDate = new System.DateTime(2999, 1, 2);
  productName = "bogus product";
  unitPrice = 99.95M;
  quantityOrdered = 5;
  stockQuantity = 50;
  categoryID = 3;
  lineItem = null;
  product = null;
}

[SetUp]
public void Init()
{
  CreateUser();
  CreateCustomer();
  CreateProduct();
  CreateOrder();
  CreateLineItem();
}

[Test]
public void TestInsertLineItem()
{
  int rows = OrderDetailData.InsertLineItem(orderID, lineItem);
  Assert.AreEqual(1, rows, "Unexpected OrderDetail row count, gasp!");
}

[TearDown]
public void Destroy()
{
  RemoveOrderLineItem();
  RemoveOrder();
  RemoveProduct();
```

```csharp
    RemoveCustomer();
    RemoveUser();
}

private void CreateUser()
{
  try
  {
    OdbcConnection dataConnection = new OdbcConnection();
    dataConnection.ConnectionString = DataUtilities.ConnectionString;
    dataConnection.Open();

    OdbcCommand dataCommand = new OdbcCommand();
    dataCommand.Connection = dataConnection;

    // Build command string
    StringBuilder commandText =
      new StringBuilder("INSERT INTO Users (");

    commandText.Append("UserName, ");
    commandText.Append("Password, ");
    commandText.Append("Role) VALUES ('");
    commandText.Append(userName);
    commandText.Append("', '");
    commandText.Append(userPassword);
    commandText.Append("', '");
    commandText.Append(userRole);
    commandText.Append("')");

    dataCommand.CommandText = commandText.ToString();

    int rows = dataCommand.ExecuteNonQuery();

    // Make sure that the INSERT worked
    Assert.AreEqual1(1, rows, "Unexpected Users row count, gasp!");

    dataConnection.Close();
  }
  catch(Exception e)
  {
    Assert.Fail("Users database error: " + e.Message);
  }
}

private void RemoveUser()
{
  try
```

```csharp
      {
        OdbcConnection dataConnection = new OdbcConnection();
        dataConnection.ConnectionString = DataUtilities.ConnectionString;
        dataConnection.Open();

        OdbcCommand dataCommand = new OdbcCommand();
        dataCommand.Connection = dataConnection;

        // Build command string
        StringBuilder commandText =
          new StringBuilder("DELETE FROM Users WHERE UserName = '");
        commandText.Append(userName);
        commandText.Append("'");

        dataCommand.CommandText = commandText.ToString();

        int rows = dataCommand.ExecuteNonQuery();

        // Make sure that the DELETE worked
        Assert.AreEqual(1, rows, "Unexpected Users row count, gasp!");

        dataConnection.Close();
      }
      catch(Exception e)
      {
        Assert.Fail("Users database error: " + e.Message);
      }
    }

    private void CreateCustomer()
    {
      try
      {
        OdbcConnection dataConnection = new OdbcConnection();
        dataConnection.ConnectionString = DataUtilities.ConnectionString;
        dataConnection.Open();

        OdbcCommand dataCommand = new OdbcCommand();
        dataCommand.Connection = dataConnection;

        // Build command string
        StringBuilder commandText =
          new StringBuilder("INSERT INTO Customers (");

        commandText.Append("CustomerID, ");
        commandText.Append("UserName, ");
        commandText.Append("CompanyName, ");
```

```
    commandText.Append("Address, ");
    commandText.Append("City, ");
    commandText.Append("PostalCode, ");
    commandText.Append("Country, ");
    commandText.Append("Phone) VALUES ('");
    commandText.Append(customerID);
    commandText.Append("', '");
    commandText.Append(userName);
    commandText.Append("', '");
    commandText.Append(companyName);
    commandText.Append("', '");
    commandText.Append(address);
    commandText.Append("', '");
    commandText.Append(city);
    commandText.Append("', '");
    commandText.Append(postalCode);
    commandText.Append("', '");
    commandText.Append(country);
    commandText.Append("', '");
    commandText.Append(phoneNumber);
    commandText.Append("')");

    dataCommand.CommandText = commandText.ToString();

    int rows = dataCommand.ExecuteNonQuery();

    // Make sure that the INSERT worked
    Assert.AreEqual(1, rows, "Unexpected Customers row count, gasp!");

    dataConnection.Close();
  }
  catch(Exception e)
  {
    Assert.Fail("Customers database error: " + e.Message);
  }
}

private void RemoveCustomer()
{
  try
  {
    OdbcConnection dataConnection = new OdbcConnection();
    dataConnection.ConnectionString = DataUtilities.ConnectionString;
    dataConnection.Open();

    OdbcCommand dataCommand = new OdbcCommand();
    dataCommand.Connection = dataConnection;
```

```
      // Build command string
      StringBuilder commandText =
        new StringBuilder("DELETE FROM Customers WHERE CustomerID = '");
      commandText.Append(customerID);
      commandText.Append("'");

      dataCommand.CommandText = commandText.ToString();

      int rows = dataCommand.ExecuteNonQuery();

      // Make sure that the DELETE worked
      Assert.AreEqual(1, rows, "Unexpected Customers row count, gasp!");

      dataConnection.Close();
    }
    catch(Exception e)
    {
      Assert.Fail("Customers database error: " + e.Message);
    }
  }

  private void CreateProduct()
  {
    try
    {
      OdbcConnection dataConnection = new OdbcConnection();
      dataConnection.ConnectionString = DataUtilities.ConnectionString;
      dataConnection.Open();

      OdbcCommand dataCommand = new OdbcCommand();
      dataCommand.Connection = dataConnection;

      // Build command string
      StringBuilder commandText =
        new StringBuilder("INSERT INTO Products (");

      commandText.Append("ProductName, ");
      commandText.Append("CategoryID, ");
      commandText.Append("UnitPrice, ");
      commandText.Append("UnitsInStock) VALUES ('");
      commandText.Append(productName);
      commandText.Append("', ");
      commandText.Append(categoryID);
      commandText.Append("', ");
      commandText.Append(unitPrice);
      commandText.Append("', ");
      commandText.Append(stockQuantity);
      commandText.Append(")");
```

```
        dataCommand.CommandText = commandText.ToString();

        int rows = dataCommand.ExecuteNonQuery();

        // Make sure that the INSERT worked
        Assert.AreEqual(1, rows, "Unexpected Products row count, gasp!");

        // Get the ID of the product we just inserted
        // This will be used to remove the product in the test TearDown
        commandText =
          new StringBuilder("SELECT ProductID FROM Products WHERE ProductName = '");
        commandText.Append(productName);
        commandText.Append("'");

        dataCommand.CommandText = commandText.ToString();

        OdbcDataReader dataReader = dataCommand.ExecuteReader();

        // Make sure that you found the product
        if (dataReader.Read())
        {
          productID = dataReader.GetInt32(0);
        }

        dataConnection.Close();

        // Create a product object
        product = new Product(productID, categoryID,
          productName, unitPrice, stockQuantity);
        Assert.IsNotNull(product, "Newly created product is null, gasp!");
      }
      catch(Exception e)
      {
        Assert.Fail("Product database error: " + e.Message);
      }
    }

    private void RemoveProduct()
    {
      try
      {
        OdbcConnection dataConnection = new OdbcConnection();
        dataConnection.ConnectionString = DataUtilities.ConnectionString;
        dataConnection.Open();

        OdbcCommand dataCommand = new OdbcCommand();
        dataCommand.Connection = dataConnection;
```

```
      // Build command string
      StringBuilder commandText =
        new StringBuilder("DELETE FROM Products WHERE ProductID = ");
      commandText.Append(productID);

      dataCommand.CommandText = commandText.ToString();

      int rows = dataCommand.ExecuteNonQuery();

      // Make sure that the DELETE worked
      Assert.AreEqual(1, rows, "Unexpected Products row count, gasp!");

      dataConnection.Close();

      product = null;
    }
    catch(Exception e)
    {
      Assert.Fail("Products database error: " + e.Message);
    }
  }

  public void CreateOrder()
  {
    try
    {
      OdbcConnection dataConnection = new OdbcConnection();
      dataConnection.ConnectionString = DataUtilities.ConnectionString;

      dataConnection.Open();

      OdbcCommand dataCommand = new OdbcCommand();
      dataCommand.Connection = dataConnection;

      // Build command string
      StringBuilder commandText =
        new StringBuilder("INSERT INTO Orders (");

      commandText.Append("CustomerID, ");
      commandText.Append("OrdersDate, ");
      commandText.Append("ShippedDate, ");
      commandText.Append("ShipName, ");
      commandText.Append("ShipAddress, ");
      commandText.Append("ShipCity, ");
      commandText.Append("ShipPostalCode, ");
      commandText.Append("ShipCountry) VALUES ('");
      commandText.Append(customerID);
```

```
      commandText.Append("', '");
      commandText.Append(orderDate);
      commandText.Append("', '");
      commandText.Append(shipDate);
      commandText.Append("', '");
      commandText.Append(userName);
      commandText.Append("', '");
      commandText.Append(address);
      commandText.Append("', '");
      commandText.Append(city);
      commandText.Append("', '");
      commandText.Append(postalCode);
      commandText.Append("', '");
      commandText.Append(country);
      commandText.Append("')");

      dataCommand.CommandText = commandText.ToString();

      int rows = dataCommand.ExecuteNonQuery();

      // Make sure that the INSERT worked
      Assert.AreEqual(1, rows, "Unexpected Orders row count, gasp!");

      // Get the ID of the order we just inserted
      // This will be used to remove the order in the test TearDown
      commandText =
        new StringBuilder("SELECT OrdersID FROM Orders WHERE CustomerID = '");
      commandText.Append(customerID);
      commandText.Append("'");

      dataCommand.CommandText = commandText.ToString();

      OdbcDataReader dataReader = dataCommand.ExecuteReader();

      // Make sure that you found the order
      if (dataReader.Read())
      {
        orderID = dataReader.GetInt32(0);
      }

      dataConnection.Close();
    }
    catch(Exception e)
    {
      Assert.Fail("Orders database error: " + e.Message);
    }
}
```

```csharp
public void RemoveOrder()
{
  try
  {
    OdbcConnection dataConnection = new OdbcConnection();
    dataConnection.ConnectionString = DataUtilities.ConnectionString;
    dataConnection.Open();

    OdbcCommand dataCommand = new OdbcCommand();
    dataCommand.Connection = dataConnection;

    // Build command string
    StringBuilder commandText =
      new StringBuilder("DELETE FROM Orders WHERE OrdersID = ");
    commandText.Append(orderID);

    dataCommand.CommandText = commandText.ToString();

    int rows = dataCommand.ExecuteNonQuery();

    // Make sure that the DELETE worked
    Assert.AreEqual(1, rows, "Unexpected Orders row count, gasp!");

    dataConnection.Close();
  }
  catch(Exception e)
  {
    Assert.Fail("Orders database error: " + e.Message);
  }
}

private void CreateLineItem()
{
  lineItem = new LineItem(quantityOrdered, product);
  Assert.IsNotNull(lineItem, "Newly created lineItem is null, gasp!");
}

private void RemoveOrderLineItem()
{
  try
  {
    OdbcConnection dataConnection = new OdbcConnection();
    dataConnection.ConnectionString = DataUtilities.ConnectionString;
    dataConnection.Open();
```

```
        OdbcCommand dataCommand = new OdbcCommand();
        dataCommand.Connection = dataConnection;

        // Build command string
        StringBuilder commandText =
          new StringBuilder("DELETE FROM [Orders Details] WHERE OrdersID = ");
        commandText.Append(orderID);
        commandText.Append(" and ProductID = ");
        commandText.Append(productID);

        dataCommand.CommandText = commandText.ToString();

        int rows = dataCommand.ExecuteNonQuery();

        // Make sure that the DELETE worked
        Assert.AreEqual(1, rows, "Unexpected Orders Details row count, gasp!");

        dataConnection.Close();
        lineItem = null;
      }
      catch(Exception e)
      {
        Assert.Fail("Orders Details database error: " + e.Message);
      }
    }
  }
}
```

Listing 15-10. *OrderDetailData.cs File*

```
#region Using derectives
using System;
using System.Collections.Generic;
using System.Data
using System.Data.Odbc;
using System.Text;
using BusinessLayer;
#endregion

namespace DataLayer
{
  public class OrderDetailData
  {
    public OrderDetailData()
    {
    }
```

```
public static int InsertLineItem(int orderID, LineItem lineItem)
{
  int rows = -1;

  try
  {
    Product product = lineItem.Item;
    OdbcConnection dataConnection = new OdbcConnection();
    dataConnection.ConnectionString = DataUtilities.ConnectionString;
    dataConnection.Open();

    OdbcCommand dataCommand = new OdbcCommand();
    dataCommand.Connection = dataConnection;

    // Build command string
    StringBuilder commandText =
      new StringBuilder("INSERT INTO [Orders Details] (");

    commandText.Append("OrdersID, ");
    commandText.Append("ProductID, ");
    commandText.Append("UnitPrice, ");
    commandText.Append("Quantity, ");
    commandText.Append("Discount) VALUES (");
    commandText.Append(orderID);
    commandText.Append(", ");
    commandText.Append(product.ProductID);
    commandText.Append(", ");
    commandText.Append(product.Price);
    commandText.Append(", ");
    commandText.Append(lineItem.Quantity);
    commandText.Append(", ");
    commandText.Append(0);
    commandText.Append(")");

    dataCommand.CommandText = commandText.ToString();

    rows = dataCommand.ExecuteNonQuery();

    dataConnection.Close();
  }
  catch(Exception e)
  {
    Console.WriteLine(e.Message);
  }
```

```
      return rows
    }
  }
}
```

Listing 15-11. *OrderDetail.cs File*

```csharp
#region Using directives
using System;
using System.Collections.Generic;
using System.Text;
#end region

namespace BusinessLayer
{
  public class OrderDetail
  {
    private int     orderID;
    private int     productID;
    private decimal unitPrice;
    private int     quantityOrdered;
    private float   discount;

    public OrderDetail()
    {
    }

    public OrderDetail(int orderID,
      int productID,
      decimal unitPrice,
      int quantityOrdered,
      float discount)
    {
      this.orderID = orderID;
      this.productID = productID;
      this.unitPrice = unitPrice;
      this.quantityOrdered = quantityOrdered;
      this.discount = discount;
    }
```

```csharp
    public int OrderID
    {
      get
      {
        return this.orderID;
      }
      set
      {
        this.orderID = value;
      }
    }

    public int ProductID
    {
      get
      {
        return this.productID;
      }
      set
      {
        this.productID = value;
      }
    }

    public decimal UnitPrice
    {
      get
      {
        return this.unitPrice;
      }
      set
      {
        this.unitPrice = value;
      }
    }

    public int QuantityOrdered
    {
      get
      {
        return this.quantityOrdered;
      }
      set
      {
        this.quantityOrdered = value;
      }
    }
```

```
  public float Discount
  {
    get
    {
      return this.discount;
    }
    set
    {
      this.discount = value;
    }
  }
 }
}
```

This concludes the test, data, and business classes. You should be able to successfully build and test the entire solution. Once you have resolved any build or test issues, you are ready to move on to the web layer.

Add Button to Check Out the Shopping Cart Contents Task

The first web layer task is to add a button to the DisplayShoppingCart.aspx so that users can start the process of placing their order. Listing 15-12 shows the updated DisplayShoppingCart.aspx code.

Listing 15-12. *DisplayShoppingCart.aspx File*

```
<%@ Import Namespace="BusinessLayer" %>
<%@ Import Namespace="DataLayer" %>
<%@ Import Namespace="System.Collections" %>
<%@ Register TagPrefix="Categories" TagName="LeftNav" Src="Categories.ascx" %>
<%@ Register TagPrefix="TopNav" TagName="TopNav" Src="TopNav.ascx" %>
<%@ Page language="c#" CodeFile="DisplayShoppingCart.aspx.cs"
        AutoEventWireup="false" Inherits="NorthwindWeb.DisplayShoppingCart" %>
<!DOCTYPE html PUBLIC "-//W3C//DTD XHTML 1.1//EN"
        "http://www.w3.org/TR/xhtml11/DTD/xhtml11.dtd">
<html xmlns="http://www.w3.org/1999/xhtml">
  <head>
    <title>Display Shopping Cart</title>
  </head>
  <body>
    <table id="Table1" cellspacing="1" cellpadding="1" width="100%" border="0">
      <tr>
        <td colspan="2" style="height: 43px">
          <TopNav:TopNav id="topnav" runat="server" />
        </td>
      </tr>
```

```
<tr>
  <td width="20%" valign="top" align="left">
    <Categories:LeftNav id="leftnav" runat="server" />
  </td>
  <td valign="top" align="left">
    <table width="100%">
      <tr>
        <th align="left">
          Product</th>
        <th align="left">
          Price</th>
        <th align="left">
          Available</th>
        <th align="left">
          Quantity</th>
        <th>
        </th>
      </tr>
      <%
        while (cartEnumerator.MoveNext())
        {
      %>
      <form action="DisplayShoppingCart.aspx"
          id="UpdateContents" method="post">
        <tr>
          <%
            lineItem = (LineItem)cartEnumerator.Value;
            Product product = lineItem.Item;
            Response.Write("<td>" + product.ProductName + "</td><td>"
              + product.Price.ToString("C") + "</td><td>"
              + product.Quantity.ToString() + "</td>");
            Response.Write("<input type=\"hidden\" name=\"availableQty\""+
            "value=\"" + product.Quantity + "\">");
            Response.Write("<input type=\"hidden\" name=\"productID\""+
            "value=\"" + product.ProductID + "\">");
          %>
          <td>
            <input type="text" size="2" name="quantity"
              value="<%=lineItem.Quantity%>">
            <%
              Response.Write(lineItem.Message);
              lineItem.Message = "";
            %>
          </td>
```

```
          <td>
            <input type="submit" value="Update Quantity">
          </td>
        </tr>
      </form>
      <%
        }
      %>
    </table>
  </td>
</tr>
<tr>
  <td colspan="5" align="center">
    <form action="CheckoutConfirmation.aspx"
        id="CheckoutConfirmation" method="post">
      <input type="submit" value="Checkout" />
    </form>
  </td>
</tr>
    </table>
  </body>
</html>
```

This will take the user to the CheckOutConfirmation.aspx page.

Create Checkout Confirmation Page Task

Now that the DisplayShoppingCart.aspx page allows the user to check out, you need to build the confirmation page called CheckoutConfirmation.aspx, as shown in Listing 15-13.

Listing 15-13. *CheckoutConfirmation.aspx File*

```
<%@ Import Namespace="BusinessLayer" %>
<%@ Import Namespace="DataLayer" %>
<%@ Import Namespace="System.Collections" %>
<%@ Register TagPrefix="Categories" TagName="LeftNav" Src="Categories.ascx" %>
<%@ Register TagPrefix="TopNav" TagName="TopNav" Src="TopNav.ascx" %>
<%@ Page Language="c#"
  CodeFile="CheckoutConfirmation.aspx.cs"
  AutoEventWireup="true"
  Inherits="CheckoutConfirmation" %>
<!DOCTYPE html PUBLIC "-//W3C//DTD XHTML 1.1//EN"
      "http://www.w3.org/TR/xhtml11/DTD/xhtml11.dtd">
<html xmlns="http://www.w3.org/1999/xhtml">
  <head>
    <title>Checkout Confirmation</title>
  </head>
```

```
<body>
  <table id="Table1" cellspacing="1" cellpadding="1" width="100%" border="0">
    <tr>
      <td colspan="2" style="height: 43px">
        <TopNav:TopNav id="topnav" runat="server" />
      </td>
    </tr>
    <tr>
      <td width="20%" valign="top" align="left">
        <Categories:LeftNav id="leftnav" runat="server" />
      </td>
      <td valign="top" align="left">
      </td>
    </tr>
  </table>
</body>
</html>
```

This creates a basic page with the top and left navigation pieces. Now when users click the Checkout button on the DisplayShoppingCart.aspx page, they go here. But you aren't displaying anything yet. Let's move on to the next task.

Display Shopping Cart Contents in Checkout Confirmation Page Task

You will need to retrieve the shopping cart that you have been building and display its contents. To do that, enhance CheckoutConfirmation.aspx as shown in Listing 15-14.

Listing 15-14. *Modified CheckoutConfirmation.aspx to Show Shopping Cart Contents*

```
<%@ Import Namespace="BusinessLayer" %>
<%@ Import Namespace="DataLayer" %>
<%@ Import Namespace="System.Collections" %>
<%@ Register TagPrefix="Categories" TagName="LeftNav" Src="Categories.ascx" %>
<%@ Register TagPrefix="TopNav" TagName="TopNav" Src="TopNav.ascx" %>
<%@ Page language="c#"
  CodeFile="CheckoutConfirmation.aspx.cs"
  AutoEventWireup="false"
  Inherits="CheckoutConfirmation" %>
<!DOCTYPE html PUBLIC "-//W3C//DTD XHTML 1.1//EN"
        "http://www.w3c.org/TR/xhtml11/DTD/xhtml11.dtd">
<html xmlns="http://www.w3c.org/1999/xhtml">
  <head>
    <title>Checkout Confirmation</title>
  </head>
```

```
<body>
  <table id="Table1" cellspacing="1" cellpadding="1" width="100%" border="0">
    <tr>
      <td colspan="2" style="height: 43px">
       <TopNav:TopNav id="topnav" runat="server" />
      </td>
    </tr>
    <tr>
      <td width="20%" valign="top" align="left">
        <Categories:LeftNav id="leftnav" runat="server" />
      </td>
      <td valign="top" align="left">
        <table width="100%">
          <tr>
            <th align="left">
              Product</th>
            <th align="left">
              Price</th>
            <th align="center">
              Quantity</th>
            <th>
            </th>
          </tr>
          <%
            while ( cartEnumerator.MoveNext() )
            {
              LineItem lineItem = (LineItem)cartEnumerator.Value;
              Product product = lineItem.Item;
              Response.Write("<tr><td>" + product.ProductName + "</td><td>"
                 + product.Price.ToString("C") + "</td><td align=\"center\">"
                 + lineItem.Quantity.ToString() + "</td></tr>");
            }
          %>
        </table>
      </td>
    </tr>
  </table>
</body>
</html>
```

Next, you need to add code to the CheckoutConfirmation.aspx.cs class to get the shopping cart from the session, as shown in Listing 15-15.

Listing 15-15. *Modified CheckoutConfirmation.aspx.cs to Get the Shopping Cart*

```
using System;
using System.Collections;
using System.Configuration;
using System.Data;
using System.Drawing;
using System.Web;
using System.Web.Security;
using System.Web.UI;
using System.Web.UI.WebControls;
using System.Web.UI.WebControls.WebParts;
using System.Web.UI.HtmlControls;
using BusinessLayer;
using DataLayer;

public partial class CheckoutConfirmation : System.Web.UI.Page
{
    protected ShoppingCart cart = null;
    protected IDictionaryEnumerator cartEnumerator = null;

    protected void Page_Load(object sender, System.EventArgs e)
    {
        if ( Session["cart"] != null )
        {
            cart = (ShoppingCart)Session["cart"];
        }
        else
        {
            cart = new ShoppingCart();
            cart.Quantity = 0;
            Session["cart"] = cart;
        }
        cartEnumerator = cart.GetCartContents();
    }
}
```

Now when the users go to this page, if they have any items in their shopping cart, those items will be displayed. But this isn't much different from the DisplayShoppingCart.aspx page. So, next you will subtotal the dollar amounts of all the items displayed.

Subtotal Shopping Cart Line Items and Display Results Task

To get the subtotal, you need to first enhance CheckoutConfirmation.aspx to display the subtotal, as shown in Listing 15-16.

Listing 15-16. *Modified CheckoutConfirmation.aspx to Show the Subtotal*

```
<%@ Import Namespace="BusinessLayer" %>
<%@ Import Namespace="DataLayer" %>
<%@ Import Namespace="System.Collections" %>
<%@ Register TagPrefix="Categories" TagName="LeftNav" Src="Categories.ascx" %>
<%@ Register TagPrefix="TopNav" TagName="TopNav" Src="TopNav.ascx" %>
<%@ Page language="c#"
  CodeFile="CheckoutConfirmation.aspx.cs"
  AutoEventWireup="false"
  Inherits="CheckoutConfirmation" %>
<!DOCTYPE html PUBLIC "-//W3C//DTD XHTML 1.1//EN"
        "http://www.w3c.org/TR/xhtml11/DTD/xhtml11.dtd">
<html xmlns="http://www.w3c.org/1999/xhtml">
  <head>
    <title>Checkout Confirmation</title>
  </head>
  <body>
    <table id="Table1" cellspacing="1" cellpadding="1" width="100%" border="0">
      <tr>
        <td colspan="2" style="height: 43px">
          <TopNav:TopNav id="topnav" runat="server" />
        </td>
      </tr>
      <tr>
        <td width="20%" valign="top" align="left">
          <Categories:LeftNav id="leftnav" runat="server" />
        </td>
        <td valign="top" align="left">
          <table width="100%">
            <tr>
              <th align="left">
                Product</th>
              <th align="left">
                Price</th>
              <th align="center">
                Quantity</th>
              <th>
              </th>
            </tr>
            <%
              while ( cartEnumerator.MoveNext() )
              {
                LineItem lineItem = (LineItem)cartEnumerator.Value;
                Product product = lineItem.Item;
                Response.Write("<tr><td>" + product.ProductName + "</td><td>"
```

```
                    + product.Price.ToString("C") + "</td><td align=\"center\">"
                    + lineItem.Quantity.ToString() + "</td></tr>");
                total += product.Price * lineItem.Quantity;
              }
           %>
          </table>
        </td>
      </tr>
      <tr>
        <td> </td>
        <td valign="top" align="right">
          Order Total:
          <%=total.ToString("C")%>
        </td>
      </tr>
    </table>
  </body>
</html>
```

Then you need to add one line of code to the CheckoutConfirmation.aspx.cs class, as storage for the subtotal. Listing 15-17 shows that enhancement.

Listing 15-17. *Modified CheckoutConfirmation.aspx.cs to Store the Subtotal*

```
using System;
using System.Collections;
using System.Configuration;
using System.Data;
using System.Drawing;
using System.Web;
using System.Web.Security;
using System.Web.UI;
using System.Web.UI.WebControls;
using System.Web.UI.WebControls.WebParts;
using System.Web.UI.HtmlControls;
using BusinessLayer;
using DataLayer;

public partial class CheckoutConfirmation : System.Web.UI.Page
{
    protected ShoppingCart cart = null;
    protected IDictionaryEnumerator cartEnumerator = null;
    protected decimal total = 0;
```

```
  protected void Page_Load(object sender, System.EventArgs e)
  {
    if ( Session["cart"] != null )
    {
      cart = (ShoppingCart)Session["cart"];
    }
    else
    {
      cart = new ShoppingCart();
      cart.Quantity = 0;
      Session["cart"] = cart;
    }
    cartEnumerator = cart.GetCartContents();
  }
 }
}
```

Now you can display the subtotal. Next, you need to add a button to cancel checking out in case users change their mind.

Add Button to Cancel the Checkout Task

For the next task, you will add a button to CheckoutConfirmation.aspx that will allow users to exit the checkout process and return to their shopping experience. Listing 15-18 shows the enhanced CheckoutConfirmation.aspx page.

Listing 15-18. *CheckoutConfirmation.aspx with a Cancel Button*

```
<%@ Import Namespace="BusinessLayer" %>
<%@ Import Namespace="DataLayer" %>
<%@ Import Namespace="System.Collections" %>
<%@ Register TagPrefix="Categories" TagName="LeftNav" Src="Categories.ascx" %>
<%@ Register TagPrefix="TopNav" TagName="TopNav" Src="TopNav.ascx" %>
<%@ Page language="c#"
  CodeFile="CheckoutConfirmation.aspx.cs"
  AutoEventWireup="false"
  Inherits="CheckoutConfirmation" %>
<!DOCTYPE html PUBLIC "-//W3C//DTD XHTML 1.1//EN"
       "http://www.w3.org/TR/xhtml11/DTD/xhtml11.dtd">
<html xmlns="http://www.w3.org/1999/xhtml">
  <head>
    <title>Checkout Confirmation</title>
  </head>
```

```
<body>
  <table id="Table1" cellspacing="1" cellpadding="1" width="100%" border="0">
    <tr>
      <td colspan="2" style="HEIGHT: 43px">
        <TopNav:TopNav id="topnav" runat="server" />
      </td>
    </tr>
    <tr>
      <td width="20%" valign="top" align="left">
        <Categories:LeftNav id="leftnav" runat="server" />
      </td>
      <td vAlign="top" align="left">
        <table width="100%">
          <tr>
            <th align="left">
              Product</th>
            <th align="left">
              Price</th>
            <th align="center">
              Quantity</th>
            <th>
            </th>
          </tr>
          <%
          while ( cartEnumerator.MoveNext() )
          {
            LineItem lineItem = (LineItem)cartEnumerator.Value;
            Product product = lineItem.Item;
            Response.Write("<tr><td>" + product.ProductName + "</td><td>"
              + product.Price.ToString("C") + "</td><td align=\"center\">"
              + lineItem.Quantity.ToString() + "</td></tr>");
            total += product.Price * lineItem.Quantity;
          }
          %>
        </table>
      </td>
    </tr>
    <tr>
      <td> </td>
      <td valign="top" align="right">
        Order Total:
        <%=total.ToString("C")%>
      </td>
    </tr>
```

```
      <tr>
        <td colspan="2" align="right">
          <form id="login" method="post" runat="server">
            <asp:Button ID="CancelButton" runat="server" Text="Cancel"></asp:Button>
          </form>
        </td>
      </tr>
    </table>
  </body>
</html>
```

Then you need to enhance the CheckoutConfirmation.aspx.cs file to handle the redirection back to the shopping experience, as shown in Listing 15-19.

Listing 15-19. *CheckoutConfirmation.aspx.cs with Redirection Added*

```
using System;
using System.Collections;
using System.Configuration;
using System.Data;
using System.Drawing;
using System.Web;
using System.Web.Security;
using System.Web.UI;
using System.Web.UI.WebControls;
using System.Web.UI.WebControls.WebParts;
using System.Web.UI.HtmlControls;
using BusinessLayer;
using DataLayer;

public partial class CheckoutConfirmation : System.Web.UI.Page
{
    protected ShoppingCart cart = null;
    protected IDictionaryEnumerator cartEnumerator = null;
    protected decimal total = 0;

    protected void Page_Load(object sender, System.EventArgs e)
    {
      if ( Session["cart"] != null )
      {
        cart = (ShoppingCart)Session["cart"];
      }
      else
      {
        cart = new ShoppingCart();
        cart.Quantity = 0;
```

```
            Session["cart"] = cart;
        }
        cartEnumerator = cart.GetCartContents();
    }

    protected void CancelButton_Click(Object sender, System.EventArgs e)
    {
        Response.Redirect("DisplayShoppingCart.aspx", true);
    }
  }
}
```

Add Button to Process Order Request Task

The last task is to add a button to CheckoutConfirmation.aspx that will act as acceptance of the user's intention to check out and process the order. First, you will add the button to the page, as shown in Listing 15-20.

Listing 15-20. *CheckoutConfirmation.aspx with a Complete Order Button*

```
<%@ Import Namespace="BusinessLayer" %>
<%@ Import Namespace="DataLayer" %>
<%@ Import Namespace="System.Collections" %>
<%@ Register TagPrefix="Categories" TagName="LeftNav" Src="Categories.ascx" %>
<%@ Register TagPrefix="TopNav" TagName="TopNav" Src="TopNav.ascx" %>
<%@ Page language="c#"
  CodeFile="CheckoutConfirmation.aspx.cs"
  AutoEventWireup="false"
  Inherits="CheckoutConfirmation" %>
<!DOCTYPE html PUBLIC "-//W3C//DTD XHTML 1.1//EN"
        "http://www.w3.org/TR/xhtml11/DTD/xhtml11.dtd">
<html xmlns="http://www.w3.org/1999/xhtml">
  <head>
    <title>Checkout Confirmation</title>
  </head>
  <body>
    <table id="Table1" cellspacing="1" cellpadding="1" width="100%" border="0">
      <tr>
        <td colspan="2" style="height: 43px">
          <TopNav:TopNav id="topnav" runat="server" />
        </td>
      </tr>
      <tr>
        <td width="20%" valign="top" align="left">
          <Categories:LeftNav id="leftnav" runat="server" />
        </td>
```

```
    <td valign="top" align="left">
      <table width="100%">
        <tr>
          <th align="left">
            Product</th>
          <th align="left">
            Price</th>
          <th align="center">
            Quantity</th>
          <th>
          </th>
        </tr>
        <%
          while ( cartEnumerator.MoveNext() )
          {
            LineItem lineItem = (LineItem)cartEnumerator.Value;
            Product product = lineItem.Item;
            Response.Write("<tr><td>" + product.ProductName + "</td><td>"
              + product.Price.ToString("C") + "</td><td align=\"center\">"
              + lineItem.Quantity.ToString() + "</td></tr>");
            total += product.Price * lineItem.Quantity;
          }
        %>
      </table>
    </td>
  </tr>
  <tr>
    <td> </td>
    <td valign="top" align="right">
      Order Total:
      <%=total.ToString("C")%>
    </td>
  </tr>
  <tr>
    <td colspan="2" align="right">
      <form id="login" method="post" runat="server">
        <asp:Button id="CompleteOrderButton" runat="server"
          Text="Complete Order">
        </asp:Button>
        <asp:Button id="CancelButton" runat="server" Text="Cancel"></asp:Button>
      </form>
    </td>
  </tr>
</table>
</body>
</html>
```

Then you will enhance the CheckoutConfirmation.aspx.cs class with a method to handle the Complete Order button click, as shown in Listing 15-21.

Listing 15-21. *CheckoutConfirmation.aspx.cs with an Order Completion Method*

```
using System;
using System.Collections;
using System.Configuration;
using System.Data;
using System.Drawing;
using System.Web;
using System.Web.Security;
using System.Web.UI;
using System.Web.UI.WebControls;
using System.Web.UI.WebControls.WebParts;
using System.Web.UI.HtmlControls;
using BusinessLayer;
using DataLayer;

public partial class CheckoutConfirmation : System.Web.UI.Page
{
    protected ShoppingCart cart = null;
    protected IDictionaryEnumerator cartEnumerator = null;
    protected decimal total = 0;

    private void Page_Load(object sender, System.EventArgs e)
    {
        if ( Session["cart"] != null )
        {
            cart = (ShoppingCart)Session["cart"];
        }
        else
        {
            cart = new ShoppingCart();
            cart.Quantity = 0;
            Session["cart"] = cart;
        }
        cartEnumerator = cart.GetCartContents();
    }

    protected void CompleteOrderButton_Click(Object sender, System.EventArgs e)
    {
        // Get the current customer
        User user = (User)Session["User"];
        Customer customer = CustomerData.FindCustomerByUserName(user.UserName);
```

```
    // Create the new Order
    int orderID = OrderData.InsertOrder(customer);

    // Do order completion stuff and redirect to OrderConfirmation page
    cart = (ShoppingCart)Session["cart"];
    cartEnumerator = cart.GetCartContents();
    while (cartEnumerator.MoveNext())
    {
      LineItem lineItem = (LineItem)cartEnumerator.Value;
      OrderDetailData.InsertLineItem(orderID, lineItem);
      lineItem.Item.Quantity -= lineItem.Quantity;
      ProductData.UpdateQuantity(lineItem.Item);
    }

    // Empty the cart
    Session["cart"] = null;

    Response.Redirect("OrderConfirmation.aspx?orderID=" + orderID, true);
  }

  protected void CancelButton_Click(object sender, System.EventArgs e)
  {
    Response.Redirect("DisplayShoppingCart.aspx", true);
  }
 }
}
```

The User class in the BusinessLayer will need to be updated. This class should look like
Listing 15-22.

Listing 15-22. *Updated User.cs File*

```
#region Using directives
using System;
using System.Collections.Generic;
using System.Text;
#endregion

namespace BusinessLayer
{
  public class User
  {
    private string userName;
    private string password;
```

```
    public User()
    {
    }

    public User(string userName, string password)
    {
      this.userName = userName;
      this.password = password;
    }

    public string UserName
    {
      get
      {
        return this.userName;
      }
      set
      {
        this.userName = value;
      }
    }

    public string Password
    {
      get
      {
        return this.password;
      }
      set
      {
        this.password = value;
      }
    }
  }
}
```

In addition, the ProductData class in the DataLayer will need to updated, as shown in Listing 15-23.

Listing 15-23. *Updated ProductData.cs File*

```
#region Using directives
using System;
using System.Collections;
using System.Collections.Generic;
using System.Data;
using System.Data.Odbc;
```

```csharp
using System.Text;
using BusinessLayer;
#endregion

namespace DataLayer
{
  public class ProductData
  {
    public ProductData()
    {
    }

    public static ArrayList GetProductsByCategory(int categoryID)
    {
      ArrayList products = new ArrayList();

      try
      {
        OdbcConnection dataConnection = new OdbcConnection();
        dataConnection.ConnectionString = DataUtilities.ConnectionString;
        dataConnection.Open();

        OdbcCommand dataCommand = new OdbcCommand();
        dataCommand.Connection = dataConnection;

        // Build command string
        StringBuilder commandText =
          new StringBuilder("SELECT * FROM Products WHERE CategoryID=");
        commandText.Append(categoryID);
        commandText.Append(" AND UnitsInStock > 0");

        dataCommand.CommandText = commandText.ToString();

        OdbcDataReader dataReader = dataCommand.ExecuteReader();

        while (dataReader.Read())
        {
          Product product = new Product();
          product.ProductID = dataReader.GetInt32(0);
          product.ProductName = dataReader.GetString(1);
          product.CategoryID = dataReader.GetInt32(3);
          product.Price = dataReader.GetDecimal(5);
          product.Quantity = dataReader.GetInt16(6);

          products.Add(product);
        }
```

```
      dataConnection.Close();
    }
    catch(Exception e)
    {
      Console.WriteLine("Error: " + e.Message);
    }

    return products;
  }

  public static Product GetProduct(int ProductID)
  {
    Product product = null;

    try
    {
      OdbcConnection dataConnection = new OdbcConnection();
      dataConnection.ConnectionString = DataUtilities.ConnectionString;
      dataConnection.Open();

      OdbcCommand dataCommand = new OdbcCommand();
      dataCommand.Connection = dataConnection;

      // Build command string
      StringBuilder commandText =
        new StringBuilder("SELECT * FROM Products WHERE ProductID = ");
      commandText.Append(productID);

      dataCommand.CommandText = commandText.ToString();

      OdbcDataReader dataReader = dataCommand.ExecuteReader();

      if (dataReader.Read())
      {
        product = new Product();
        product.ProductID = dataReader.GetInt32(0);
        product.ProductName = dataReader.GetString(1);
        product.CategoryID = dataReader.GetInt32(3);
        product.Price = dataReader.GetDecimal(5);
        product.Quantity = dataReader.GetInt16(6);
      }

      dataCommand.Close();
    }
    catch (Exception e)
    {
      Console.WriteLine("Error: " + e.Message);
    }
```

```csharp
    return product;
}

public static ArrayList SearchForProducts(string searchString)
{
  ArrayList products = new ArrayList();

  try
  {
    OdbcConnection dataConnection = new OdbcConnection();
    dataConnection.ConnectionString = DataUtilities.ConnectionString;
    dataConnection.Open();

    OdbcCommand dataCommand = new OdbcCommand();
    dataCommand.Connection = dataConnection;

    // Build command string
    StringBuilder commandText =
      new StringBuilder("SELECT * FROM Products WHERE ProductName LIKE '%');
    commandText.Append(searchString);
    commandText.Append("%'");

    dataCommand.CommandText = commandText.ToString();

    OdbcDataReader dataReader = dataCommand.ExecuteReader();

    while (dataReader.Read())
    {
      product = new Product();
      product.ProductID = dataReader.GetInt32(0);
      product.ProductName = dataReader.GetString(1);
      product.CategoryID = dataReader.GetInt32(3);
      product.Price = dataReader.GetDecimal(5);
      product.Quantity = dataReader.GetInt16(6);
      products.Add(product);
    }

    dataConnection.Close();
  }
  catch (Exception e)
  {
    Console.WriteLine("Error: " + e.Message);
  }

  return products;
}
```

```
public static void UpdateQuantity(Product product)
{
  try
  {
    OdbcConnection dataConnection = new OdbcConnection();
    dataConnection.ConnectionString = DataUtilities.ConnectionString;
    dataConnection.Open();

    OdbcCommand dataCommand = new OdbcCommand();
    dataCommand.Connection = dataConnection;

    // Build command string
    StringBuilder commandText =
      new StringBuilder("UPDATE Products Set UnitsInStock = ");
    commandText.Append(product.Quantity);
    commandText.Append(" WHERE ProductID = '");
    commandText.Append(product.ProductID);
    commandText.Append("'");

    dataCommand.CommandText = commandText.ToString();

    int rows = dataCommand.ExecuteNonQuery();

    dataConnection.Close();
  }
  catch (Exception e)
  {
    Console.WriteLine(e.Message);
  }
}
}
}
```

This should complete all the tasks for the Display Checkout Confirmation user story. But remember that a story is not complete until the customer says so. That is where the acceptance test for this user story comes into play.

Acceptance Testing

The acceptance test for a story is defined by the customer and automated (if possible) by the acceptance tester. Our customer defined the acceptance test for the Display Checkout Confirmation user story as follows:

- Click a Checkout button on the Display Shopping Cart page to check out.

- Display a Checkout Confirmation page that lists all the items currently in the shopping cart.

- See a subtotal dollar amount of the order.

- When a Continue button is clicked on the Checkout Confirmation page, the order should be built and handed off for processing.

- A Cancel button should also be displayed on the Checkout Confirmation page. When clicked, that button should take the user back to the Display Shopping Cart page.

Developing the Remaining User Stories

This iteration has four other user stories. As in the first iteration, they are being developed in parallel with the Display Checkout Confirmation user story, which we focused on here. Each user story has its own acceptance tests written by the customer and automated by the acceptance testers, where possible.

The developers switch pairs at least once a day. They take a test-driven approach with the remaining user stories, just as with the user story described in this chapter.

All the developers keep track of the time they spend on the tasks that they picked for this iteration. When the tracker comes around (at least twice a week), the developers report the actual time they have spent on their tasks.

You can download the source code for this iteration from the Source Code area of the Apress website (www.apress.com).

Coach's Journal

During this iteration, I noticed that the team is getting better at pairing. The pairs were better at switching who was on the keyboard and who was not. I also saw that the team members are getting more acclimated to their environment, and that overall communication is starting to occur more frequently and openly.

Also, the acceptance testers are getting more comfortable with testing early rather than later. The acceptance testers were extremely helpful in working with the customer to define the acceptance tests and determining what could be automated.

As in the last iteration, I spoke with our customer frequently to make sure that he was comfortable with what was going on during the iteration. When our customer had concerns or questions, I addressed them immediately. This iteration, our customer became keenly aware of a need for securing the website during the ordering process. I sat down with him, and we discussed several options that he had in this area. I can see that he is already thinking about security stories for the next release.

Summary

By now, you should be getting a feel for the XP process. You have seen how to take a test-driven development approach to coding. You have witnessed how an iterative approach can provide a lot of feedback in the form of unit and acceptance tests. Daily stand-ups and the graphs and charts generated by the tracker create a better environment for communication. All of this communication allows the team members to better gauge where they are at meeting their targets.

You are well on your way down the XP path.

APPENDIX A

■ ■ ■

Preparing Your Development Environment

This appendix explains how to prepare your environment for the implementation section of this book (Part 3). It provides step-by-step instructions for setting up Visual Studio and the database for the examples in the book.

Visual Studio Setup

To follow along with the examples in Part 3 of this book, you need to create a Visual Studio solution named Northwind that contains four projects; DataLayer, BusinessLayer, NorthwindWeb, and TestLayer. Each of these projects contains logically separated classes associated with the database objects, business objects, web objects, and unit tests. This solution will host your entire application.

Creating the Northwind Solution

The Northwind solution will act as the container of all of the projects. To create your new solution, follow these steps:

1. In Visual Studio, select File ➤ New ➤ Project.

2. In the Project Types pane, select Other Project Types, and then select Visual Studio Solutions. In the Templates pane, select Blank Solution.

3. Enter Northwind for the solution name. Enter (or browse and select) the location where you would like to save the solution. Your New Project dialog box should look similar to the one shown in Figure A-1. Click the OK button.

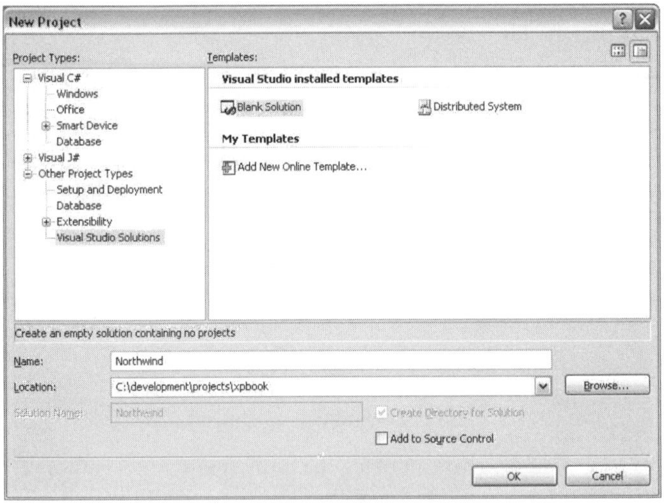

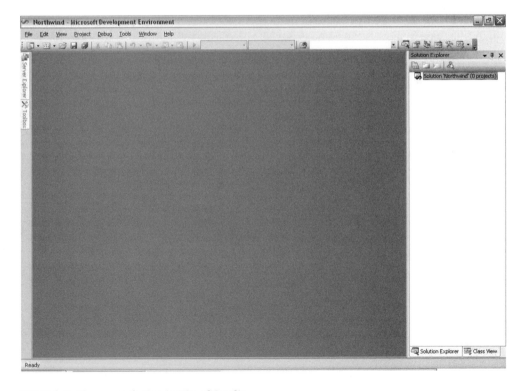

Figure A-1. *Creating the Northwind solution*

Your Visual Studio environment should now look similar to Figure A-2. At this point, you have a new solution named `Northwind`, which can be found in a directory named `Northwind`, stored in the directory you selected as its location.

Figure A-2. *The new solution in Visual Studio*

■**Note** As you may have noticed, the name of our solution is the same as the ever-present and often over-used Microsoft Northwind database. This is because the application covered in Part 3 of this book focuses on pushing the Northwind database to the Web.

Creating the DataLayer Project

The DataLayer project will contain all of the classes related to database connectivity. To create this project, follow these steps:

1. Right-click Northwind in the Solution Explorer, select Add, and then select New Project.

2. In the Project Types pane, select Windows under Visual C#. In the Templates pane, select Class Library, as shown in Figure A-3.

Figure A-3. *Creating the DataLayer project*

3. Enter DataLayer as the name of the project, and then click the OK button.

You now have a new Visual Studio project named DataLayer, which is displayed in the Solution Explorer, as shown in Figure A-4. You can find the physical contents of the project in the <SolutionLocation>\Northwind\DataLayer directory.

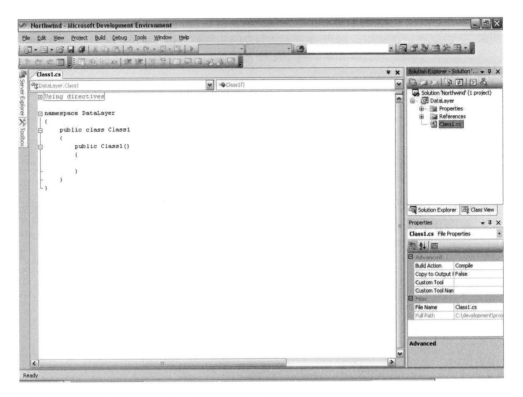

Figure A-4. *The DataLayer project added to the solution*

■Note As you create each of the projects in your solution, you will notice that an empty class named
Class1 (or something similar) has been created in each project. This is default Visual Studio behavior and
can be ignored for now.

Creating the BusinessLayer Project

The BusinessLayer project will contain all of the classes related to business logic. To create this
project, follow these steps:

1. Right-click Northwind in the Solution Explorer, select Add, and then select New Project.

2. In the Project Types pane, select Windows under Visual C#. In the Templates pane,
   select Class Library.

3. Enter BusinessLayer as the name of the project, as shown in Figure A-5, and then click
   the OK button.

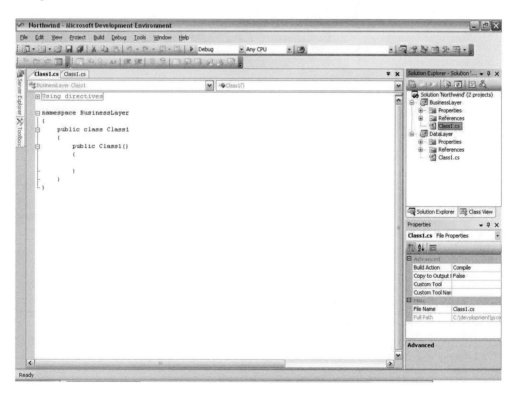

Figure A-5. *Creating the BusinessLayer project*

The Solution Explorer now displays the DataLayer and BusinessLayer projects, as shown in Figure A-6.

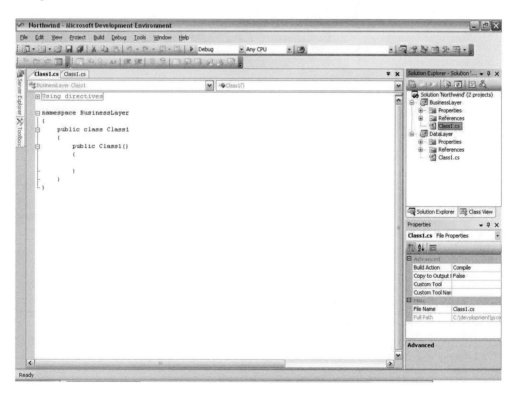

Figure A-6. *The BusinessLayer project added to the solution*

Creating the NorthwindWeb Project

The NorthwindWeb project will contain all of the classes related to the web layer of the application, including ASP.NET, HTML, and any other web-related files.

Follow these steps to create the NorthwindWeb project:

1. Make sure that Internet Information Services (IIS) is running and listening to the default HTTP port of 80. (If you need help figuring out how to get IIS up and running, refer to Microsoft Help.)

2. Right-click Northwind in the Solution Explorer, select Add, and then select New Website.

3. In the Project Types pane, select Visual C#. In the Templates pane, select ASP.NET Web Site.

4. Enter a location that ends with NorthwindWeb for the web project, as shown in Figure A-7, and then click the OK button.

Figure A-7. *Creating the NorthwindWeb project*

After you click the OK button, Visual Studio will communicate with IIS to create the new website. When this process is complete, you should have a new Visual Studio project named NorthwindWeb displayed in the Solution Explorer, as shown in Figure A-8.

■**Note** When you examine your newly created web project, you will notice some default web application files. These files can be ignored for now.

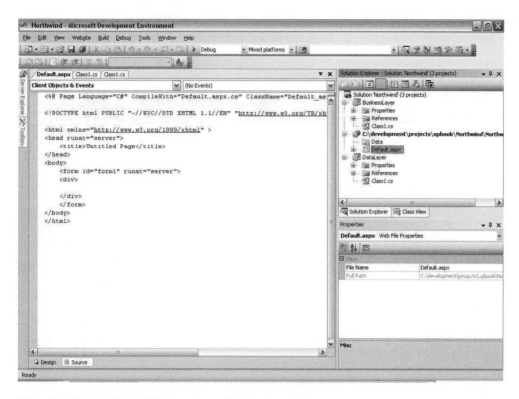

Figure A-8. *The NorthwindWeb project added to the solution*

Creating the TestLayer Project

The TestLayer project will contain all the source code for unit testing. For this book, you will be using a testing framework called NUnit (covered in Chapter 7), which supports test-first development. This particular framework provides a graphical user interface (GUI), so you will know if your tests are passing.

Download NUnit from www.nunit.org. After you have downloaded NUnit and installed it, you will need to configure it to work with Visual Studio, as follows:

1. Right-click Northwind in the Solution Explorer, select Add, and then select New Project.

2. In the Project Types pane, select Windows under Visual C#. In the Templates pane, select Class Library. Enter TestLayer as the project name, and then click the OK button.

3. Right-click TestLayer in the Solution Explorer and select Properties. Then select the Debug tab on the left side of the window.

4. Make sure the Configuration drop-down list is set to Active (Debug). In the Start Action section, select Start External Program and enter C:\Program Files\NUnit 2.2.2\bin\nunit-gui.exe (assuming you installed NUnit in the default location). In the Start Options section, enter TestLayer.dll in the Command Line Arguments text box. Your Properties window should look like the one shown in Figure A-9.

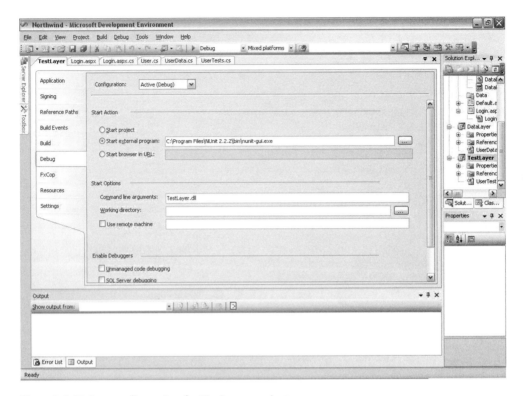

Figure A-9. *Debug configuration for TestLayer project*

You have set up NUnit to automatically launch when you run the TestLayer project. When you start the debugger, NUnit will be launched and the Visual Studio debugger will automatically be attached to the NUnit process. Let's walk through a simple example.

Running a Unit Test

This exercise simply demonstrates how to add a unit test to a project and run the unit test. Building test cases is covered in Chapters 7, 13, and 15.

1. Right-click TestLayer in the Solution Explorer, select Add, and then select Class.

2. Choose Class from the Templates pane.

3. Name the class CategoryTests.cs and click the Add button. This will create and display the CategoryTests class with the following code:

```
#region Using directives

using System;
using System.Collections.Generic;
using System.Text;
```

```
#endregion

namespace TestLayer
{
  public class CategoryTests
 {
    public CategoryTests()
    {

    }
  }
}
```

4. Right-click the `TestLayer` and select Add Reference.

5. In the Add Reference dialog box, click the Browse tab. Navigate to the NUnit application's `bin` directory, which is located at `C:\Program Files\NUnit 2.2.2\bin` (if you installed NUnit in the default location).

6. Select the following DLLs: `nunit.core.dll`, `nunit.extensions.dll`, `nunit.framework.dll`, `nunit.uikit.dll`, `nunit.util.dll`, and `nunit-gui-runner.dll`. Then click the Open button.

7. Verify that the NUnit DLLs are listed in the Browse tab, as shown in Figure A-10, and then click the OK button.

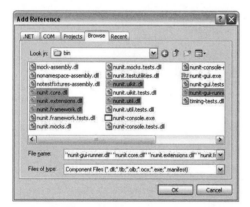

Figure A-10. *Adding NUnit DLL references*

8. Change the code to look like this:

```csharp
#region Using directives;

using System;
using System.Collections.Generic;
using System.Text;
using NUnit.Framework;
using BusinessLayer;

#endregion

namespace TestLayer

{
  [TestFixture]
  public class CategoryTests
  {
    Category  computerCategory;

    [SetUp]
    public void Init()
    {
      computerCategory = new Category(1,  // Category ID
        "Computer",                       // Category Name
        "Computer related stuff.");       // Category Description
    }

    [TearDown]
    public void Destroy()
    {
      computerCategory = null;
    }

     [Test]
    public void GetCategoryName()
    {
      string  computerCategoryName = computerCategory.CategoryName;
      Assert.IsNotNull(computerCategoryName, "The category name was null,
            gasp!");
      Assert.AreEqual("Computer", computerCategoryName, "Got the wrong
            category name, gasp!");
    }
  }
}
```

9. Add a C# file to the BusinessLayer project called Category.cs.

10. Change the `Category.cs` file code to look like this:

```
#region Using directives

using System;
using System.Collections.Generic;
usinf System.Text;

#endregion

namespace BusinessLayer
{
  public class Category {
    private int categoryID;
    private string categoryName;
    private string categoryDescription;

    public Category(int categoryID, string categoryName,
        string categoryDescription)
    {
      this.categoryID = categoryID;
      this.categoryName = categoryName;
      this.categoryDescription = categoryDescription;
    }

    public string CategoryName
    {
      get
      {
        return this.categoryName;
      }
    }
  }
}
```

11. Right-click the `TestLayer` project and select Add Reference.

12. Click the Projects tab, select `BusinessLayer` from the list, and click the OK button.

13. Right-click the `TestLayer` project and select Set as StartUp Project. The `TestLayer` project name will now appear in bold.

14. Select Build ➤ Build Solution (or press Ctrl+Shift+B).

15. Select Debug ➤ Start (or press F5). This will bring up the NUnit window, as shown in Figure A-11.

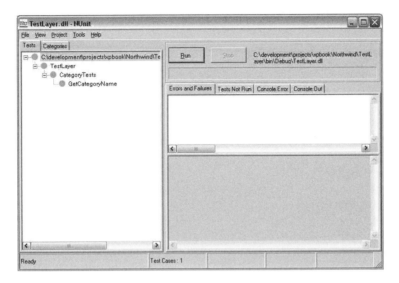

Figure A-11. *The NUnit window*

16. Click the Run button.

17. If everything went correctly, you should see a green bar under the Run button, and the testing tree on the left should have all green circles, as shown in Figure A-12. Click the window's close box to exit NUnit.

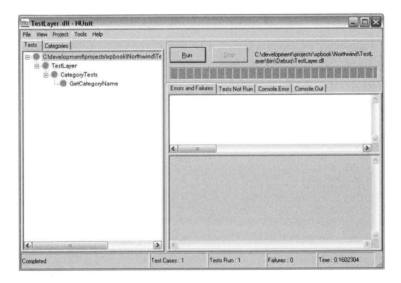

Figure A-12. *Results of running the test*

Don't be worried if you don't understand everything in the source code files you just created. Chapters 7, 13, and 15 explain how these files work. This example is very trivial and not optimized in any way. However, it does start to give you an idea of what a testing framework does.

The Database Setup

For this book's examples, you also need to configure the Northwind database. This involves setting up the Open Database Connectivity (ODBC) data source and associating that data source with Visual Studio Solution Explorer.

■Note When deciding on the type of database to use in our examples, we went back and forth several times. We thought of using Microsoft SQL Server or the Microsoft SQL Server Database Engine (MSDE), but ended up using Microsoft Access because we could package the complete database in our source archive. You can find a copy of the Northwind.mdb file in the source code archive for this book at the Apress website (www.apress.com).

Setting Up the ODBC Data Source

First, you need to set up an ODBC data source that references the database. To configure an ODBC data source, follow these steps:

1. Extract and copy the Northwind.mdb database file to a local directory on your hard drive (for example, C:\xpnet\database\).

■Note In our examples, we are assuming that you are using Microsoft Windows XP. If you are not, then you will need to adjust these instructions accordingly.

---

2. Open Control Panel, select Administrative Tools, and launch the Data Sources (ODBC) application. You will see a dialog box similar to the one shown in Figure A-13.

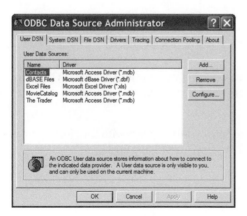

Figure A-13. *The ODBC Data Source Administrator dialog box*

3. Select the System DSN tab and click the Add button to open the Create New Data Source dialog box, as shown in Figure A-14.

Figure A-14. *The Create New Data Source dialog box*

4. Select the Microsoft Access Driver and click the Finish button.

5. In the ODBC Microsoft Access dialog box, enter Northwind in the Data Source Name field, as shown in Figure A-15. Then click the Select button.

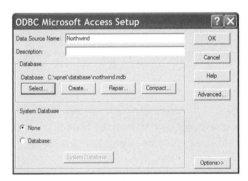

Figure A-15. *The ODBC Microsoft Access Setup dialog box*

6. Enter the path to the location of your Northwind.mdb file and click OK. The ODBC Microsoft Access Setup dialog box will show your changes. Click OK to commit your changes.

7. The ODBC Data Source Administrator dialog box appears with the Northwind data source in the list. Click the OK button to close this dialog box.

Connecting to the Database

Now that you have an ODBC data source referencing the database, you can set up a new Visual Studio data connection. Follow these steps to connect to the Northwind database:

1. Open the Northwind solution, and then open the Server Explorer, if it is not already visible. (Choose View ➤ Server Explorer or press Ctrl+Alt+S to display the Server Explorer.)

2. Right-click Data Connections in the Server Explorer and select Add Connection.

3. Click the Provider tab and select Microsoft OLE DB Provider for ODBC Drivers, as shown in Figure A-16.

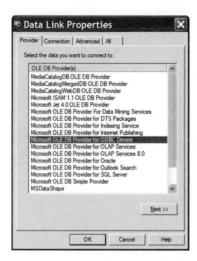

Figure A-16. *Selecting the Microsoft OLE DB Provider for ODBC Drivers*

4. Click the Connection tab and select Use Data Source Name. Select Northwind in the first drop-down list. Then click OK.

If you expand the Data Connections node in the Server Explorer, you will see a connection for ACCESS.C:\xpnet\database\northwind.admin. If you expand the Northwind database, you will see icons for Tables and Views, as shown in Figure A-17. These are parts of the Northwind database.

Figure A-17. *The Server Explorer with the new data connection*

Browsing the Database

Let's take a quick look at the database itself. Follow these steps:

1. Open the Server Explorer and expand the ACCESS connection. You should now see new entries showing the Tables and Views nodes (see Figure A-17).

2. Expand the Tables node. A list of all the tables in the database will be displayed, as shown in Figure A-18.

Figure A-18. *Tables in the Northwind database*

3. Right-click the Products table and select Retrieve Data from Table. This will retrieve all the data in the Products table in the Northwind database and display it in a spreadsheet form, as shown in Figure A-19.

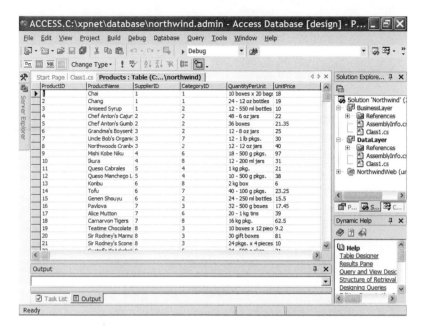

Figure A-19. *The Products table*

You can add delete and change data directly from this form. You can also use this same process to view any table in the database.

You now have set up your environment for the examples in this book. You created the appropriate Visual Studio solution and projects, configured NUnit, and finally configured your Microsoft Access data source, which holds the database that you will be using in the examples.

■ ■ ■

.NET C# Coding Conventions

When all of the developers on your XP team are working on the same code, as is the case with collective code ownership, you don't want each of them changing the code appearance to suit their individual styles. This would be a tremendous waste of time. So, by agreeing on a coding standard at the beginning of the project, you will increase the productivity and communications of the team.

If you dig through the Visual Studio online documentation, you will find a scattering of information pertaining to coding conventions that Microsoft recommends for C#. That documentation is much too vague and does not cover all of the coding conventions that would be needed on a daily basis.

This appendix presents a compilation of all the coding conventions we use when creating .NET applications. As much as possible, we try to follow the coding conventions that the Visual Studio tool uses when autogenerating code. We do this so that we will not be fighting with the tool. But, as you may have already discovered, Visual Studio is not always consistent. The suggestions in this appendix should help you with a starting point for your XP team's coding conventions. Feel free to tailor your conventions to your team's preferences.

Coding conventions can turn into holy wars if you let them. Don't go there. Remember that working software is what is important to a customer, not which line has a brace. If your team is having a hard time deciding on the coding convention, the coach should have the final word.

Coding conventions are not of any value if you don't use them. Make sure everyone understands the conventions and uses them. When new developers join the team, make sure they get a copy of the coding conventions and understand the conventions. If you are the coach, make sure the team is using the coding conventions by visually inspecting the code.

Naming Conventions

What is in a name? Names are used to label and describe things. The more descriptive the name, the better understanding we have of what the name means. *Bicycle* is a name used to describe a human-powered lightweight vehicle with two wheels and seat. If we use the name *full-suspension mountain bike*, you get an even more detailed understanding of what we mean.

Object-oriented languages like C# allow developers the flexibility to name classes, methods, fields, and so forth more descriptively. Don't be afraid to use longer names for these sorts of things, if it leads to greater clarity. Use whole words instead of abbreviations. Communication is a fundamental XP value, so communicate when naming.

.NET has two major types of letter cases: Pascal and camel. In Pascal case, the first letter of the first word in the name you are creating is uppercase, as well as each subsequent word used within the same name, as in `ThisIsPascalCase`. Using camel case, the first letter of the first word is lowercase, and then you use uppercase for each subsequent word within the same name, as in `thisIsCamelCase`.

Hungarian notation is a means whereby a type description is used within the name to give a hint as to the type of the thing being named. We use this style sparingly within our .NET coding conventions. You will find it used for naming classes that extend the `Exception` base class, as in `IllegalArgumentException`, and for suffixes to GUI components, as in `submitButton`.

You will use naming conventions in C# for many items. Table B-1 shows the various naming conventions we use.

Table B-1. *Naming Conventions*

Item	Case	Example	Notes
File	Pascal case	`DatabaseConnector`	Use nouns to describe classes.
Class	Pascal case	`DatabaseConnector`	Class names should match the names of the files in which they are defined.
Interface	Pascal case	`IDatabaseConnector`	Interface names begin with an `I`.
Method	Pascal case	`CalculateBalance`	Use verbs to describe methods. Note that Visual Studio is not consistent with this naming convention.
Private and protected instance field	Camel case	`private float accountBalance`	
Public instance field	Pascal case	`CustomerName`	
Private and protected class field	Camel case	`protected static int numberOfAccounts`	
Public class field	Pascal case	`public static bool HasGoodCredit`	
Static final	All caps	`public static final decimal MINIMUM_BALANCE = 100`	
Local Variable	Camel case	`string accountNumber = FindAccountByCustomerName (customerName)`	
Parameter	Camel case	`public void GetCurrentBalance (string accountNumber)`	
Property	Pascal case	`public string AccountNumber { get { return accountNumber; }} return accountNumber;`	

Item	Case	Example	Notes
Namespace	Pascal case	`namespace DataLayer`	
Unit test method	Pascal case	`TestFindAllCustomers`	Start the test method name with the word Test.
Unit test setup method	Pascal case	`Initialize`	
Unit test teardown method	Pascal case	`Destroy`	
Solution	Pascal case	`NorthwindTrader`	
Project	Pascal case	`DataLayer`	

Indentation

You can configure Visual Studio to use either tabs or spaces for indentation, as well as set the number of character units to indent. We used two spaces as unit of indentation for this book in order to make the code more readable on a page. Our day-to-day convention is to use four spaces as the unit of indentation.

Line length is also important for readability. Try to restrict lines to no longer than 80 characters. When you need to wrap lines that are longer than 80 characters, here are some rules you should follow:

- Break before the operator
- Break after a comma
- Line up parentheses

Declarations

When declaring class fields, instance fields, or local variables, declare only one per line. When making several declarations together, align the field or variable names. For local variables, you should initialize the variable when you declare, unless you need to perform some other action, like a computation, before you can initialize the variable.

Declarations should be placed at the top of the class or method in which they are declared. This will make the declarations easier to find later. One exception to this rule is the declaration and initialization of a local variable within a for loop.

Statements

There are several types of statements in C#. Each line should not contain more than one statement.

For if, if-else, and if else-if else statements, always use braces:

```
if (boolean condition)
{
  statements;
}
```

```
if (boolean condition)
{
  statements;
}
else
{
  statements;
}
```

```
if (boolean condition)
{
  statements;
}
else if (boolean condition)
{
  statements;
}
else
{
  statements;
}
```

You should also always use braces for for, foreach, while, and do-while statements:

```
for (initialization; boolean condition; update)
{
  statements;
}
```

```
foreach (type declaration in IEnumerable)
{
  statements;
}
```

```
while (boolean condition)
{
  statements;
}
```

```
do
{
  statements;
}
while (boolean condition);
```

In return statements, do not use parentheses unless they make the return value more obvious:

```
return myList;
return myList.count();
return;
```

Here is the form we use for switch statements:

```
switch (expression)
{
  case constant-expression:
        statements;
        break;
  default:
        statements;
        break;
}
```

We use the following form for try-catch-finally statements:

```
try
{
  statements;
}
catch (exception)
{
  statements;
}

try
{
  statements;
}
catch (exception)
{
  statements;
}
finally
{
  statements;
}
```

Comments

You can use several kinds of comment types in C#. Table B-2 shows an example of each type and when to use it. If you are creating excessive amounts of comments in your code, this is an indication of poorly written code. Consider refactoring the code to make it more understandable and so that it requires fewer comments.

Table B-2. *Comment Types*

Type	Example	When to Use
Documentation	`/// <summary>This class represents a bank account</summary>`	Use to document classes and methods.
End of line	`int myCounter = 0; // Keeps track of how many times this method has been called`	Use to describe the purpose of something that may not be clear.
Single line	`// Here is where we gather account data`	Use to describe the purpose of the thing or block of code to follow. Used by Visual Studio to comment out lines of code.
Multiline	`/* . . . */`	Use to comment out a block of code, or when describing the purpose of the code that follows takes several lines.

White Space

White space, while ignored by the compiler, improves readability by separating logical units of code.

One blank line should always be used in the following situations:

- Between methods

- Between a declaration and a statement

- Between logical sections of code

- Before a single or multiline comment

Blank spaces should always be used in the following situations:

- A keyword followed by a parenthesis

- After a comma in a parameter list

- Before and after mathematical operators

- Within a for statement, breaking up the three logical sections of the statement

Solution and Project Organization

Every solution will have the following projects:

- The business project holds only business objects.

- The data project handles database and other legacy systems access for the purpose of retrieving or updating data.

- The presentation project handles all views that are needed by the end user to use the system.

- The test project holds all the unit tests for the application.

■ ■ ■

XP Resources

XP is a young process and therefore constantly changing. This appendix lists additional resources that will help you keep track of the evolution of this exciting methodology. Who knows—you may even find yourself actually contributing to this evolution.

Websites

Visit the following websites for information about Agile methodology in general, XP specifically, and testing software:

- Agile Alliance (`www.agilealliance.com`): This is a great resource maintained by the Agile Alliance, which is a nonprofit group focused on the promotion of agile software development and helping organizations adopt those concepts.

- The New Methodology (`http://martinfowler.com/articles/newMethodology.html`): This is Martin Fowler's website, which describes the move to Agile methodologies and provides an overview of some of these methodologies.

- XProgramming.com (`www.xprogramming.com/`): This website, by Ron Jeffries, is an excellent resource for information about XP. The site contains articles about the state of XP, techniques, tips, and reports. You will find XP-oriented testing and software tools and applications. The site also offers a plethora of documentation, including the original C3 papers, which capture the spirit of that exciting first XP project.

- Extreme Programming Wiki (`http://c2.com/cgi/wiki?ExtremeProgrammingRoadmap`): This is Ward Cunningham's site, which is focused on capturing and maintaining XP discussions and evolution. It provides a great roadmap to just about every XP topic that you can think of, including the different practices, a list of who's who in XP, and much more.

- XPlorations (`www.xp123.com/xplor/`): This is Bill Wake's website, which provides a series of articles describing various characteristics of XP.

- XP User Groups (`www.c2.com/cgi/wiki?CategoryXpUsersGroup`): Check out this site for a list of XP user groups around the world.

- NUnit (www.nunit.org/): This website hosts the NUnit unit testing software.

- .NET Mock Objects (http://sourceforge.net/projects/dotnetmock/): This is the site of the SourceForge .NET Mock Objects project—a generic unit testing framework used when developing .NET unit tests with mock objects. The current project is pretty light on documentation. It should improve as the project evolves.

Mailing Lists

You may want to join the following mailing lists:

- Extreme Programming (http://groups.yahoo.com/group/extremeprogramming/): This is a Yahoo forum discussing XP practices and principles.

- Extreme Programming Jobs (http://groups.yahoo.com/group/xp-jobs/): This is just what it sounds like—a Yahoo user group focused on finding and posting jobs related to XP.

- Extreme Programming User Groups (http://groups.yahoo.com/group/xpusergroups/): This is a Yahoo user group that focuses on sharing ideas between XP user groups. This group is not for discussions on XP itself.

- JUnit Mailing List (http://groups.yahoo.com/group/junit/): This group is focused on Java unit testing, but it does have some good discussions about test-driven development. If you are not looking for explicit .NET topics, you may want to take a look at this group.

- NUnit Mailing List (http://groups.yahoo.com/group/nunit/): This is a relatively new list that is focused on NUnit and test-driven development.

Conferences

Several conferences cover XP practices. Unfortunately, the URLs for these conferences keep changing every year. So, you should perform a search on XP conference to get the latest URLs for these types of conferences. As examples, two conferences that have been held in the past are XP Agile Universe (www.agile2006.com) and XP Day (www.xpday.org).

Index

You Need the Companion eBook

forums.apress.com

FOR PROFESSIONALS BY PROFESSIONALS™

JOIN THE APRESS FORUMS AND BE PART OF OUR COMMUNITY. You'll find discussions that cover topics of interest to IT professionals, programmers, and enthusiasts just like you. If you post a query to one of our forums, you can expect that some of the best minds in the business—especially Apress authors, who all write with *The Expert's Voice*™—will chime in to help you. Why not aim to become one of our most valuable participants (MVPs) and win cool stuff? Here's a sampling of what you'll find:

DATABASES
Data drives everything.

Share information, exchange ideas, and discuss any database programming or administration issues.

INTERNET TECHNOLOGIES AND NETWORKING
Try living without plumbing (and eventually IPv6).

Talk about networking topics including protocols, design, administration, wireless, wired, storage, backup, certifications, trends, and new technologies.

JAVA
We've come a long way from the old Oak tree.

Hang out and discuss Java in whatever flavor you choose: J2SE, J2EE, J2ME, Jakarta, and so on.

MAC OS X
All about the Zen of OS X.

OS X is both the present and the future for Mac apps. Make suggestions, offer up ideas, or boast about your new hardware.

OPEN SOURCE
Source code is good; understanding (open) source is better.

Discuss open source technologies and related topics such as PHP, MySQL, Linux, Perl, Apache, Python, and more.

PROGRAMMING/BUSINESS
Unfortunately, it is.

Talk about the Apress line of books that cover software methodology, best practices, and how programmers interact with the "suits."

WEB DEVELOPMENT/DESIGN
Ugly doesn't cut it anymore, and CGI is absurd.

Help is in sight for your site. Find design solutions for your projects and get ideas for building an interactive Web site.

SECURITY
Lots of bad guys out there—the good guys need help.

Discuss computer and network security issues here. Just don't let anyone else know the answers!

TECHNOLOGY IN ACTION
Cool things. Fun things.

It's after hours. It's time to play. Whether you're into LEGO® MINDSTORMS™ or turning an old PC into a DVR, this is where technology turns into fun.

WINDOWS
No defenestration here.

Ask questions about all aspects of Windows programming, get help on Microsoft technologies covered in Apress books, or provide feedback on any Apress Windows book.

HOW TO PARTICIPATE:

Go to the Apress Forums site at **http://forums.apress.com/**.

Click the New User link.